Fashion and Age

Fashion and Age
Dress, the Body and Later Life

Julia Twigg

B L O O M S B U R Y
LONDON • NEW DELHI • NEW YORK • SYDNEY

Bloomsbury Academic

An imprint of Bloomsbury Publishing Plc

50 Bedford Square
London
WC1B 3DP
UK

1385 Broadway
New York
NY 10018
USA

www.bloomsbury.com

First published 2013

British Library Cataloguing-in-Publication Data
A catalogue record for this book is available from the British Library.

ISBN: HB: 978-1-8478-8696-5
PB: 978-1-8478-8695-8

Library of Congress Cataloging-in-Publication Data
A catalog record for this book is available from the Library of Congress.

Typeset by Apex CoVantage, LLC, Madison, WI, USA
Printed and bound in Great Britain

Contents

List of Illustrations

Figures

Tables

Acknowledgements

This book occupies a special place in my life and academic development, allowing me to bring together and reflect on aspects of my life and self normally separated. At an academic level, I have long been interested in the ordinary and the day-to-day, and the ways experiences and social practices at this level offer routes to explore larger questions. I have pursued these themes in fields such as food and drink, in a study of vegetarianism; bathing and washing, in a study of personal care; and now dress, in this study of its role in the lives and experiences of older women and in new, related work on dementia and the materiality of dress. Running through all these areas has been a concern with questions of embodiment and its role in the lived reality of people's lives. This book also touches on a second academic concern of mine which has been to bring wider perspectives to bear on the territory of ageing. For too long, later years have been analysed through the lens of social welfare, with an emphasis on frailty and dependence and, often, with an objectifying and distancing gaze. Although I have done work within this social welfare tradition—and still value it— I am pleased to have the opportunity this new work has given me to address a wider conception of age and its social significance, bringing to bear on it new literatures and new analytic concerns. At a more personal level, this study has also let me pursue, for the first time academically, a long-established interest in the history of dress. This has brought me great pleasure and allowed me to indulge in aesthetic and historical concerns that have been part of my life but have not been expressed academically. I did my undergraduate degree in history and in many ways, it remains my first love intellectually. Lastly as an older woman myself—I am in my sixties—I have encountered many of the dilemmas in relation to dress analysed in this book: tensions in the way I should or might like to present myself, sadness at the loss of certain sorts of engagement with fashion, but also continuity in an enduring involvement in this pleasurable aesthetic realm.

I am grateful to the many respondents in the study, particularly the older women who so generously shared their views and experiences with me. The interviews with them were enlightening, enjoyable and at times very funny. I am especially grateful to the three respondents who were willing to be part of a more extended study exploring their earlier lives. Hearing them talk about and reflect on their lives and the role of dress in them was a fascinating and at times moving experience. I am particularly grateful to them for allowing me to reproduce their images. I would also like to thank respondents in the magazine and fashion industries who gave of their time and expertise, enabling me better to understand the ways age is understood in these media and design contexts. Visiting their offices and design studios was a fascinating and novel experience for me and brought many insights into the fashion worlds they inhabit.

I would like to record my thanks to the various funding bodies that generously supported this work. ESRC provided the funding for the main research study, Clothing, the Body and Age. ESRC has also funded a related, though different study on dementia and dress. The Nuffield Foundation provided funding for an earlier scoping study on clothing and frail elders. The British Academy supported a small secondary data analysis of the Family Expenditure Survey, looking at spending on clothing, cosmetics and hair from 1960 to 2005. This was undertaken in conjunction with Dr Shinobu Majima of the University of Gakushuin. I am very grateful to her for academic expertise, analytic insight and enthusiasm. She was an ideal colleague.

I would like to thank Posy Simmonds for generously allowing me to use without cost her wonderful cartoon 'A lifetime in babywear', which so brilliantly conveys the interplay between bodily and cultural ageing. The cartoon was originally published in *Followers of Fashion: Graphic Satires from the Georgian Period,* Hayward Publishing, London 2000. 'Life and age of woman' is printed courtesy of the Library of Congress. Figures 5.1–5.7 are printed by permission of the study respondents. Figures 6.1 and 6.2 are printed courtesy of Condé Nast.

Chapters in this book draw on articles including 'How does *Vogue* negotiate age?: fashion, the body and the older woman', published in *Fashion Theory* in 2010; and 'Adjusting the cut: fashion, the body and age on the UK high street', published in *Ageing & Society* in 2012. 'Dress and the narration of life: women's reflections on clothing and age' was published in A. C. Sparkes (ed.) *Auto/Biography Yearbook 2009, BSA Auto/Biography Study Group* and 'Fashion and age: the role of women's magazines in the constitution of aged identities' in V. Ylänne (ed.) *Representing Ageing: Images and Identities.* I am grateful to the publishers for allowing me to draw on these.

I have presented aspects of this work at numerous conferences and events. I am grateful to the universities who have supported me in doing so: Copenhagen, Roskilde, Stockholm, Helsinki, Jyväskylä, Linköping, Lleida, Toronto, Oxford, Lancaster, Manchester, Brunel and Newcastle.

I would like to thank my own university, the University of Kent, for giving me the intellectual space in which to develop these ideas, and for providing a supportive and enabling environment. I would particularly like to thank many good colleagues in the School of Social Policy, Sociology and Social Research and in research services, particularly Phil Ward.

I am particularly grateful to the many friends and colleagues who have assisted in aspects of this work and who have offered support and encouragement, especially Helen Charnley, Avner Offer, Wendy Martin, Stephen Katz, Sara Arber, Sonja Iltanen-Tähkävuori, Chrissy Buse, Judy Mummery, Jan Clare Side and Annie Kenyon Edwards. Most of all, however, I would like to thank my partner, Martin Peach, for all his support and encouragement over many years.

– 1 –

Introduction

Fashion and age sit uncomfortably together. Fashion inhabits a world of youthful beauty, of fantasy, imagination, allure. Its discourses are frenetic and frothy; its images glamorous and—above all—youthful. Age by contrast is perceived as a time of greyness, marked by retirement from display or engagement with the erotic and style conscious. It is associated with a toned-down, self-effacing presentation. Historically age has been seen as a time for shifting one's focus away from worldly concerns towards more heavenly, spiritual ones, a passage in life marked less by preoccupation with surface and display, and more with inner essence. Even in a period like ours, when such directly religious themes have lost much of their cultural purchase, the idea that later years are a time for reflection and interiority, rather than extravagance and display, has not altogether gone. And, of course, from the perspective of the fashion world itself, age is not just peripheral to fashion but positively erosive of it. Age is at war with its central values, as Time's claw destroys the youthful beauty on which it rests.

In this book, however, I explore the ways these two fields can be and are linked, using the territory of clothing and age to explore central questions in modern culture. Is the nature of later years changing under the impact of social and demographic change, and how has this affected how old age is imagined, experienced and understood? Do older people feel differently about their lives now? What role might spheres of cultural production like fashion and dress play in such changes? How indeed do fashion and the fashion world treat old age? The grey market is recognized as increasingly significant economically. Are consumers seeing changes in the way the commercial world responds to this? Older people are often characterized as frustrated shoppers unable to find their desires reflected in the market. Is this so, and why? There are deep ambivalences experienced here by both customers and retailers, as the fashion world attempts to walk the tightrope of ageism, producing goods that are aimed at this market, but without being overtly labelled as such. Indeed, this is a cultural field that is permeated by the language of 'moving younger'. Why is this so, and do such impulses reflect the aspirational nature of consumption rather than any real change in the cultural location of age? What part does age play in the dynamic of fashion transmission itself, and has it replaced social class in the ordering of this?

I will explore these questions in a series of chapters that examine the responses of older women themselves; the media, in the guise of fashion editors and journalists;

and the fashion industry, in the form of design directors for major clothing retailers. These chapters draw on new empirical work. But before doing so, I will reflect in this chapter on the ways in which the study of ageing and dress contributes to a range of academic debates, helping to shift the framework within which these are discussed, as well as bringing new material and insights to bear on them.

Shifting the Debate

Fashion studies has long ignored the subject of age, prioritizing the avant-garde and ultra fashionable, thus reflecting the values of the fashionable world in its own analyses. Fashion operates here as an exclusionary term that is applied only to the epicentre of the industry and its extension in the media. This tendency has been reinforced by the influence of cultural studies, which has similarly focussed on a small, ultra-fashionable core, albeit at the same time extending its analyses to include more edgy, subcultural influences. As a result fashion studies only addresses a limited part of the market for dress. It remains preoccupied with the youthful and transgressive; and there has been remarkably little work that addresses older people or the processes of age. Beyond forty in this literature, there is silence. But this is to exclude a significant proportion of the buying and clothes-wearing population.

Addressing questions of age, therefore, can expand the remit of fashion studies, opening it up to wider influences and sources, transcending its current narrow base. Above all discussing these questions repositions fashion studies nearer the lived reality of people's dressed lives. Age allows us to think about clothing and dress as everyday practices engaged in by everyone, part of the mundane business of social reproduction, rather than special activities confined to the fashion-conscious elite and governed by its particular fashion-oriented preoccupations. Such an approach has, of course, long been prominent in social anthropology, and those parts of dress studies that have explored the lived reality of dress as part of the wider material turn in sociology; and this book draws on such influences, which will be explored further in the next chapter.

Studying clothing and age also allows us to examine the role of dress in the constitution of social difference. Age is one of the master identities, a key dimension of difference, and yet one that sociology has by and large neglected, preferring to focus its attention on categories such as gender, class, race and sexuality. Sociology largely treats age as something 'obvious', lying beyond the social, embedded in physiology, pertaining to the fields of medicine or social welfare, and essentially uninteresting. As a result, we are in much the same position now with regard to age as we were forty years ago in relation to gender, which was similarly neglected, naturalized in the body, treated as obvious, so ubiquitous indeed that we could not see its power. Since then, of course, we have come to recognize the centrality of gender to all aspects of the social world. A similar shift in understanding needs to occur in relation to age. It too is one of the key structuring principles within society, ordering and ranking people, shaping their experiences, determining the ways in which they are evaluated and judged, limiting and enabling their development. It intersects with other social categorizations in significant ways, so that the ways in which ageing is experienced and understood are closely affected by cross-cutting identities, particularly gender and social class. Both of these have a significant impact on the field of dress.

Clothes are central to how we present ourselves at the individual and social levels. We recognize who people are through the medium of their dress. We are indeed so accustomed to reading a category like gender from dress that we forget the degree to which it rests on conventional dress codes, rather than direct information about the sexed bodies that lie beneath. Dress thus acts to naturalize social divisions. In a similar way we read socioeconomic status from styles of dress, noting not just the material expense or condition of clothing, but also the subtlest differences of presentation and style. British clothing codes are indeed significantly linked to social class. Other social divisions or categories are similarly made manifest through dress. Clues as to sexuality, for example, are frequently found, particularly with the emergence in the twentieth and twenty-first centuries of distinctive codes indicating lesbian or gay identity, as well as the continuance of more subtle indicators.

Age too is made manifest in distinctive clothing styles. In the chapters that follow I explore the long tradition of age ordering in dress. By this I mean the systematic patterning of cultural expression with regard to dress according to an ordered and hierarchically arranged concept of age. These processes are not confined to old age, but operate across the life course. Age ordering is clearly visible in childhood where the link between clothing and age status can be seen very clearly, though it also intersects with the development of the body: clothes for a three-year-old are different in cut and style from those for a teenager. These associations, and their interplay with the corporeal, continue through the life course, changing and developing as other aspects of identity and the body change, until in later years the emergence of a distinctive set of clothing norms related to age can be observed. Though the character of these is always culturally contingent, shifting with historical developments in dress and fashion, certain commonalities or enduring features mark out such dress: darker, duller colour; looser, longer cut and, for women in particular, more covered-up, self-effacing styles. To a degree these features reflect changes in the body that occur with age or, most important, their social interpretation. They also reflect, however, the wider cultural estimation of older people and their position in society, embodying at the sartorial level evaluations and judgements concerning their worth and status. I explore the meaning of this patterning of dress, together with assertions that it is no longer relevant, more fully in subsequent chapters when I address age ordering and its putative demise as part of the wider reconstitution of ageing.

Exploring clothing and dress also brings into view aspects of life that are significant for many women, but that have not always received attention within the Academy. As Dyhouse says, 'much of women's social history is embedded in clothes, cosmetics and material culture' (2010: 7). Addressing clothing and dress thus foregrounds aspects of women's culture that have sometimes been obscured and denigrated. One of the experiences that I have had in undertaking this research has been the way the topic has been greeted with enthusiasm by middle-aged and older women who have expressed pleasure in finding matters of direct interest and concern to them reflected in academic work. I have had similarly warm messages from fellow women academics, though their comments have sometimes been hedged around by guilt at displaying interest in such matters. As Tseëlon (2001) and others have commented, to be interested in dress places one on the edges of seriousness, threatening connection with the narcissism and triviality traditionally assigned to women. As a result, many women who occupy senior or professional positions are cautious in expressing interest in dress.

Exploring the role of dress, however, makes visible areas of life that are important to many women. This is not to assume that all women are interested in these matters, but it is to recognize that many are, and moreover that these aesthetic spheres play a significant part in the constitution of identities in Western culture. Whilst feminist work of the second wave tended to be critical of such interest, seeing fashion as implicated in women's subordination, with the rise of postmodernism, feminism has been more willing to acknowledge the role of areas like dress in self-fashioning, recognizing the aesthetic pleasure that such cultural spheres offer women; indeed this recognition is one of the defining features of postmodern feminism. There is now an acknowledgement within feminist writing of the inescapability of matters of dress and of the presentation of the body, so that the dream of second-wave feminism of transcending such matters has gone: there can be no 'natural' dress, any more than there can be a 'natural' body. Cultural constitution in some form is inevitable. With this has come a more open acknowledgement of the potential importance of these areas of expressivity for many women. Fashion is for many a source of joy and uplift. There is aesthetic pleasure to be derived from colour and textile, from the feel and look of dress. It can be positive and life-enhancing, as much as oppressive and objectifying. Dress also has a significant part to play in the process of being visible, of occupying social and cultural space in a confident manner. This is particularly significant in the context of age where older women can find themselves becoming invisible culturally, no longer seen or noticed. This is in contrast with the experience of youth where young women can find themselves and their bodies hypervisible, constituted oppressively in an omnipresent male gaze. For older women, however, and to some degree older men too, the struggle is to be seen at all. Here dress, especially if chosen and worn in a confident and positive manner, can be part of an assertion of value, a repudiation of invisibility.

This book largely addresses the situations of women. In doing so it reflects the wider cultural association of women with fashion and dress, which have traditionally been constituted as feminized fields, their discourses and practices primarily embodied in the lives of women. But matters of dress are not absent from the lives of men: men too are involved in the day-to-day business of choosing and buying clothes. Indeed from the perspective of material culture or the anthropologically influenced traditions that inform this study, they are as much involved as women in questions of dress and its role in identity formation: it is just that the practices are less visible and more entrenched and the codes more conservative. Many of the strictures in relation to dress and older women apply also to men: the adoption of duller, more covered-up styles; the retreat from sharper, ultra-fashionable dress. But the pressure is less overt and the condemnation of transgression less harsh. This reflects the different nature of clothing codes in relation to men and women at all ages, but it also points to the ways in which gender operates differentially in relation to the presentation of the body.

Exploring the role of clothing and dress allows me to unpack some of the ways gender operates at an embodied level. Age has different effects on the lives of men and women; and clothing is an arena in which we can explore this. Women's lives at all stages are more closely policed with regard to appearance than is the case with men. This carries forward into ageing, where the visible signs of age act to erode a woman's cultural status earlier. For men, particularly middle-class men, signs of age like greying temples and lines can enhance their standing, pointing to sources of power and status associated with age. Women, by contrast, are subject to judgements that require them to meet the youthful ideal. Normative femininity is formed around an image of youthfulness. This is a central part of its construction, and any derogation from it erodes a woman's status, calling into question her membership of the category, so that ageing is experienced by many women as a form of cultural exile from femininity itself. These judgements pertain most strongly to appearance, but they leak across into the field of dress. In the chapters that follow I examine the specific ways in which age and gender intersect in clothing norms, looking in particular at the differential and gendered ways these apply to women, specifically in the harsher moral judgements that are made with regard to their appearance and their failure to meet the norms of youthful femininity, or their transgression in attempting to do so through 'unsuitable', overly youthful dress.

Clothing and dress can also contribute to debates around the role of the cultural economy in shaping the nature of people's lives under high modernity, specifically through the ways in which the media and the commercialized world of goods act upon people's understandings and experiences of age. Ageing is culturally contingent, shaped by a complex of material, social and symbolic influences, among which are increasingly those of consumption culture. The media and the fashion industry are actively engaged in presenting new ways of being to older people. Design needs to be understood here as a normative process in which implicit assumptions are made about the meanings and values encoded in cultural goods. The fashion industry acts as a cultural mediator, interpreting the times to its customers, and in doing so proposing new ways of being an older person, though of course the language of 'old' and 'older' is always avoided in this consumption-oriented, aspirational culture. Magazines aimed at this sector see a significant part of their role as advising women how to negotiate what is seen as the tricky territory of later years, showing them how to adjust their changing appearance to make it more acceptable, and by implication younger, and how to select clothes that are age appropriate, not too young or too old, successfully displaying continuing engagement with the cultural practices of normative femininity. Clothing retailers are similarly engaged in proposing new ways of being older. They are closely interested in the grey market, and, recognizing its potential, have attempted to draw it into the fashion arena. Traditionally older people's dress has been sourced from slowly evolving lines on the edges of the fashion market, but increasingly retailers have aimed to integrate the older market more fully into the mainstream, proposing newer, fresher, more fashionable looks for older people, and with them a faster fashion cycle. As a result, the lives and bodies of older people have increasingly been colonized by the concept of fashionability. These developments have largely been presented in positive terms, expanding the social opportunities of older people, increasing their cultural visibility, but they have a darker, more negative potential also. New opportunities bring new expectations, new requirements in relation to the presentation of the body, which is increasingly made subject to forms of governmentality that require individuals to display the active repudiation of age through engagement with consumption practices like fashion. As a result, though fashion offers an opportunity of cultural integration to older people, it does so at a price. Linking oneself to the fashion cycle with its rhythm of the seasons and constant representation of looks does offer older women tropes of renewal in a cultural context where these are few, but these tropes intersect with the bodily experience of ageing in ultimately discouraging ways, pointing up the ways in which renewal no longer works in the way that it once did.

Through dress we can also engage with debates around the role of embodiment in culture. All cultures dress the body in some form; and clothing and dress are central to the ways bodies are managed and expressed. They are the vestimentary envelope that presents the body in a social setting. As a result there is a constant interplay between the body and dress, with the two operating dialectically: dress works on the body, imbuing it with social meaning; while the body is a dynamic field that gives life and fullness to dress (Entwistle 2000: 327). Dress thus allows me to explore some of the complex ways the body is present within culture. This is particularly significant in the context of society's understandings around age. The body is indeed central to ageing: it is through changes in the body that we come to recognize our own and other's ageing. But age is also culturally contingent: its meanings and experiences shaped by the discourses, practices, norms and values of the surrounding culture. Among these are norms and practices in relation to dress, many of which reflect ideas about the body and its presentation. Clothing thus allows us to address the mediation between bodily and cultural forms of ageing, exploring how the culture of ageing is in part shaped by embodied experience, at the same time as addressing the ways cultural fields like dress play a part in the embodied constitution of age.

Focussing on clothing and dress also helps shift the ways in which researchers think about age academically, widening the context within which it is analysed. Until recently, age was primarily discussed in the context of social welfare, with a heavy emphasis on frailty and decline. But new academic influences are changing this. Over the last decade, partly in response to the wider cultural turn across the social sciences, there has been a concerted effort to look at later years in a different way, one that encompasses wider themes, theories and methodologies. Under the label of *cultural gerontology,* this has addressed later years as a whole, providing what has previously been absent—a proper sociology of old age. Though sociology often refers to age and its increasing significance in modern society, it rarely engages with the topic in a wholehearted way. As a result there is little real sociology of age. Cultural gerontology is in effect providing this, drawing in a wider range of theorizing, including work influenced by postmodern and poststructuralist analyses, expanding the subject matter of age to include topics like consumption, leisure and the media, as well as analytic areas like embodiment and the visual. This book contributes to this development, aiming to widen the range of discourses within which the experience of ageing is caught, as well as offering new fields in which to explore the lives of older people and the ways they are shaped by culture. The new gerontology has also drawn in work from other academic traditions, notably the arts and humanities, with revived interest in subjectivities and identities as expressed in novels, painting and cultural production generally. These have been joined by a renewed historiography of age that looks beyond the earlier focus on frailty, dependence and the institutions of the welfare state to uncover the historical experiences of people in their later years. Once again these developments are reflected in this book.

Age as a social category has itself expanded, with the tendency to shift the chronology of 'later years' back into late middle age. As a result 'age studies' now starts in the fifties. These processes have the potential to reach further back, as analysts increasingly acknowledge the significance of age as an ordering principle throughout the life course. When and how ageing is deemed to set in also varies in different cultural fields. As we shall see in relation to high fashion, ageing arrives early, certainly by the late twenties. In the related field of appearance, women begin to experience pressure around the signs of age promoted by the cosmetics industry from their late thirties. These processes intersect with other social categorizations such as gender and class. Women, for example, are commonly believed to age earlier than men; they are certainly subject to more stringent evaluation in relation to their appearance and failure to meet the youthful norm of femininity. Social class operates similarly to protect elite groups, enabling them to remain longer within the mainstream category of 'not yet old'.

Clothing and dress also allow researchers to address debates around the reconstitution of age. Across both academic and popular accounts, there is a pervasive belief that the nature of old age—or later years as it is often conceptualized in this debate—has undergone significant change over the last thirty years. This is partly the product of changing demographics that mean that older people represent a growing proportion of the population. Living into old age is also now the majority expectation. It also reflects wider social change in relation to the life course in which stages of life have become more fluid and less clearly defined. Together these features have produced a sense that later years today are different, constituted in different ways, more flexible and contingent than was in the case in the past. With this goes a belief that older people are in some sense 'younger' than in the past, with their lives more integrated culturally with those of the mainstream. Fields like consumption are seen as significant arenas in which such integration has occurred. Clothing and dress thus offer fields within which we can explore these debates. Is the dress of older people still as age-ordered as it was in the past? Have the norms governing appropriate dress in relation to age weakened, or shifted? Has everyone 'moved younger' in their dress so that, in the language of the media, sixty is the new fifty or forty?

By studying the material reality of dress I can also contribute to debates around the politics of ageing. There is a long history whereby discrimination and prejudice are expressed at the level of the body. We are familiar with this in the expression of misogyny in relation to women and their bodies, and racism in relation to ethnic minorities, but it is also true in relation to old people. At a profound level, ageism is a bodily based form of oppression carried forward at a visceral level in responses to the appearance of old people. It is this that underpins the pervasive culture of anti-ageing, as older people attempt to avoid diminished status by trying to fight off the visible appearance of age that will expose them to cultural erosion and discrimination. Though facial and bodily appearance are at the centre of these concerns, clothing can also play a part in entrenching or mitigating these judgements, as seen in the pervasive drive to 'move younger' in terms of dress.

Clothes are thus implicated in the politics of age through their larger role as bearers of cultural meaning. As Barnard (1996) suggests, clothes are ideological. They encode values through which individuals are ranked and judged; and they mark out and naturalize hierarchies of power and status. This includes those in relation to age; and it is clear that there are aspects of the dress traditionally associated with age that carry such meanings—the dull, drab, dark, self-effacing, don't-look-at-me styles associated with age that express marginalization, withdrawal and secondary status. Ageing is a political process. Challenging these clothing norms can thus be read as a challenge to the political status of older people in the widest sense.

Clothing and age thus resonate through a number of important debates. In the chapters that follow I explore these further, unpacking the ideas, experiences and assumptions that underlie them, relating them to evidence from a range of sources, including the voices of older women themselves, the commentary of journalists, and the views and experiences of design directors in clothing companies.

−2−

Clothing, Fashion and the Body

In this chapter I explore the ways fashion, clothing and dress have been theorized, focussing in particular on the intersections between clothing and identity and their relevance to questions of age. I look at the ways in which dress operates as part of the micro social order and the distinctive significance of age in this. I also examine the role of age ordering in dress, and the commonly expressed idea that this is no longer significant in the way it was in the past. Lastly, I suggest that age has become incorporated into the structures of fashion itself, replacing the previous dominance of class as an engine in the diffusion of styles.

Fashion, Clothing and Dress

The focus of this book is clothing and dress rather than fashion itself. In general fashion denotes a particular sort of dress—the fashionable or the fashion-related—or a particular aesthetic realm—that of fashion and the cultural forces that create it. It is an exclusionary term containing a sense of forms of dress that are not considered fashion, though the boundaries of these are variably drawn, so that for some, fashion ends at the inner core of cutting-edge designers, and for others it extends to the more style-conscious parts of the mainstream. In general, however, the old are not considered to fall within fashion's orbit, or to do so only weakly or contentiously. As a result, *fashion* is a somewhat problematic term to deploy in this study, suggesting a field from which older people are largely excluded.

The term is also problematic because of the negative sense that attaches to it in traditional academic circles and beyond. Fashion here stands for the trivial and superficial. There is a widespread sense in the Academy that fashion is a shallow subject not meriting serious analysis. As Tseëlon (2001) notes, to engage in research on dress is to place oneself on the fringes of academic respectability. Mainstream sociology indeed inherited many of the prejudices against fashion found in the work of earlier puritan and moralistic writers, who saw it as a species of vanity focussed on external surface not inner essence. Sociology, with its bias towards rationality and the masculine-defined worlds of work and the public sphere, carried this negative evaluation forward into its own value system, treating subjects like fashion as lightweight and superficial. These subjects' association with the feminine further undermined their status; and as Entwistle (2000) notes, there are parallels here with the initial disregard within sociology of topics like the body and emotion. More recently, however, with the rise of cultural studies and the shift towards the postmodern themes of identity and agency, and with the new emphasis on the visual, some of the negativity around fashion as a subject has gone. Cultural studies has, however, displayed its own limitations through its emphasis on the edgy and transgressive, reproducing the values of the youthful elite in its own analyses. As a result the range of identities it has explored is limited, and older people are generally excluded from the field.

Despite this negativity, sociology has engaged with a concept of fashion, and in doing so, it has given it a distinctive meaning. Fashion, from the time of Simmel (1904/1971), has predominantly been theorized within sociology as the cycle of continual, institutionalized change associated with the development of industrial or consumption-oriented Western societies. Though encompassing novelty and change in relation to all cultural goods, dress has come to exemplify the process, so much so that the word *fashion* has itself come to denote clothing and the clothing industry. The link between fashion and modernity has been widely theorized by, among others, Lipovetsky (1994), though the association has been criticized for being less uniform or direct than he and others suggest. Many historians of dress indeed argue that the origins of fashion lie earlier, in the emergence of court society in Burgundy in the late Middle Ages (Steele 1997); and some have questioned the perception of fashion as a distinctively Western phenomenon, suggesting that it is found in other cultures too (Craik 1994).

Fashion can also be understood in terms of the complex of material and cultural production which forms it and in which economic, technological, commercial and aesthetic influences all operate. Fine and Leopold (1993) conceptualize this as the Fashion System, the nexus of commercial, design and media influences that together provide the principal sources of changing aesthetic judgements about clothes, determining choices available in the market and providing the goods to satisfy these. This system, Entwistle (2000) argues, provides the raw materials for most everyday dress, both in the sense of the garments themselves and in the discourses and aesthetic ideas about them. All aspects of dress in the West are to some extent influenced by it. It is, however, not the only source, and other socially entrenched ideas, including ones in relation to age, mediate its influence.

As a result, the sources of meaning in dress are more plural and complex than the classic sociological model of centre and periphery suggests. Recognizing this, Polhemus and Proctor (1978) developed the concept of 'anti-fashion'. They pointed to the range of dress that does not aspire to be part of fashion, and indeed rejects overt connection with it, pointing to fixed or slowly evolving forms of dress that are outside its realm and that uphold tradition and symbolize the values of the social order. Davis (1992) extended the term to express the rejection of fashion, whether from the perspective of opposition or studied neglect; and he outlined cultural styles such as 'feminist protest', 'countercultural insult' and 'conservative scepticism'. The last he regards as the blandest form of anti-fashion, though also the most economically significant because it is so pervasive. Crane (2000) quotes a survey that reported that half of American women said they were not interested in fashion; and of the third that said they were, the majority were young. Lack of interest in fashion is, therefore, fairly widespread, especially among the middle-aged and older. *Anti-fashion* is, however, not a wholly satisfactory term because it mixes up oppositional subcultures and conservative elites disengaged from and feeling superior to the realm of fashion. But the point that lies behind it is well made, and is particularly relevant to groups like older people, especially men, who largely inhabit this conservative world of anti-fashion.

Fashion writing itself has traditionally ignored older people. The fashion literature, like the fashion industry, is concerned with spectacle, display and creativity; it celebrates the edgy, the fashionable, the erotic and the transgressive. And it disproportionately focusses on elite forms of dress like haute couture or the work of cutting-edge designers (Evans 2003). The bulk of mainstream, day-to-day clothing receives relatively little analysis. This is all the more so in relation to older people's dress, which is almost wholly ignored in writing about fashion. Part of the reason for this relates to the values of the fashion world itself. Fashion is strongly—perhaps inherently—youth-oriented. It is beautiful, young bodies that designers aspire to dress and that are featured throughout the Fashion System. It presents an idealized world in which age does not feature, or in which it represents a dereliction, a corruption of the vision, a falling-off and failure, something to be excluded and ignored. Ageing here takes on the character of Kristeva's (1982) abjection, something to be feared, repelled, cast into darkness. From the perspective of mainstream fashion, age is simply not attractive or sexy; and comments from the editor of *Vogue,* as we shall see, confirm and naturalize this sense. Fashion is indeed closely linked to the erotic—so much so that for some theorists the constant play of eroticism is the engine force of fashion and the key to its meaning and deep appeal. Older people, particularly women, are regarded as beyond the erotic, indeed, particularly in the eyes of the young, beyond sex itself. Their clothing choices are, therefore, deemed of little interest to students of fashion: indeed to extend the analysis to this group would, in the eyes of many commentators, degrade the essence of fashion itself.

Social anthropology, by contrast, has a long history of taking clothing and dress seriously. Dress here is understood as encompassing more than simply clothing, extending to the wider assemblage of items into looks. The ways in which clothing is worn, the body styles deployed, as well as the dress objects themselves, have been the subject of a considerable literature within anthropology, reviewed by Hansen (2004) and Crane and Bovone (2006). The tradition has received further impetus from the wider material turn in anthropology and sociology in which clothing and dress have been part of the creation and attribution of symbolic values to material culture. Miller and others have explored the ways material objects like the physical surroundings of the home become significant in meaning-making, representing aspects of distributed personhood (Miller 1987, 1998; Küchler and Miller 2005; Guy et al. 2001; Weber and Mitchell 2004; S. Woodward 2007). Dress can be part of this.

The emphasis on clothes as material objects finds echoes in museum-based dress studies which has similarly treated garments or accessories as concrete texts (Taylor 2002, 2004; Beaujot 2012). Such object-based scholarship focusses on how the cut, styling and fabric reveal aspects of their meaning—the ways they have been abraded by work, shaped around the body and its changes, adapted and recut for pregnancy or age. In this 'pathological' approach (Breward 2003: 64), garments are no longer the pristine objects of the museum tradition, but living evidence of the embodied physicality of dress. Though this study does not attempt to engage with clothes in quite that way, such approaches serve as reminders of the significance of the materiality of dress and its interrelationship with the body. The cut and drape of clothes reflect assumptions about the sorts of bodies that will inhabit them, so much so that these can be read across from the physical objects to those who will or did occupy them. An example of such an approach is found in work of the Finnish design academic Iltanen-Tähkävuori who used the concrete reality of a series of garments as a starting point to interrogate assumptions made by designers about the individuals—in her case older people and those with dementia—who would wear them (Iltanen 2005; Topo and Iltanen-Tähkävuori 2010; Iltanen-Tähkävuori et al. 2012). Designers in the study initially asserted that age did not matter in their design practice, but as they handled and analysed the concrete garments, the implicit assumptions they held about age began to emerge. Clothes designed for the mainstream older market do reveal themselves through their cut and fit; indeed one of the ways it is possible to identify retailers who are addressing this market is through examining the cut of their clothes. Those aimed at the older market tend to be cut more generously, longer and looser, and for women, with lower bust seams and for men, higher rise in the trousers. The nature of dress is thus shaped by the bodies and lives of the people who wear it. This understanding helps to shift the focus of analysis away from the abstract, mind-centred accounts that have typified much fashion theory, which shares a bias towards abstraction characteristic of postmodernism and its influence on body studies more generally, and towards a more concrete engagement with the lived, material reality of dress as worn by the majority.

The textiles used can also be significant. The garment industry is itself a very material field, centred around the production of physical objects in the form of clothing and rooted in the developments of the textile industry, which has, particularly during the twentieth century, developed a range of new, scientifically based textiles (Handley 1999; Hibbert 2001; O'Connor 2005, 2011). Some of these—Crimplene, Spandex—have particular symbolic resonance in relation to age. Crimplene, developed by Du Pont, was originally part of the scientific miracle of the 1960s, but by the 1970s it had become a byword for unfashionability. As Schneider (1994) shows, it was held in particular distain by young middle-class Americans who, as part of the wider turn to nature in the 1970s, became enchanted by the virtues of natural fibres and were repelled by its bright 'plastic' qualities. With its indestructible washability, it has become inextricably associated with elderly women in care homes. As a result, for many women in the study, it has become the fibre to dread (though such is the ever-shifting nature of fashion that Crimplene recently experienced a minor revival in the youthful avant-garde). Lycra, also developed by Du Pont, by contrast retained its positive associations. O'Connor (2011) has explored its distinctive role in the bodily experiences of the baby boomer generation where it emerged initially as part of the dancewear and aerobics trend of the 1980s, but was borne forward into later decades by its role in allowing stretch and give for figures that began by the 2000s to age, losing their firmness and welcoming more elastic, forgiving fabric. The anthropological tradition of reading the meaning from the object, reflected in O'Connor's account, allows me in a similar way to explore some of the unarticulated links that lie between forms of dress that are thought appropriate for the very old and the very young. The dress of the very young and the very old is similar in terms of materials, colours and fastenings, with bright pale colours, easy-clean fabrics and elastic cut. I return to these links between babyhood and age later in this chapter.

Consumption and the Dream of Renewal

Clothes can also be theorized in terms of consumption culture. Early analyses of consumption were dominated by Marxist approaches that saw it as epiphenomenal, something secondary to production, resting on the stimulation of false needs and unauthentic desires and undermining true feelings and real experiences (Aldridge 2003; Paterson 2006). In the writings of the Frankfurt school in particular, consumers were presented as cultural dupes manipulated by capitalism; and there are links here with second-wave feminism and its identification of fashion as inauthentic and distorting. More recently, however, work on consumption has taken a more neutral approach, treating it as an everyday act within modern culture. Work by Douglas and Isherwood (1979) took forward analyses that present consumption as a symbolic practice, a form of expression that makes visible and stable the category of culture. Miller (1998) in particular has reasserted the tradition whereby objects are recognized as having cultural significance as well as use, so that consumers, rather than being cultural dupes, are agentic beings actively engaged in fashioning self and identity through material things, and in this way recovering the object from the alienated process of production (Dant 2007). This approach is particularly relevant for accounts such as this that focus on the lived reality of dress.

Consumption rests on the stimulations of new desires; and fashion through its origins in competitive emulation acts to deliver this. Clothing has thus played a central role in the development of consumption culture. At a historical level, the textile industry is one of the engines of the Industrial Revolution that produced consumer society. Clothing and dress are also central elements in the planned obsolescence of consumer society; indeed they epitomize these processes, for without the systematic institutionalized change exemplified in fashion, there would be no impetus to buy more goods, particularly in areas like clothing where in the wealthy West most people already possess more than is sufficient for their material needs. These processes of planned obsolescence and the material resources needed to support them are, however, at the heart of the growing critique of the world economy in ecological terms, something that is itself reflected in growing uneasiness in the fashion industry around ecological issues, evidenced in Marks & Spencer's recent campaign encouraging the return of garments as a basis for new purchases.

At the heart of the rhetoric of fashion is the language of renewal and rebirth. Clothes offer the possibility of constant renewal of the self; indeed part of the excitement and joy of fashion comes from this capacity. Fashion provides what one of the journalists in the study called 'a lift... a bit of a tonic'. This sense of renewal, resting on the re-presentation of the self, underlies the way people use shopping as means to enhance themselves and their mood, as well as to extend their sense of self through the acquisition of material goods (though this also has malignant versions in the form of compulsive buying (Lee and Mysyk 2004)). The language of the seasons that permeates the fashion system and around which it is structured reflects this sense of constant renewal, the capacity of fashion to promise how consumers might, in Larkin's words, 'begin afresh, afresh, afresh' (1988: 166).

But this intersects with the experience of age in complex and ultimately discouraging ways, as changes in the body and appearance mean that the processes of renewal begin to falter. Each new season presents new modes, but increasingly ones that may not flatter or fit. As Featherstone and Hepworth (1991) note in their celebrated account of the Mask of Ageing, the body as it ages finds it increasingly difficult to enact a youthful inner self. As a result there is a growing discordance between the processes of fashion renewal and the physical basis for them in the form of the ageing body. The discordance is not total, and the promised renewal continues to work, but to a lesser degree and with disquieting subtexts.

These influences, of course, only operate for those interested in engaging with fashion, which many older people, especially men, are not. For them, what is more significant is the attraction, not of new, but old clothes, and of established forms of dress that leave the individual free *not* to engage with the realm of consumption. This sense of disengagement underlies much of the conservatism that marks the dress of the old, where the changes of the fashion cycle have ceased to exert their cultural pull. Indeed, many older people give up buying clothes to any great extent because they feel that they already have enough to 'see them out'. This encourages the widely held view among marketers that the old as a group are relatively uninterested in consumption and are, as a result, a poor focus for marketing.

Clothing and the Body

Clothing is intimately linked to the body. As Entwistle notes, no culture leaves the body unadorned, so that clothes are one of the means whereby bodies are made social, given identity and meaning. Dress needs to be understood as, in Entwistle's words, 'situated body practice' (2000: 11). Getting up and dressed is thus a process of preparing the body for the social world, both an intimate experience of the body and a public presentation of it. But when we get dressed we do so within the bounds of a culture and its particular norms. We even see the body through the conventions of dress, as Hollander (1978) showed in her historical analysis of the nude in painting, in which she showed how the shape of the nude body is determined by the clothes that it is *not* wearing: nudes representing dressed bodies, but without their clothes. Dress thus works on the body, imbuing it with social meaning; while the body is a dynamic field that gives life and fullness to dress. The two operate dialectically (Entwistle 2000: 327). Dress lies on the margin of the body, marking the boundary between self and others, individual and society. This boundary is intimate and personal, yet also cultural and collective, structured by social and moral pressures.

Though the intersections between the body and its social presentation are relevant to all ages, they take on particular significance in relation to age. To a large extent we experience our own and others' ageing through changes to the body; and these intersect with norms about dress. I explore these processes more fully in the next chapter and in the empirical ones that follow, though noting here how dress needs to be understood as part of a set of wider processes disciplining the body, constraining and enabling its expression. As such, it can be interpreted in Foucauldian terms, forming one of the ways bodies are discursively produced and made subject to the exercise of bio power, made subject to forms of governmentality. Dress acts on the body, rendering it meaningful. We can see this very clearly through dress codes of the workplace or uniforms in hospitals or prisons (Ash 2010) whereby bodies are disciplined and rendered docile and productive. In relation to age, similar modes of disciplinarity apply, in particular through the imposition of codes that express and shape ideas about what it is to be old.

Dress, thus, forms part of the micro social order. As such it is subject to discourses of morality, frequently spoken of in moral terms: good, bad, faultless, correct, vulgar, tarty, cheap. Like food, dress attracts a language that reaches beyond the phenomena being described, encompassing a powerful moral charge. There is an overdetermined quality to these descriptions that draws strength from the ways clothing, like food, is a cultural field concerned with the body, its expression and control. How we look is linked to how we will be judged; and bodies that do not conform to the rules of dress flout the conventions of a culture, risking exclusion, scorn and ridicule (Entwistle 2000). Being correctly dressed is thus an element of engaging successfully with the social world. Entwistle (2000) notes the unease and anxiety that attach to failing to meet the standards required by the moral order of the social space; and individuals feel vulnerable and embarrassed if their dress lets them down through laddered tights, drooping hems or other failures of appearance.

This moral ordering in dress bears down on older people in distinctive ways. We can identify three of these. The first relates to the threat of dereliction that attaches to later years. Here, lapses of dress can take on new and threatening meanings. Stains, visible food marks, gaping buttons, marks and tears become not just offences against performance norms of the social space, but signals of a larger social and moral decline. If ignored they can threaten the standing of an older person and his or her capacity to remain part of mainstream society. The bodies of older people are thus judged more strictly and more negatively than those of the young. There is no longer the possibility, in the context of age, of Herrick's 'sweet disorder of the dress': the erotic possibility of the disorder celebrated by the poet evaporates with age, to be replaced by untidiness—or worse—dereliction. Older people thus find themselves caught within a harsher moral climate in relation to dress—harsher that is, if they want to resist the reduced and changed identities that such failings signal. Remaining well-dressed, or at least acceptably so, thus becomes part of maintaining an acceptable presence as an older person.

Disciplinary discourses also operate differentially in the forms of dress thought appropriate—or more significantly inappropriate—for older people to wear. I explore these processes more fully in the section on age ordering and in the chapters that follow, but simply note here the moral force that attaches to such judgements and their roots in ideas about the body and its management. Most of the rules relating to dress in age reflect underlying assumptions about the body and its evaluation, most frequently in the form of avoiding excessive exposure through short skirts, low necks and strappy tops. One of the most powerful discursive formations for older women is the traditional cultural trope of 'mutton dressed as lamb'. An old-fashioned phrase, whose culinary referent is now largely lost, it is still widely recognized and used as a term of control, policing women's appearance and disciplining their bodies (Fairhurst 1998; Holland 2004; Hurd Clark et al. 2009). The behaviour it castigates is dressing in an inappropriately youthful way, but underlying this is the meaning of an inappropriately sexual way (Fairhurst 1998). It was alluded to and recognized in a number of the study interviews; and it even appeared in the interview with the editor of *Vogue*. The term is most commonly applied to women in late middle age, and it has connotations of looking tarty, like an old slag or slapper. The references to prostitution reinforce the sexual nature of the condemnation, and the sense that is related to expressions of sexuality deemed inappropriate and disruptive of the moral order. It is a gendered phrase only applied to women: like many sorts of sexual condemnation, there is no equivalent for men, once again reinforcing the ways age, gender and sexuality intersect.

There is a third and additional way in which the bodies and dress of older people are made subject to disciplinary discourses, and this relates to new demands around bodily presentation and appearance. The body in the West has increasingly become, in Shilling's (2003) words, 'a project', a source of personal identity and focus for disciplinary practices aimed at this-worldly forms of meaning, displacing the older disciplinary and ascetic practices of religion. We can observe this in the slim, toned, fit body ideal (as well as in malignant versions in terms of eating disorders and wide-spread body anxiety, notably among young women (Bordo 1993; MacSween 1993; Gimlin 2002). It is reflected also in consumption practices. As part of this, new moral demands are placed on older people in regard to their appearance. I explore these new modes of govermentality more fully in the next chapter. As a result, however, it is no longer acceptable simply to be and look old. Increasingly the requirement is to discipline the body in ways that show commitment to resisting age, through such strategies as strenuous dieting or beauty practices. Clothing and dress can be part of this, with the spread of new expectations that older people—women especially—will remain up to date and fashionably dressed, and with that part of the mainstream.

Gender and Dress

Clothing and dress are strongly gendered fields. As a result, much of the writing on dress has been heavily influenced by feminism. Feminists of the second wave, however, tended to be critical of fashion and its impact on the lives of women. Fashion was seen as imposing oppressive forms of gender identity, embodying practices designed to objectify and limit women, locking them into defensive and inauthentic forms of presentation (Friedan 1963; Greer 1971; Daly 1979; Evans and Thornton 1989; Bartky 1990; Jeffries 2005). It distorted the natural body through subordinating practices like high heels and corsets, reducing women to objects of a sexualizing gaze, rendering them unable to act effectively in the world. It diverted women's energies into trivial questions of appearance and reinforced negative stereotypes of women as ever-changing, inconstant and narcissistic. More recently, feminists influenced by postmodernism have taken a less negative view, recognizing the inescapability of matters of style and cultural formation in relation to the body and appearance. They have also been more willing to see fashion as part of a distinctive women's culture, an area of pleasure and expressivity that goes beyond the reproduction of patriarchy and capitalism (E. Wilson 1985).

It remains the case, however, that dress is closely implicated in the reproduction of gender. For many theorists (E. Wilson 1985; Davis 1992; Tseëlon 1995; Entwistle 2000) gender is indeed the central preoccupation of fashion; and it forms one of the most clearly marked aspects of dress across most cultures. As Kidwell and Steele (1989) show, the complex interplay of gender is at the heart of many clothing styles. Clothes reflect the body at the same time as they obscure it, being widely used to hide sexual difference in the strongly biological sense, while pointing up and signalling it through assumptions concerning gender in clothing codes. Clothing thus acts to deliver gender as self-evident or natural, when it is in reality a cultural construct, reproducing gender as a form of body style and reinforcing the complex interplay between sexed bodies and gendered identities. Fashion thus plays a critical part in the way femininities (and masculinities) are rendered, played out, resisted and understood (Holland 2004), contributing to a set of gendered behaviours and practices that are themselves fluid, shifting and contextual.

A range of earlier work has explored the ways the female body is unfinished business, regarded as deficient in its natural form, unsatisfactory, requiring constant vigilance and repeated beauty work for it to be made acceptable and feminine. For Bartky (1990, 1999) and others, fashion and beauty practices are modes of body discipline, producing self-regulating female subjects through the demonstration of control over the physical body. Body management becomes a means of normalizing and disciplining the female body, ensuring its innate unruliness is tamed and made acceptable. In terms of dress, Davis (1992) points to the dual character of such disciplinary processes through the example of the modern bra, which both conceals and enhances the female sexual form, constituting the female body in a directly erotic form at the same time as controlling and obscuring it.

This moulding of the female body into acceptable social forms is also found in relation to age. Beauty practices, especially anti-ageing ones, are part of the process of producing an acceptable form of woman in later years—still feminine, still displaying engagement with the disciplinary practices of femininity, yet in a toned-down way that accepts the lesser claims to attention and regard. In relation to clothing this means still wearing feminine or fashionable dress, showing that the individual is still involved, still trying to present a good appearance, and not falling into the dangers of neglect and potential dereliction. It can involve showing a continuing commitment to fashion in the form of the trends of the high street, but without straying into overly youthful dress. As Hurd Clarke and colleagues comment in their study of older Canadian women:

> By clothing their bodies deliberately and in accordance with socially sanctioned prescriptions, the women effectively managed the impressions of others through the projection of a happy, healthy and cogitatively intact self. (2009: 724)

Acceptable dress was thus a means of maintaining status in the context of its erosion.

In this book I focus largely on women. The empirical study on which it draws (see appendix) was confined to older women. This reflects the reality of the older population, which is predominantly female. (Ironically it is older men who have been somewhat neglected in academic studies of age recently.) Primarily, however, it reflects the way fashion is constituted as a feminized field, whose discourses are differentially embodied in the lives of women: women shop for clothes more frequently and spend more (on average half again compared with men); they engage more fully with the subject through the popular media; and, most significant, they are associated culturally with the ideas of fashion and appearance. Most writing on fashion and dress, whether popular or academic, centres on women. Taking women as the focus also provides a link across to the extensive body of work influenced by feminism concerning the body, appearance and gender.

Men have traditionally been excluded from the territory of fashion. Within modern Western hegemonic masculinity, fashion is seen as a somewhat uneasy, even dangerous territory. Active interest in it is traditionally regarded as effeminate, associating men with the triviality or narcissism of women. Masculine identity, Crane (2000) suggests, is traditionally constituted as fixed and innate, and conscious attempts to construct identity through clothing are thus viewed as suspect, implying something lightweight or insubstantial. This is despite the rich history of men's use of dress (notably in uniforms and formal dress) to denote identity and signal status. Indeed until the period of the Great Renunciation from the second half of the eighteenth century when men renounced brightly coloured and embroidered silks for sober woollen garments (Flugel 1930), the dress of elite men was as flamboyant and splendid as women's (McNeil and Karaminas 2009). These strictures have eased somewhat recently with the emergence of metrosexual man; and younger men are now more openly engaged with fashion and appearance. However, it remains the case that older men are largely disengaged from fashion as a cultural field.

This is not to say that clothing and dress are irrelevant to their lives. Indeed from an anthropological or material culture perspective, they cannot be. Older men also get dressed, make choices about their appearance, present their bodies in culturally distinctive ways and express consumption choices in the market. Men's dress is at least as culturally coded as that of women; indeed in many ways the codes are stricter and more closely defined, the range within which they operate narrower, so that a slight adjustment of cut or detail, of tone or texture, can signal right or wrong dress for a particular person or social group. Men's clothes, however, are less governed by fashion and its volatility. There is a slower fashion cycle, with more garments falling into the category of slowly evolving staples rather than fashion goods. There is a lesser aspiration to look fashionable, indeed doing so can carry negative connotations. This closer coding and slower evolution of styles means that it is in some ways easier to observe certain dynamics in relation to clothing and age, in particular the significance of age as a replacement for class in the dynamic of fashion and the diffusion of styles. We shall explore this more fully below.

Men are, however, subject to many of the same norms in regard to dress and age that women are, though in milder form. Older men too learn to avoid styles deemed too youthful by virtue of their fashionability, showiness or exposure of flesh, though as I noted earlier the dominant codes for men's dress mean that these elements are more muted than is the case for women. They thus share in some of the negative evaluations of the body and age encoded in dress for older women.

Men's status, however, is less tied to their appearance than is the case with women. There is not the same requirement that they present themselves in their dress in terms of heterosexual appeal, an aspect that remains a powerful element in women's dress. Men by contrast, particularly middle-class men, dress to exhibit power and status. (Though the latter is not absent from women's clothing, it is expressed differently.) This means that dress and age are differently constituted for men and women. Older men still can (to some extent) draw on forms of dress that express embodied status, for example the suit; whereas for older women there is greater discordance between their presentation and the youthful ideal that dominates dress codes and that is a crucial part of the constitution of femininity in the modern West. Normative femininity is youthful, and this means that the changes in appearance that occur with age erode the status of women in a much more direct way.

Clothing, Identity and Social Order

Dress, as Entwistle (2000) notes, plays an important part in the mundane business of reproducing social order, and there is a long-established link in dress studies between clothing and social identity. Clothes are indeed, as Breward (2000) notes, one of the ways social difference is made concrete and visible. I have noted this already in relation to gender, but I need also to recognize its role in other forms of social difference. The most notable of these is, of course, the link with social class. From the time of Veblen (1899) and Simmel (1904/1971) onwards, sociologists have explored the way clothing operates as part of class identity, with fashions diffusing down the social hierarchy as they are successively adopted and abandoned by elites and as lower groups take them up. Competitive class emulation is thus the engine of fashion, understood here as institutionalized, systematic change. Bourdieu (1984) offered a more nuanced account of these processes of class distinction and diffusion in which dress is seen as an aspect of cultural capital, part of how elites establish, maintain and reproduce their positions of power, reinforcing relations of dominance and subordination through their capacity to define what is fashionable or correct and to abandon it once it becomes mainstream and commonplace.

More recently, the democratization of fashion and the rise of street styles have challenged the dominance of class in sociological accounts of fashion, introducing more plural sources of style and allowing for bottom-up accounts of meaning and value in dress, as well as diffusion of styles (Davis 1992; Crane 2000). The coterminosity of social and cultural elites has also been questioned. As a result, other dimensions of social identity are increasingly emphasized. There is a growing sense that different meanings in relation to dress are significant and other dynamics are in play in the diffusion of styles.

The emphasis on street styles and bottom-up sources has sometimes led to fashion and identity being theorized in subcultural terms, in which clothing and body styling acts as markers of the boundaries of the group, or, in Polhemus's term, 'tribe', a means of stabilizing identity and registering belonging (Polhemus 1994; Evans 1997). Hebdige (1979) indeed regarded consumption as central to subcultural identity. Such approaches focus on youth culture, street styles and transgressive, countercultural modes; and they are rarely applied to conventional or dominant groups, though York's account of Sloane Ranger (York 1980; York and Barr 1982) and Le Wita's analysis (1994) of the French haute bourgeoisie is a notable exception. Older people do not fit easily or well into such subgroup analysis, which classically focusses on groups that can be regarded as deviant or in some degree oppositional. Though attempts have been made to interpret age as a form of deviant identity, the analogy remains strained. Though perhaps deviant in their marginalization from the mainstream, older people are not oppositional in culture, and it is not helpful to regard older styles as adopted for countercultural effect or to assert a deviant identity.

Dress is also significant in relation to other forms of social difference, for example sexuality. There is now a considerable literature on gay and lesbian fashion and its role in articulating the emergence of distinctive and visible subgroups around the expression of sexuality, particularly as it emerged in the twentieth century (Rolley 1993; Holliday 2001). Similar work has explored the ways race and ethnicity interact with norms of fashion, underpinning distinctively ethnic forms of dress, as well as the complex interactions between modes and styles associated with migrant cultures and their variation, expression and counter expression in the countries of adoption and subsequent descent (Khan 1993; Tulloch 2002; Tarlo 2010). Dress has also been analysed in terms of national identity, most typically in the form of distinctive national or regional dress and its codification and entrenchment as part of the history of nationalism. In the case of England, with its early move to an urban industrial society, such regional or national styles are largely absent, though Breward and colleagues (2002) in their *Englishness of English Dress* identify distinctive national traditions in clothing. Dress can also signal identity in terms of personal character or interests: a bookish disposition; an orientation to the arts or cultural interests; an enjoyment of sport or allegiance to a particular club or association. Dress can thus play an important part in signalling or erasing elements of identity, and is capable of exhibiting a complex of closely nuanced meanings.

Dress has also been theorized in semiotic terms, whereby clothing is presented as a linguistic code—a means whereby people send messages about themselves. Barthes (1985) presented a celebrated account of the Fashion System in such structuralist terms. But if clothing is a code, it is an inexact one. Empirical work suggests that meanings are not always fixed or shared, with the link between the intention of the wearer and the interpretation of the observer far from straightforward or apparent (Feinberg et al. 1992). Davis (1992) suggests clothing is a code, but one with what he terms 'low semanticity'; he argues we should regard it as an aesthetic rather than a linguistic code, communicating ambiguity and complexity. Steele makes a similar point likening the messages of dress to music as 'expressive in an indirect, allusive way' (1989: 6). As will be noted in Chapter 4, respondents in this study did not find it easy to articulate what their clothes said about them or their identities. Like with other cultural goods, the meanings of dress are immanent and hidden, subject to masking, interpretation and uncertainty.

Clothing and identity have also been theorized in terms of performativity, emphasizing their role in processes of self-realization and presentation. Judith Butler's (1993) work on drag and the performativity of gender has been particularly influential here. Such analyses have the advantage that they capture the dynamic interaction of self, body and dress, acknowledging the embodied nature of clothing as it both expresses identity to the outside world and acts back on and reinforces it for the individual at a directly physical level. Clothed bodies thus become as Craik (1994) suggests 'tools for self management', part of how we perform our identities, while also acting back on the self, reinforcing and endorsing the identity we perform. This is easy to see in terms of, for example, military uniforms and the ways they buttress a particular version of embodied masculinity; or the role of high heels and tight skirts in relation to sexualized femininity. Certain forms of dress thus permit or discourage certain forms of body performance. It is not just that clothes have particular meanings, but that they impose body styles that are themselves expressive and have the capacity to act back on the individual. This is as true of age as other social categories. High-heeled, thigh-high boots—not traditionally part of the performance of age—do not just look different from a knitted shawl drawn round the shoulders—epitomizing age—they also impose a different body stance. What you wear affects how you feel and to some degree how you will behave.

This sense of performativity is captured in the comments of a woman in her late seventies in an earlier study (Twigg 2010). Wearing conventional, elegant dress, she explained, was for her more comfortable than jeans or other garments conventionally associated with ease. She recounted how a young woman had challenged her:

> somebody once said—some young thing said—very emphatically, quite aggressively, 'Well what we insist on these days is comfort'. By which she meant really things not fitting properly, so she could move around. And I thought about this and I thought,... I'm comfortable sitting like this, conventionally in a chair with a back to it, but once you get people sprawling about in jeans, so then—I mean this skirt isn't confining, but it sort of encourages you not to sprawl about too much. But once they wear bifurcated garments that encourage sprawling, they do that, and so then you get these sofas that, you know, they're just sort of splodges that don't support you. And people, sort of, all over the place. And this, they regard as comfort. Well, that's fine if they're comfortable, but what they seem unable to grasp is that I, sitting like this, am also perfectly comfortable...Comfort isn't only physical, it's being mentally at ease also.

This quotation conveys very well the embodied identity of a certain sort of older woman. Reflecting the habitual manners of the individual, it is about being in the world and the continuity of that with identity and selfhood, expressed in and through performance. I explore the performativity of age further in the next chapter.

The Lived Experience of Dress

These understandings link to the growing tradition in sociology that explores the lived experience of dress and the ways clothes are contextualized, particularly in women's lives (Guy et al. 2001; Weber and Mitchell 2004; S. Woodward 2007). In emphasizing the voices of women, such approaches have parallels with reception studies in media research, refocussing analysis away from the production of goods and meanings and towards their consumption and interpretation. Most accounts of fashion or the fashion system present top-down movements of meaning from the cultural world, to goods that are inscribed with meanings that are then transmitted to the purchasers. Work by Guy and Banim (2000) and others, however, aims to reverse that flow of meaning, showing how clothes are deployed by individuals to create meaning and identity in their lives. Though they accept, in line with mainstream feminist analysis, that the fashion system is restrictive and can be oppressive, Guy and Banim argue that women can and do reappropriate and subvert the meanings carried in clothing. Weber and Mitchell (2004), in their account of 'dress stories', similarly aim to show how dress can be an entry point for personal and private autobiography, a springboard for the narration of personal memories. Such approaches chime with the new emphasis on consumption as a continuing process, something that is not confined to the moment of purchase, as it is in most marketing or economic analyses, but extending over time, part of a wider analysis of how consumers *become* through the process of *doing*. It also links to an analysis of consumption that presents it as performative, emotional and felt, in which consumers become through the process of enacting—by thinking through and with the body (Mansvelt 2009).

Sophie Woodward (2007), in her account of why women wear what they wear, has explored what she terms 'the wardrobe moment', the process whereby women reflect on what they are going to wear and how it embodies—or does not embody—their sense of self. Older women face a distinctive version of the wardrobe moment as they ponder the degree to which garments do or do not suit their changed bodies as they age. For Woodward, clothing is part of the process of extending the self in and through material objects, that draws on Gell's account of 'distributed personhood'. Clothing thus allows people to engage with questions of identity in a concrete, material way, seeing the self in externalized form. For Miller this process assumes an almost Hegelian quality whereby dress becomes a means through which the self is discovered and created in an ongoing process of self-actualization. Where the fusion between the self and the outfit is fully successful, the 'objectification' in Miller's terms (the word is not used pejoratively) is complete; where unsuccessful, it produces dysjunction, unease and self-consciousness. Clarke and Miller (2002), in their ethnography of shopping for clothes, reveal the anxiety this process can produce. Drawing on fieldwork in a North London street, they point to the uncertainty and unease many women feel when faced with the aesthetic and social choices contained in clothes. They note how this aspect of anxiety and unease has been ignored in the mainstream fashion literature with its celebratory emphasis on expressivity and self-fashioning.

The dominant account in fashion theorizing, particularly that influenced by postmodernism, is indeed in terms of choice and agency (Finkelstein 1991; Polhemus 1994), and it chimes well with how fashion is presented within consumption culture, in which there is an emphasis on creating a unique and individual version of the self through consumption goods. But these aspects of choice and agency in dress—as in other things—are greatly overstated. It is notable in modern society how similar people in fact appear. This is partly because individuals shop in a market shaped by mass production and the Fashion System (Fine and Leopold 1993), but it also reflects the truth that the range of people's self-expression is fairly narrow. At least as significant as agency and choice are the principles of conformity and order. Wearing the right clothes, the appropriate dress for the occasion, fitting in rather than standing out, are the dominant concerns of most people. As Simmel long ago pointed out, fashion needs to be understood in terms of the competing desires for social equalization and for individual differentiation, the interplay between the wish to fit in and to stand out (Simmel 1904/1971), in which, I would suggest, the first is in many ways the more significant. Indeed Clarke and Miller (2002) argue that postmodern fluidity and optionality are a source of anxiety as much as of pleasure and agency, with the wish to choose the right clothes and fear of choosing the wrong dominating many women's shopping choices. Franklin also notes the irony of how 'the increasing emphasis on individuality does not encourage us to create uniquely beautiful looks for ourselves' (2001: 138).

Clarke and Miller (2002) situate what is happening in relation to dress in the context of the long-term decline in the West of social structures supporting normative behaviour. Drawing on Habermas, they argue that modernity has produced conditions whereby the authority of institutions is eroded, and with it rules of conduct and behaviour. This has produced a fragmented culture, marked by anxiety as much as freedom, offering new opportunities for framing the self, for playing with identity and its instability, but also new uncertainties and anxieties. As a result, individuals are burdened with the task of creating meaning, and with it, normativity, for themselves. In relation to clothing, this is reflected in the decline of fashion authority, the easing up of rules about what might be worn and by whom. This has particular implications for the situations of older people, in some senses freeing them, but at the same time imposing new demands.

Davis (1992) argues that we need to understand clothes in terms of the interplay between personal and social identity. We are all actively engaged in the articulation of our identities, but in the context of powerful collective currents that impinge on our sense of self. Fashion addresses itself to these collective elements, acting upon the instabilities of social identity at both an individual and a collective level. This is what gives it its cultural force. His approach emphasizes the ambiguity and instability that lie at the heart of dress; an analysis shared by Tseëlon (1995). Davis focusses largely on gender, but his argument applies as much to age. He reminds us of the essential ambiguity and uncertainty that underlie many forms of cultural production, and of the need to retain these in our analyses, something of relevance when addressing questions of resistance and performativity in the next chapter.

Age Ordering

We have seen how clothing and identity are linked, most strongly in the case of the master identities of gender and class, though also in other dimensions of social difference such as ethnicity and sexuality. But such perspectives are rarely extended to age. But is not age also one of the master identities? How we are perceived, who we socialize with, how we are judged and ordered socially are all crucially determined by our age or our location within an age categorization. We should not, therefore, be surprised to find such distinctions expressed in dress.

The clearest way to highlight this is through the concept of 'age ordering'. By this I mean the systematic patterning of cultural expression according to an ordered and hierarchically arranged concept of age. It can clearly be seen in relation to children, where at least since the late eighteenth century, and often earlier, children have worn distinctive age-related forms of dress. The degree to which childhood is marked out in this way has varied historically (Paoletti and Kregloh 1989; N. Marshall 2008), but it is associated in particular with the Romantic movement and the new cult of childhood that emerged in the nineteenth century with its emphasis on children as social beings in their own right, expressed through distinctive dress. Cook (2004) traces this development in the early twentieth century with the emergence of retailing, particularly based in department stores, specifically aimed at children. More recently the trend has been for children's clothes to be less, rather than more, distinctive, with the spread to young girls in particular of adult female styles as part of a more general extension of consumption culture to this group.

In relation to old age, there has been a similar pattern of structured expectations, expressing norms about what is appropriate—or more significantly, inappropriate—for people as they age. Such patterning is observable historically in manuscripts, portraits, woodcuts and book illustrations; and it is vividly present in classic pyramidal images of the Ages of Man or Woman, in which dress is used to convey social and bodily change across the life course (Thane 2005). Dress codes in the past were more clearly linked to social status, both in terms of position in the social hierarchy, exemplified in sumptuary legislation that enforced such links legally, and categorization in terms of the life course, so that a woman's status as a young girl,

Figure 2.1   The life and age of woman displaying the interplay between the body, age and dress

married woman or widow was marked by her dress. Age-coded dress was part of this. Though always subject to historical specificity, certain features recur in relation to dress and age: more covered-up styles, higher necklines, tighter-drawn linen and longer skirts. When skirts became short in the 1920s, many old women retained their long length; and indeed skirt length remains a diagnostic feature of dress for older women. Colours tend to be darker or more sombre: many older women in the past moved permanently into a version of mourning. For men a similar pattern of longer means older obtained historically, with older men adopting the long robe in contrast to the short hose of the young. They might still wear rich materials, if among the elite, at least up until the eighteenth century, but they often also adopted darker, more sober colours. We can see this in sixteenth-century Augsburg merchant Matthaus Schwarz's depiction of his life in dress through eighty-eight illustrations of himself wearing different outfits in which there is a clear trend in his later years to darker, more covered-up dress in contrast to the elaborate and colourful outfits of his youth (Braunstein 1992; Rublack 2010).

There is, thus, clear evidence for age ordering in dress in the past. But does it still obtain? There is certainly a widespread view today that age ordering is obsolete, or at least in major decline. It is often asserted, particularly in the media, that older people need no longer dress distinctively, as they did in the past, and that they are now free of such restrictions. This argument largely centres around the persistence of norms that separate out the dress of older people and that emphasize a need to tone down, to avoid showy, dramatic styles or colours and to adopt quieter, more sober and self-effacing forms. Many of these traditional prohibitions on dress for older women relate to the body and its exposure in ways that make claims in relation to sexuality.

In the chapters that follow I explore the evidence for this more fully; and in doing so, I look in particular at this account of age in terms of toning down. But this is not the only way age-related styling can be observed and understood. There are other age-coded forms in play. Lurie (1992), for example, draws attention to the widespread adoption by American elders in particular of a distinctive resort or leisure wardrobe marked by bright colours and soft, loose shapes. It clearly contrasts with the traditional associations of age with sobriety and self-effacement. These trends, however, need to be understood in the context of the wider rise of casual dress, which has become the predominant form of dress, outside white collar office wear, for the majority of the population. Casual dress has its origins in exercise or sportswear. In this it follows a long-established pattern of diffusion whereby styles enter the clothing lexicon from the world of sport and are then integrated into the mainstream, taking on more formal properties and meanings. Laver (1950), for example, traces the evolution of men's formal wear from its origins in the English riding jacket of the late eighteenth and early nineteenth centuries, through the tailored coat, to the formal dress suit of white tie and tails. More recently the process can be observed in relation to anoraks, which entered the clothing system in the 1950s as smart ski wear, but by the late twentieth century became the principal form of outerwear worn on the high street. The current diffusion of dress from exercise wear into casual dress in the form of track suits, trainers, layered garments and fleeces is the most recent version of this long-established pattern. One of the ways to understand the diffusion of such dress to older people is in terms of the dynamic whereby age has come to operate as a diffusional structure within the fashion system. I will explore the role of this structure more fully below.

For Lurie, however, there remains something distinctively childish about such leisure dress, with its toddler shapes, bold patterns and bright, fresh colours. Its adoption by older people, especially older men, signals a life at play, no longer constrained by the norms of business dress with its emphasis on the sober, dark and structured. These sports clothes allow for body movement, and with it body spread. Elastic waistbands and Spandex fabrics, made possible by the technical development of textiles, can accommodate changes, but in subtle ways that maintain integration with mainstream younger clothing through the metaphor of sport. But they are also clothes that signal a return to the comfort and ease of babyhood exemplified in their toddler-like shapes and asexual styles. In this, however, they point darkly to another future, that of the residential or nursing home, where easy-clean, easy-wear clothing becomes the norm,

A Lifetime of Babywear:

6 mnths - 3 yrs

3-7 yrs

8-14 yrs

14-35 yrs

35-50 yrs

50-70 yrs

70 yrs+

THE SEVEN AGES *of* MAN

Figure 2.2   A lifetime in babywear displaying the interplay between the body, age and dress, by Posy Simmonds. Courtesy Posy Simmonds/The Hayward Gallery

and where fully adult dress gives way to clothing that is easy for the staff to manage with its elastic waists, pull-on trousers and artificial fabrics (Twigg 2010).

Age coding can, however, take on other forms. There is, for example, a style that can be termed 'sweet old lady' dress. A distinctive style characterized by floral patterns, soft fabrics, frills, high necks and long sleeves, it represents an enduring mode and not just clothing that is out of date (though such is the nature of fashion that it is periodically in vogue, usually identified by terms such as *granny style*). Klepp and Storm-Mathisen, in their Norwegian study of dress beliefs of young and middle-aged women, note the existence of this style. They found that women in their forties, as well as avoiding dress deemed too young, were concerned to avoid styles seen as too old. These were exemplified by

flowered dresses, pleated skirts, white lace blouses and mauve coloured garments; in other words, thoroughly feminine clothing and accessories that are devoid of sexual connotations…have a lot in common with the 'chaste young girl's fashions' that the mothers of the teenagers wish their daughters would wear, but which the girls themselves absolutely refuse to wear. (2005: 335)

In British context, these clothes echo an almost wholly obsolete age-related style in the form of 'jeune fille dress' worn by young women up until the 1960s. This was a significant style in the period before youth fashion took off, which placed the control of clothing in the hands of the young themselves, enabling the more direct expression of sexuality. The key features that unite jeune fille and old lady dress are pretty femininity and the avoidance of the erotic. We will note the relevance of this style for M&S's Classic range in Chapter 7.

A third age-related style is that of Mother of the Bride. This is one of the few positive cultural tropes in relation to clothing for older women. This is significant since, as noted earlier, age-appropriate dress is largely defined negatively in terms of what should not be worn. Mother of the bride outfits are a distinctive form of day wear, typically a dress and coat or dress and jacket, in other words a whole outfit, often worn with a hat. They tend to be dressy, somewhat elaborate, often involving lace or embroidery. Their most distinctive characteristic is the colour range: typically clear, light, fondant colours—pinks, turquoises, lilacs—that echo the traditional hues of bridesmaids. They are positive colours, never black, grey or office neutrals. They are thus marked by being traditional, feminine, pretty and upbeat in feeling. Shops specializing in such dress can be found in most towns in Britain. They clearly relate, as the style name suggests, to the burgeoning wedding market which has exploded over the last three decades in the United Kingdom with the growth of elaborate weddings, stimulated initially by the broadcasting of royal marriages, but carried forward on the wave of celebrity culture and growing affluence among the general population. Their remit is, however, wider, and they are also worn at a range of special events in Britain: garden parties, unveilings and charity occasions, particularly those involving the royal family.

The last point is an important part of their meaning. Female members of the royal family are the epicentre of this style. They are typically worn at civic or charitable events endorsed by the royal family—as well as, of course, at race meetings. They are also linked to hats, which in Britain have become specialized items almost wholly confined to such events and kept alive as a style by them, in contrast to other countries where this clothing code is less current. Mother of the bride outfits thus draw strength from their subterranean connections with the royal family, representing the traditional old-fashioned values female members of the royal family, particularly the Queen, are felt to embody. As such they are closely linked to what has been the most successful aspect of the monarchy in the twentieth and twenty-first centuries—its links to the charitable sector (Proshaska 1995), embodying as they do important aspects of civic life and of the family. Such forms of dress have particular resonance for older women, providing one of the few sources of positive dress images for them. This is particularly clear in relation to the Queen, whose photograph is ubiquitous in residential homes and day centres, where she provides a positive image of an older woman still in the public realm—something many older people find themselves excluded from—the centre of love and attention, in a wholly dignified way. Such images counteract self-effacement and cultural invisibility, but in a way that is completely consonant with traditional, conservative values. As examined in Chapter 6 on magazines, these functions are also performed by celebrities in the form of older actresses.

Age-related dress thus clearly persists, though in more complex ways than the simple account in terms of toning down might suggest. In subsequent chapters I explore more fully the idea that old age is undergoing a cultural shift and that this has implications for cultural fields like dress. In Chapter 4 I explore the views of older women themselves, seeing how they both endorse and challenge the persistence of age coding. In Chapter 6 on magazines, I look at how a new ideal of agelessness has replaced the earlier emphasis on the structural position of older women, and how this is reflected in the way fashion is presented to the older market within mainstream magazines like *Vogue*. I shall also observe, in line with the analyses of Sophie Woodward (2007) and Clarke and Miller (2002), how the new freedoms produce new anxieties and how this is reflected clearly in magazines aimed at older women who see a central part of their role as helping readers navigate the difficult new territory around dress. I also explore the evidence suggesting older people have themselves become more integrated into mainstream culture through their consumption choices, so that their dress is less marked by age and more by lifestyle and other personal choices. In Chapter 7 I present the views of design directors who work in this field and who clearly believe that the current generation of older people are in some sense different; though I also register in the next chapter the degree to which the mythology of the baby boomer generation has exaggerated the effects of this cultural shift.

Across these areas of debate, however, there is a persistent sense that older people are 'moving younger', that they are dressing younger, adopting younger styles and behaving in ways that suggest there are no longer the cultural barriers that there were in the past between different stages of life. There is, however, a different way we can understand this persistent language of moving younger, and this is in terms of the dynamics of fashion itself in which, rather than older people moving younger, styles are diffusing older. I explore this in the next section.

Age as the New Style Diffusion

I noted earlier the classic sociological accounts from Veblen (1899) and Simmel (1904/1971) onwards which have analysed fashion as a tool of class competition, part of a dynamic of competitive emulation and display in which styles are taken up and abandoned by elites as they are transferred down the social hierarchy. Elites thus display their distinction through repeatedly marking themselves off from lower orders (Bourdieu 1984). Recently, however, the dominance of class in the dynamic of fashion has lessened with the development of a new, more plural system. Crane (2000) argues that a consumer-based fashion system has succeeded the old class-based one and that this has allowed for greater stylistic diversity. Instead of being oriented to elites, fashion now incorporates the tastes and concerns of social groups at all levels. As part of this shift, youth has replaced class as the engine of fashion. Clothes intended for younger age groups are becoming increasingly differentiated from those oriented towards middle-aged adults. As a result in Europe as well as the United States, age has become one of the most important factors in selling clothes (Crane 2000). In contrast to the 1950s, industrial fashion today is oriented primarily towards the young. Crane suggests that this age segmentation will increase:

> Instead of the upper class seeking to differentiate itself from other social classes, the young seek to differentiate themselves from the middle aged and the elderly. As trends diffuse to older age groups, younger age groups adopt new styles. (2000: 198)

Although the analysis centres on youth, her insight is relevant to old age also.

By this interpretation, age ordering has not gone. It is still significant; it simply has taken on a new form. Rather than denoting social position as in the past, it is now caught up in the dynamic of fashion itself. What we are observing, therefore, is not that the dress of older people is moving younger, but that styles are diffusing older as they pass from the centre of fashionability in the youth market to the periphery in the older one. It is this that underlies the sense that ultra-fashionable styles look 'odd' or 'unsuitable' or 'ridiculous' or 'sad' on older people. The sharpness of their fashionability has to be blunted before they can be adopted by older wearers. Thus in the 1980s, leggings initially emerged on the fashion scene promoted by Vivienne Westwood, carrying a sense of shock and sexual frisson, then moved into the youthful mainstream, and from there on to middle-aged housewives on peripheral housing estates, thus making the diffusional journey both in terms of age and class (until, of course, they were revived again in the youthful market in conjunction with smocks in the mid 2000s from whence they once again have diffused to the mainstream). There is a parallel here with Laver's (1937: 40) celebrated account of the fashion cycle, in which styles move from being indecent ten years before their time, daring one year before, chic in their time, dowdy three years later, hideous twenty years after, amusing thirty years after, romantic a century later and beautiful a century and a half later; though since the 1930s, the cycle has speeded up. Part of the diffusion to the status of dowdiness and out-of-dateness relates to age as styles are repeatedly abandoned by the young and taken up by the old. Freitas and colleagues (1997), for example, in their study of college-aged young people's views, found that they associated styles for older people with being out of date, and were keen to mark themselves off from them. From the perspective of these younger people, clothes are not homogeneous in terms of age, whatever middle-aged people may like to imagine. Klepp and Storm-Mathisen's (2005) Norwegian study similarly shows the centrality of age in relation to dress from the perspective of the young and middle-aged.

Sometimes the process of style diffusion also contains a cohort effect, with the meaning of styles altering with the ageing of the cohort that wears them. For example, in the 1950s tweed sports jackets were worn by young men in the United Kingdom—undergraduates or young teachers—and associated with a youthful, easygoing approach. In photographs they appear conservative now, but that was not their meaning in the 1950s and 1960s. With a red woollen tie, they signalled a certain radicalism. By the 1980s tweed jackets—classically in grey herringbone—had become standard wear for conservative, middle-aged male academics, representing sober, sensible garb that stopped short of the formality of a suit. By the early twenty-first century, the tweed jacket and tie had gone from the world of work and is now found in older people's clubs and retirement homes, worn by men in their seventies and eighties. A parallel pattern occurs in relation to pleated skirts for women. Young and fresh in the 1950s and 1960s, they become increasingly age coded, until by the early 2000s, they were emblems of age; retailers like Jaeger in the United Kingdom refuse to stock them because they 'age the range' (though as part of the ever restless nature of a fashion, they are currently enjoying a slight revival at the younger end). Anoraks and fleeces, particularly when combined with feminine colours and embroidered details that draw on sweet old lady style, are similarly subject to the process of 'moving older'.

Conclusion

Clothing and age intersect in complex and culturally contingent ways. Dress is an important field in which identity is expressed and negotiated; and I have noted its significance in relation to master identities like gender and class. But I have also argued that these perceptions need to be extended to age. I have outlined some of the cultural connections currently made between age and dress, noting how they reflect enduring cultural evaluations of age and ones that are in the process of changing. In particular I have suggested that age has come to perform a distinctive and new function within the fashion system, operating as a dynamic principle in the diffusion of styles, and with that in the processes of fashion itself understood as systematic institutionalized change. In the next chapter I develop these themes further in the specific context of theorizing about age.

–3–

Ageing, Embodiment and Culture

Though ageing is a bodily process, it only becomes meaningful in the context of culture. In this chapter I address a set of central questions around the ways age is performed and experienced in current culture, exploring how these intersect with questions of dress. I focus in particular on the argument that the nature of later years is changing and that consumption lifestyles play a part in this. But before doing so I need to address age as a key social division or master identity.

Age as a Social Division

Age is one of the key social divisions ordering and ranking individuals within society. Like gender, race, class, sexuality or disability, it is a master identity, governing how we are perceived, ranked and evaluated. Until recently, however, age has not received the same attention as other social categories. It has been neglected by sociologists who—reflecting the wider ageism of the culture—have implicitly regarded it as uninteresting, taken for granted, lying in some sense beyond the social, pertaining to the territory of medicine or welfare. Calasanti and Sleven (2006) rightly berate sociology for its pernicious failure to theorize age relations despite their significance for central sociological questions of inequality and power. Age is often omitted from the debate on intersectionality (Anthias 2001; Valentine 2007; Calasanti 2008), which foregrounds divisions of class, gender, race and sexuality. And yet age is highly significant for the complex ways these social divisions intersect and for related questions of power, inequality and esteem.

Age operates both as an ordering principle in society and as a dimension of power and status. Individuals and groups are accorded identity and status on the basis of their positions in the age order. This prescribes appropriate obligations and behaviours across the life course. Among these, as noted in Chapter 2, are expectations in relation to dress. But age relations are not simply a form of social ordering. Like other social divisions, they embody relations of power and domination, forming part of a nexus through which groups gain identity and power in and through their relations with others. As with gender, class and race, esteem and worth are hierarchically distributed. Youth is prized, so that, as Kathy Woodward (1991) argues, we are not judged by how old we are, but how young we are not. Old age thus becomes a form of dereliction, a loss, a movement away from the ideal. The old, in the perspective of dominant culture, represent a disruption of the visual field (Furman 1997, 1999). Like the disabled or abnormal, they represent the Other, evaluated as 'less than', so that ageing becomes a version of Goffman's (1968) 'spoilt identity'. Age relations thus need to be seen as systems of inequality that privilege the not old at the expense of the old. Just as racism implies an unexamined whiteness and disability an unexamined ableism, ageism signals the presence of an unexamined and privileged category of normative youth and middle years (R. Butler 1969; Bytheway 1995; Calasanti 2003; Sandberg 2008).

Calasanti and Slevin (2001) argue that old age needs to be seen as a distinct stage of life, not just the additive result of events occurring over the life. It not only exacerbates other inequalities but is a social location in its own right, conferring loss of power for those designated old regardless of their advantage in other hierarchies. Discrimination and exclusion based on age thus lie across and intersect with other inequalities, as the old are marginalized and lose power on the basis of their age. We can observe this across a range of fields. Older people, for example, find it harder to get jobs, and their exclusion from the labour market undermines their full citizenship; medical staff take their views less seriously, consult them less often and limit their treatment; and they suffer from wider cultural disparagement in relation to their appearance, as evidenced in the vast industry of anti-ageing through which older people attempt to improve their cultural status. These processes of marginalization are carried forward into norms in relation to dress.

We need thus to recognize that ageism is, as Laws (1995) argues, a bodily form of oppression. Meanings of a largely negative sort are read onto the aged body, which are then used to justify exclusionary practices, underwriting the presentation of the old as essentially Other. Discrimination in relation to age—as in other categories—has an embodied, visceral quality to it. These elements have been most frequently explored in relation to racism (Gunaratnam and Lewis 2001; Ahmed 2002), but they apply to ageism also, as is clear from work in medical sociology that has exposed negative attitudes among nursing and care staff towards the bodies of the old and the way this underlies discriminatory practice. Such embodied, visceral responses can be seen also in relation to the appearance of older people, which is a key site for the expression of ageism, as Hurd Clarke (2011) has analysed in relation to facial appearance, and Ward and Holland (2011) in relation to hair. These feelings are internalized by individuals themselves, as I highlight in the chapter that explores the voices of older women, where some respondents speak of their bodies in ways that assume they are sources of disgust to wider society, so that hiding and covering them up with dress and retreating from view is taken to be the best response from the perspective of everyone.

Age differs from other social divisions in that, in time, individuals will move across its category boundary. The young will eventually become old; and those who practice ageism, unlike sexism or racism, will someday be its victim (Andrews 1999; Irwin 1999). Ironically this does not produce a positive response based on solidarity. As Andrews (1999) notes, what separates ageism from sexism and racism is the element of self-hatred. The person stereotyped is the person they will become. As a result age has not, by and large, become the basis of identity politics as other forms of difference have. As Gilleard and Higgs (2000) note, older people, particularly those who are healthy and have high social capital, resist appeals to aged status: their aspiration is to stay 'young' and to hold on to their status within mainstream culture. By the time they have unequivocally moved into the category of the 'old', their capacity to challenge oppression or mobilize opposition has been undermined by frailty.

Dress plays a part in relations of power. As Barnard (1996) argues, clothes are ideological, part of how social groups establish, sustain and reproduce positions of power and relations of domination and subordination. Such cultural processes enable relations of inequity to appear natural, proper and legitimate. We can see this most clearly historically in the widespread phenomenon of sumptuary legislation, whereby brightly coloured, embroidered, silken or otherwise highly valued dress was restricted to the social elite and denied to lower orders. Up until the end of the eighteenth century, power was expected to be splendid. In this way clothes play a part in inequalities of social rank, making exploitation by one class of another appear natural and proper (Barnard 1996: 196). These perceptions have largely been developed in relation to class and gender, but they apply to age also. Chapter 2 examined aspects of the dress of older people that can be said to be ideologically formed, suggesting subordination and social exclusion—the grey, drab, self-effacing, shabby dress associated with age. This reflects the wider ideology of ageism, underwriting at a visible bodily level the structural exclusion and poverty experienced by many older people. Here there is a direct link between cultural analyses and the arguments of the structured dependency theory, exemplified in the Political Economy School (Estes 1979; Phillipson and Walker 1986; Townsend 1986; Estes and Binney 1989; Arber and Ginn 1991; Phillipson 1998), which have exposed the degree to which features of old age are the product of social and political processes and choices that structure the material conditions of later years. A fundamental part of the cultural dynamic of age rests on the structural denigration and exclusion achieved by such political and social policies, with the result that drabness and greyness of dress, arising in part from poverty, act to naturalize and obscure what are essentially social and political processes.

There are parallels here in the forms of dress thought appropriate for people living in asylums and long-stay institutions in the past. For example it was common in learning disability hospitals in the United Kingdom until the 1970s for inmates to wear bulk-purchased or hospital-manufactured clothing (Linthicum 2006). With their harsh textiles, unflattering cut and studied avoidance of fashion or sexuality, these clothes sent messages about how those living in such institutions were to be seen. Worn in prescribed ways, with hair and limbs correctly disposed, they imposed a particular stance, produced a particular body, so much so that getting residents into normal, mainstream clothing was an important element in the project of normalization through social role valorization (Wolfensberger 1972; Brown and Smith 1992). In the past clothes for older people displayed some of the same characteristics, shabby, loose, dull, down at heel, so that dissolving the boundaries between dress for the aged and the mainstream can similarly be seen as a political project, part of improving the cultural location of older people.

What Counts as Old?

Old age is conventionally deemed to start with retirement (that is how it is defined, for example, in UK and other government statistics), and is predominately conceptualized as a state of dependence and frailty. More recently, however, under the influence of wider social change, these assumptions have been challenged and to some degree destabilized. Changing demography has greatly expanded the period post retirement (though rising retirement ages are due to eat into this), opening up the new cultural territory of the Third Age, which increasingly looks very similar in character to late middle age. As a result there is an growing tendency to read the 'later life' back into the fifties, a process endorsed by growing fluidity over retirement, which has the effect of further blurring the transition into 'old age'. These processes of drawing age back into the fifties, however, need to be set against the countervailing tendency of reading age as something that now occurs later than in the past, so older people are seen as in some sense 'younger' than in the past.

Ageing, however, also needs to be understood as a process that operates throughout the life course, which is not confined to old age. How it operates, when it is deemed to kick in, varies across different cultural spheres. For example, in high fashion, ageing sets in very early, certainly by the late twenties. Similarly in the spheres of cosmetics and face creams, anxieties about the visible signs of ageing begin to appear from the thirties onwards, actively promoted by the cosmetic companies (Coupland 2003, 2009; Hurd Clarke and Griffin 2007, 2008; Hurd Clarke 2011). It operates differentially in relation to gender, with the common perception that women 'age' younger than men: a belief that has its roots in their evaluation in the sphere of appearance, and carried forward in practices like their exclusion from the media at significantly younger ages than their male counterparts. It operates in a similarly differential way in relation to class, with higher-status and more affluent individuals to some degree protected from its erosions, allowing those of higher social status to avoid the assumption of aged status for longer. Judgements about when old age starts are also affected by the age of the observer (Abrams et al. 2009). 'Old age' is thus a fluid, contextually contingent, cultural category that overlaps and intersects with other social and cultural structures.

Changes in the academic field of gerontology, exemplified in the rise of cultural gerontology, have also endorsed the tendency to read 'age' back into the fifties. In doing so, they have expanded the field of gerontology markedly, bringing into play new subject matter such as consumption, leisure, appearance, sport, literature, as well as new theorizing that draws in postmodernist and poststructuralist perspectives and work within the arts and humanities (Cole 1992; Katz 1996, 2005; Gullette 1997, 2011; Basting 1998; K. Woodward 1999, 2006; Gilleard and Higgs 2000). The study of later years has been greatly enriched by this repositioning of the subject. At the political level, it has enabled a shift towards a more sympathetic account of old age in which the subjectivities of older people are foregrounded and the objectifying discourses of frailty and social welfarism less dominant. In general I concur with this widening of the territory of old age, and its reconceptualization in terms of 'later years'; indeed the empirical study on which this book draws took fifty-five as its starting point.

In expanding ageing to encompass those in their fifties and older, however, we need to recognize that there are significant differences within this age span and that the body is at the heart of many of these. What women wear in their eighties and nineties is not just the product of cultural expectations, but also reflects changes at a bodily level. I explore these more fully in Chapter 7 by looking at how retailers respond to changes in the body and the requirements these place on style and cut. In a similar way if we look at the media's discourses of dress, the preoccupation with resisting age, with remaining part of the shopping mainstream, the somewhat frenetic account of being still fashionable that characterizes their treatment of this area, this relates to a distinct stage of ageing, one that indeed reflects the preoccupations of women journalists and readers in late middle age rather than those in their seventies and eighties. Hurd Clarke (2011) similarly notes, in relation to questions of appearance, how women of advanced age find the more pressing issues of health and functioning displace earlier concerns rooted in the beauty ideology. We need, therefore, to recognize that there are significant structural differences to be acknowledged within the category of 'old age'.

The Reconstitution of Ageing

The new sense of fluidity over when later years are deemed to start itself reflects changes in the cultural location of old age. Proponents of the reconstitution of ageing thesis argue that later life is in the process of changing under the impact of a series of interconnected developments that have occurred across Western society over the last fifty years (Phillipson 1998; Blakie 1999; Gilleard and Higgs 2000). Rising life expectancy and declining family size have produced a dramatic demographic shift. Between 1901 and 2003 the proportion of the UK population aged over fifty increased from 15 to 30 per cent, and is projected to rise to 41 per cent in 2031 (Tomassini 2005). Similar figures are found in the United States and other Western countries. With this has come changes in the nature of the life course. The normative life course entrenched in the early years of the twentieth century (Anderson 1985), and persisting in the West broadly until the 1980s, has been destabilized. This was based on a relatively secure pattern of education, followed—for men—by full-time, life-long work in the same occupation, often the same organization, accompanied by marriage, family formation and eventually retirement. Women followed a slightly different trajectory. But in the late twentieth and early twenty-first centuries, this has been replaced by longer and more fragmented periods of education and training, with the possibility of looping back; more flexible forms of work and portfolio careers; higher and more persistent rates of female labour market participation; greater fluidity in personal relationships, with partnering and repartnering; earlier, more flexible and longer retirement. Together these changes underpin the sense that later years are no longer the clearly defined or scripted period of life they once seemed, and that traditional age ordering within society has been weakened, with stages of life, and behaviour appropriate to them, less clearly prescribed.

Under conditions of post- or late modernity, it is argued, there has also been a shift in locus of identity from production to consumption. Traditional formations of class and gender—and to a degree age—have become less central, as identities become more fluid, more optional, less socially entrenched and more the product of agency and choice (Giddens 1991; Bauman 2000). Patterns of consumption become increasingly significant in the narrative of self and the formation of social identities, as they come to perform an integrative function within an individuated culture, acting to integrate people within a common culture of lifestyle. With the decline in secondary institutions there is a shift towards a more neoliberal experience of the self in which freedom to choose and to express the self through choice is increasingly promoted as a key value. This affects the constitution of old age, which moves from being a relatively fixed state to one more marked by flexibility and optionality (Phillipson and Biggs 1998). As we shall see this is reflected in the magazine presentation of fashion and older women and in the comments of design directors. Here consumption offers older people the possibility of counteracting the cultural exclusion traditionally associated with age, as they join younger cohorts in pursuing the same cultural trends. Of course, this dream of integration rests on the possession of resources. Though in the period from the 1960s the incomes of some pensioners in the United Kingdom have risen, many remain in poverty. This has produced a dual trend, towards greater heterogeneity among older people, combined with greater similarity in relation to the general population. Ian Jones and colleagues (2008) suggest that this dual pattern extends to cultural identity, with some elders joining younger cohorts in their spending patterns and self-identity while others remain tied to older patterns of deprivation and exclusion.

These shifts underlie the emergence of the Third Age as a new cultural space. Presented as a period post retirement, freed from the constraints of work and, to some degree, family responsibility, it is marked by leisure, pleasure and self-development. Though defined as a state rather than chronological age, it roughly maps onto the fifties to seventies. The concept has been criticized for describing the lives of only a section of older people—the affluent middle class—and for presenting an aspirational version of their lives; for projecting all the difficulties of old age into a dark Fourth Age of disability and decline; and, through its emphasis on choice and agency, for implicitly providing ideological support for a neoliberal restructuring of the welfare state and its support for older people (Phillipson 1998). The Third Age with its roots in consumption imagery also encodes other dimensions of social difference or advantage, for example ethnicity (this is a largely white world) or relationship status (this is a vision of coupledom).

Some theorists (Öberg and Tornstram 1999, 2001) have suggested that the period is better conceptualized in terms of an extended plateau of late middle years that only ceases with the irruption of ill health and disability. They suggest that modern cultures are marked by a declining salience of age ordering at all stages of life, with adulthood an increasingly undifferentiated period between childhood and frail old age.

Within this narrative of change, the baby boomers feature prominently. At a popular level they present a handy term to encapsulate a series of social changes. For the media they provide attractive images that allow them to rehearse the imagery of the 1960s yet again. It is notable how often discussion of changes regarding age are framed in terms of the distinctive qualities of the 1960s generation (though many of the features described belong more to the early 1970s—understood here as the Long Sixties (Marwick 1998)). At a visual level, the 1960s were peculiarly youth-oriented. This is particularly true of the fashions of the period, exemplified in the United Kingdom by the designs of Mary Quant and the appearance of models like Twiggy. They valorized a prepubescent look, with knock knees, panda eyes, flat-barred shoes, short skirts and smock shapes. The media in presenting issues around clothing and age recurringly feature this period and make the link to the baby boomer cohort. There is a widely held assumption in the media that the ageing of this cohort will be different: it will not want to adopt the frumpy age-related dress assumed to be the pattern of previous generations. Surely the women who pioneered the mini skirt, journalists repeatedly ask, will not want to sink into knitted tops and pleated skirts: they will insist on retaining youthful styles and engagement with mainstream fashion. I examine the truth of this assertion in subsequent chapters.

Academic accounts of the baby boomers often reflect this media view, presenting them as a 'special' generation (Gilleard and Higgs 2000; Biggs et al. 2007). Edmunds and Turner (2002) describe them as a 'strategic generation in aesthetic, cultural and sexual terms...the first...to live through a time when mass consumer revolution transformed popular taste' (quoted by Phillipson 2007). Gilleard and Higgs in particular have presented them as cultural pioneers, the generation who invented youth culture and went on to develop lifestyle-oriented consumption culture. Others have depicted them in less flattering terms, as a narcissistic generation greedy in its appropriation of resources and selfish in its pursuit of hedonistic individualism (Stewart and Torges 2006; Willetts 2010). Yet others have described them in terms of the shift to post-scarcity values (Inglehart 1997).

This account, however, presents analytic problems. The underlying demography is not as straightforward as is sometimes assumed and varies significantly among different Western countries (Phillipson 2007). In the United States, the home of the 'baby boomer' terminology, there was a sustained surge in births from the mid 1940s to the mid 1960s. In some European countries (Finland) (Karisto 2007), there was a peak immediately after the war; in others (Germany), there was no significant surge at all. The United Kingdom had a distinctive pattern of two separate peaks, one in the late 1940s, the other in the mid 1960s. Baby boomer terminology is usually associated with the first, formally known as the Bulge.

I have suggested in other work analysing consumption patterns on clothing and related goods that the baby boomers are not as distinctive a cohort as has been claimed. It is true that their spending patterns in the United Kingdom do show greater engagement with consumption, but the effect is really one of historical period, the product of general social and economic change, rather than the impact of a distinctive cohort (Twigg and Majima 2013). A better way to understand the phenomenon is as a shorthand for 'the current generation of better-off people in late middle to early old age', roughly those in their mid fifties to early seventies, so what the term really indicates is the current cohort of Third Agers. This explains the loosely used demographics. It also underlies the implicitly classed nature of the term. When thinking of a baby boomer we do not envisage a working-class pensioner living on a low income. Baby boomer suggests something different. It is an upbeat, successful term that aims to put psychic distance between the current generation and images of dependence and decline that have traditionally marked ageing. This construction is a significant element in the media fascination with the boomers, especially what they term the 'alpha boomers'. The phenomena is well captured in Zoomers (Boomers who Zoom), an elite, wealthy group identified and promoted by the Canadian *Zoomer* magazine. Stephen Katz and Barbara Marshall have explored the ways older lives are constituted in terms of such heroic forms of anti-ageing (Marshall and Katz 2002; Katz 2005). These then are carried through in a mass of promotional literature, for pensions, holidays, commercial goods, which presents active, healthy, good-looking elders having a wonderful time and fully integrated in the commercialized world of lifestyle (I. Jones et al. 2009). Consumption here offers opportunities to resist the cultural marginalization traditionally associated with old age though—as always—it requires income to do so.

Ageing, Gender and the Body

In its earlier stages, social gerontology traditionally avoided the topic of the body, regarding an emphasis on it as retrogressive, locking the subject into biological essentialism, reinforcing the dominant discourses of ageing, both popular and scientific, that regard it as 'all about the body' and its decline. Emphasizing the body also seemed to threaten the gains of the Political Economy School and its understanding of how old age is socially constructed in which crucial features of the experience of age are structured by sociopolitical factors rather than biological ones. A focus on the body was also perceived as potentially demeaning to older people. There is a long history according to which subordinated groups—women, black people—are represented in terms of their bodies, effectively reducing them to their bodies. Focussing overtly on the bodies of older people seemed to reinforce such processes of objectification and disparagement (Twigg 2006). More recently, however, under the impact of new theorizing in the sociology of the body and the wider cultural turn, social gerontology has begun to address bodily themes. The body is now recognized as a key nexus in age studies, with ageing understood as the product of a complex interplay between bodily and cultural factors (Cole 1992; Katz 1996; Öberg 1996; Gullette 1997; K. Woodward 1999, 2006; Tulle-Winton 1999, 2000; Calasanti and Slevin 2001; Andersson 2002; Twigg 2006; Hurd Clarke and Griffin 2007, 2008; Sandberg 2011). The body is itself increasingly understood, in Grosz's (1994) terms, as an 'open materiality', neither wholly inscribed by culture nor simply a product of nature, but lying on the borders between. As a result the significance of the body in ageing needs to be acknowledged, but in ways that are neither essentializing nor oppressive. There are parallels here with debates in feminism that have similarly sought to engage with the embodied difference of sex, but in ways that do not entrench oppressive readings that diminish and limit women. In a similar way the role of the body in ageing should be recognized, but without reducing old age to it.

Modern media culture is intensely youth-oriented. We are surrounded by representations and images in which the body is presented in youthful, idealized form, offering an unattainable level of perfection. The damaging effect of these images on younger women has been widely critiqued by feminists such as Bordo (1993) and Wolf (1990) in terms of the beauty ideal and its malignant effects, evidenced in the pervasive body dissatisfaction that has become the norm among modern Western women. Women are taught to feel insecure about their bodies, constantly monitoring them for imperfections and engaging in forms of improvement and self-surveillance (Bordo 1993). For radical feminists like Bartky (1990) these processes represent a form of patriarchal oppression that sets up culturally sanctioned means of judging women, and then by finding them deficient, acts to immobilize their capacity to resist. Holstein (2006) notes the irony that while women have achieved greater status as agents than ever before, they are faced by an escalating set of expectations in relation to their bodies. These pressures are not confined to younger women, but have spread to older women, who increasingly find themselves interrogating their mirrors for the signs of decline that will erode their cultural status (Gullette 1997, 1999). Older women are thus not just subject to the traditional male gaze of patriarchy, but the additional gaze of youth that evaluates them in terms of the ways their bodies fall short of the youthful ideal.

These processes have intensified over the last fifty years with the rise of new techniques of self-surveillance which have put the ageing body under review in ways that were not the case in the past. The ubiquity of mirrors and the arrival in the twentieth century of the bathroom as a specialized space where the whole body could be observed lit and naked have facilitated new levels of self-surveillance and monitoring. The widespread availability of digital photographs and their arrangement and preservation in media forms such as Facebook encourage new forms of personal re-view, including of changing appearance. Here photographs act, as Sontag argues, in complex ways, undermining rather than preserving identity, ultimately testifying to time's relentless melt (Hockey and James 2003).

Such pressures in relation to ageing need also to be set in the context of new forms of governmentality, expressed in the rise of healthism, a set of cultural norms that enjoin personal responsibility to individuals for the creation and maintenance of healthy bodies. Linked to the positive health messages found in health education, they reflect the wider neoliberal transfer of responsibility away from the collective to the individual and the growing focus of public policy on individualized solutions. Under this regime, there is a shift in the focus of ascetic work on the body, away from religious or spiritual goals that characterized it the past towards material ones in the form of the creation of the marketable self, capable of being a vehicle for successful consumption (Turner 1984; Featherstone and Hepworth 1991). Failure to look fit, toned and slim here becomes a new sign of moral laxity, evidence of failure to exert proper discipline over the body. Ageing adds additional pressure, with the visible signs of ageing becoming a mark of personal failure and—particularly for women—letting yourself go. As Furman (1997) showed in her account of older women in a New Jersey beauty salon, failure to present an acceptable appearance represented a deeper failure to maintain the disciplinary practices of normative femininity and as such threatened their standing in a socially conservative community.

Under late capitalism these anxieties form the basis for a vast anti-ageing industry centred on the dread of looking old (Gilleard and Higgs 2000; Katz 2005). The cos-metics and pharmaceutical industries in particular have identified anti-ageing prod-ucts and the 'mature' market as key sectors for development; and their advertising has become one of the most powerful ways in which the face of ageing is constructed and reinforced, reflecting and amplifying the ageist ideology that permeates Western culture (Coupland 2003, 2009; Hurd Clarke 2011). Adverts tell women that they need to battle against ageing through beauty work and that youthfulness is vital to their so-cial visibility and cultural worth. Hurd Clarke (2011) shows how, as procedures like Botox injections or cosmetic surgery become available, they are promoted and mar-keted in such a way that they are normalized, becoming essential tools in the achieve-ment of proper femininity. The market thus does not simply respond to demand, but actively shapes it, creating new ways of being older, new normativities in relation to appearance and behaviour. Social status or education is no protector in this culture of body dissatisfaction and age anxiety. Hurd Clarke (2011) found that women of higher socioeconomic status were more involved in, concerned about and dissatisfied with their physical appearance than were women of lower socioeconomic status. They are also more likely to have internalized healthist norms that hold individuals morally responsible for the status of their bodies.

At the visual level, older women often report becoming invisible, sidelined and at times literally no longer seen in a culture focussed on the young (Greer 1991;

Gullette 1997, 2011; Gibson 2000; Holstein 2006; K. Woodward 2006). This sense is reinforced by the erasure of age—particularly female age—from the media: older women TV presenters, for example, find their careers ended prematurely with signs of age; women actors find it increasingly difficult to secure good parts. Hurd Clarke notes the descent into social oblivion and loss of social privilege reported by older women on the basis of their changed physical exteriors, and the ways this erodes their full citizenship (2011: 135). As Kathy Woodward (1999) comments, the older female body is both invisible—in that it is no longer seen—and hypervisible—in that it is all that is seen.

Pollock has explored this theme in the context of the Western tradition of art, taking as her focus Canova's celebrated sculpture of the Three Graces. She argues that the female nude of Western art enshrines an ideal of 'timeless beauty', presenting a body that is timeless both in the sense that it is an ideal which traverses historical time and in the sense that it denies time. The eternally youthful female figures that people Western art are, for her, fetish objects held in 'transtemporal permanence' and denied histories or futures. Their function is as a defence against decay, death and the temporality of life. They represent the stasis of time but crucially they do so through the perfection and idealization of Woman in terms of perpetual youthfulness. Pollock notes in particular the absence of 'figurations of the maturing of the feminine in and through time', so that when high art does address the ageing female body, as in Rodin's 'She who was once the beautiful helmet maker's wife', it presents an image of fear. 'Old women in art are there to terrify us as a *momento mori*, juxtaposing as scary witches, hags, old bags to the soft fullness of the one moment of female desirability: youth' (2003: 193). The visual tradition of high art thus feeds into the cultural understanding of the female body, entrenching the ideal of femininity as only existing in its true essence in the form of youth, so that age is disconnected from this essence.

Contemporary femininity is thus constructed in such a way that it implicitly rests on a norm of youthfulness. That is a central part of its meaning: to be feminine is to be youthful. Indeed Robert Wilson's somewhat infamous attempt to promote Hormone Replacement Therapy in the 1960s was entitled *Feminine Forever* (1966). Ageing is experienced here as a steady movement away from this normative status and the social prestige that attaches to it. This underlies the pattern of injunctions in regard to appropriate dress for age: the requirements that older women cover up and tone down; the condemnation of exposure of the body, particularly in ways that make claims to sexual allure; the sense that ultra-fashionable dress is 'pathetic' or 'sad' on the old. It underlies the sense that overtly feminine, pretty dress 'no longer works' and is inappropriate for women as they age because it exposes the contrast between the normative expectations written into the garment and the body that displays it. It contributes to the sense of cultural exile many older women report, particularly those who at earlier stages of their lives took part in and enjoyed the cultural practices of femininity, many of which are embodied in the sphere of fashion. Here old age is experienced as a form of exile and exclusion from the feminine, from aesthetic self-fashioning, indeed from sexuality itself. I will examine in the next chapter how this underlies the sadness and discontent expressed by some women in the study.

In the creation of a normative feminine appearance, the cult of slimness plays a part. During the twentieth century, the body ideal in the West shifted from the earlier emphasis on voluptuous curves and maternal fullness towards an ideal based on youthful slimness. The current body ideal for women is toned, fit and youthful (Bordo 1993; Sterns 1997). Within the elite fashion world, it approaches the androgynous and prepubescent in its rejection of fleshliness. Concerns have been raised about the implications of this ideal for young women, with the widespread incidence of eating disorders (Bordo 1993; MacSween 1993), but it affects older women too, producing a dynamic whereby the pursuit of slimness becomes a significant anti-ageing technique. Many women, after menopause, put on weight. Flesh also becomes differently disposed about the body: more towards the middle and the bust. These shifts become more marked with advancing age, creating the classic appearance of the elderly body. Flesh also loses its tone with age, no longer forming the basis for potentially voluptuous curves, presenting instead flesh that sags and spreads unless held in by restrictive underwear. In the past this was achieved by corsets and foundation garments; today by a mass of commercially available shapewear based on Lycra and other control fibres. These changes in the body make it hard to fit into fashionable dress, which is cut for a young figure. As the editor of UK *Vogue* commented:

> No matter how much you might want to be fashionable, or how much you're prepared to wear really quite fashionable things, you will find it hard to fit them.

The fashionable norm, just like the feminine norm to which it closely relates, is youthful. Only the radical eradication of flesh can restore the older body nearer to the youthful norm. The women in the study who were most elegantly and fashionably dressed were those who had extremely slim bodies. But this required either the imposition of radical disciplinary practices of dieting or the possession of a body that is naturally extremely thin, approaching the androgynous, in earlier years. We thus have the paradox that being able to achieve the youthful fit of fashionable dress, and with it normative femininity, rests on *not* having an ultra-feminine body earlier in life.

These pressures are not confined to women. Men suffer from them too, though to a lesser degree, since their status traditionally is less closely tied to their appearance. Ageing is also believed to set in later for men. Whereas women's status in terms of appearance begins to decline in late youth or early middle age, men's status largely remains unaffected, protected by other sources of cultural esteem and power associated with work. Indeed signs of middle age in men—greying temples, smile lines—are often viewed positively since they are associated, for middle-class men in particular, with economic and cultural status. To this degree Connell's (1995) hegemonic masculinity can be said to be 'mid aged' as well as middle class, white and heterosexual, in that these together represent the dominant, 'unmarked' state within

Western capitalist societies against which other identities are formed. With retirement, however, some male sources of esteem and power decline. Katz and Marshall (2003) have explored the pressure on men to remain 'forever functional' in the form of sexually potent in the commercialized anti-ageing culture, where it is presented as a signal of status and continued belonging to the privileged group. The men pictured in such anti-ageing adverts translate the achievement orientations of the labour market into recreational consumption in their pursuit of symbols of continuing vigour. Calasanti and Slevin (2001) note, however, that men retain aspects of their favoured position within the gender order, as evidenced in their capacity to 'move younger' through partnering with younger women.

At a subjective level, however, the evidence in relation to gender and body image is less clear. Some work suggests that men in fact suffer from greater erosion of body image and self-esteem in age than women, who appear to develop better strategies for dealing with these (Baker and Gringart 2009). Scandinavian work reports that older women have higher levels of body satisfaction than do younger women, because they are no longer subject to the stringent body norms applied to young women. As a result older women reported as good or better levels of body satisfaction as men, reversing the well-established pattern of earlier years (Öberg and Tornstam 1999; Daatland 2007, 2008). Krekula (2007) in her study of the views of women over seventy-five suggests some of the complexity and ambivalence of women's evaluation of their bodies in age. The women did use negative words to describe changes to their bodies such as wrinkles and slackness of figure, but at the same time they spoke with pride about their 'dressed-up body', which was the focus of pleasure, esteem and adornment. Krekula suggests that it is fruitful to distinguish conceptually between the physical body, which pertains to wrinkles and loss of appearance, and the body as an embodied identity claim: 'it is possible to understand how these women describe their bodies with pride when they convey identity claims, and at the same time, talk about bodily changes with negative words' (2007: 166).

Successful Ageing and the Dream of Agelessness

Against the predominately negative cultural presentation of age, there have been a series of attempts to reframe the process or the state more positively. Variously termed 'successful', 'positive' or 'affirmative' ageing, these aim to provide positive, upbeat and optimistic narratives. But as many have pointed out, such accounts are not always as benign as they suggest. Katz in particular critiqued the ways positive ageing has been appropriated by commercial interests, which have translated its potentially radical message into a vehicle for commercial development, in which timeless, postmodern accounts of ageing are aligned to new frameworks for growing older based on consumerism. Quoting Hepworth, he notes how positive and negative ageing are 'socially constructed moral categories reflecting the prevailing social preference for individualised consumerism, voluntarism and decentralisation' (2001: 29). Successful ageing intersects with class, as the possession or otherwise of resources affects who can and cannot age well (Calasanti and Slevin 2001). To a significant degree it is constructed against groups who fail in the endeavour: derelict, ill 'no hopers' who have abandoned the disciplinary demands of fitness and success. Onto these groups all the feared aspects of old age are projected. Work by Hazan (1994) and Degnen (2007) has explored the ways older people themselves internalize ageism and set up a dynamic of Othering whereby the status of being old is kept at bay through the construction of others who represent that stigmatized state and who come to represent the abject version of old age.

In this context of ageism, 'agelessness' is sometimes presented as a way forward. As a cultural ideal, agelessness is widely promoted in the media, especially in relation to fashion, where it is the current ideal presented by *Vogue* magazine. But as Andrews argues, the dream of agelessness is, once again, not as positive as it might at first seem. She suggests that it rests on a false dualism in relation to the body and the self that encourages older people to eradicate their own histories, denying who and what they are by virtue of having lived long lives. It thus represents an internalization of society's devaluation of older people, resting on a form of resistance in which individuals attempt to separate themselves from the stigmatized group through a 'desperate plea for personal exceptionalism' (1999: 306). But trying 'to pass' in this way ultimately means participating in your own erasure; it is bound to fail since it is targeting the ultimately impossible task of transforming the self rather than addressing the real source of problem in the wider ageist culture.

Performativity and Resistance

I noted in Chapter 2 how age, like other forms of dressed identity, can be interpreted through the lens of performativity. Age here is seen as on a parallel with Judith Butler's (1993) account of gender, a product of repeated stylized acts. Laz (1998, 2003) argues, however, that we should see age in terms not of performance, but 'accomplishment', something we 'do', on a parallel to West and Zimmerman's concept of doing gender as a 'routine, methodical and recurring accomplishment embedded in everyday interaction'. Gender, as in Butler's account of performance, is seen as an achieved property of situated conduct, and this approach helped shift the understanding of gender from matters internal to the individual, towards the interactional and institutional areas. Laz argues that we need to see age in a similar way, as something that is continually accomplished. She prefers *accomplished* to *performed* because the latter implies a capacity to stop performing, and with that an essence or true nature underlying the performance. It also implies that the performance is deliberate and purposive. But age—as so many writers have pointed out—is not optional in this way. We cannot stop ageing, and to regard it wholly as performative is misleading. Seeing age as an accomplishment, as something collective and interactive, does allow us scope to explore the role of cultural goods like clothes in the way it is accomplished and made manifest in culture.

But ambiguity arises in relation to age with regard to exactly what is performed or accomplished. Are older people doing or performing age? Certainly there can be aspects of this in their behaviour, as individuals adopt manners and styles thought appropriate to their age; and this can extend to choice of dress. It is perhaps easiest to identify in relation to aspects of the role that have status or might be embraced positively—for example a grand or stately manner and the dress that goes with this. Performativity as a concept suggests an element of volition and choice in its expressivity; and it often implies something against the cultural grain, certainly self-conscious and perhaps challenging, as its intellectual locus in Judith Butler's work on drag and gender suggests. This challenging quality is part of its attraction to writers like Kathy Woodward (2006). A clear example of such performativity in relation to age is the Web site Advanced Style, illustrating older people living in New York wearing very highly styled, ultra-fashion-conscious dress (Cohen 2012). It is a self-conscious, edgy, performative look that makes sense in an urban centre like New York. But a question remains as to what they are performing. Is it indeed age, or an alternative vision of age? Or is it youth? The reason these clothes are so striking is that they are disruptive of expectations of what older people should and should not wear. There is a discordance between the high styles and the ageing bodies that display them. There is thus a limit to performativity. Identities are not wholly optional, the product of agency and performance, but are in large measure culturally assigned. This is particularly so with identities like race and age that are made manifest in bodily appearance, where individuals are accorded limited optionality. You cannot choose not to be black or not to be old. Wearing very youthful styles will not produce a youthful identity, rather the reverse, drawing attention to and pointing up the contrast between the youthful style and the ageing body that wears it.

Some of the same tensions around agency and volition are found in the concept of resistance, though here the intellectual origins are different, lying in Foucault and his conception of power. For Foucault power and resistance are dialectically constituted, with each new formation of disciplinary power creating the countervailing possibility of resistance encapsulated in his celebrated dictum: 'Where there is power, there is resistance' (1990). But the basis for this resistance was never adequately theorized in his work; and to that degree it is not possible to say where, or in what circumstances, it might or might not emerge, nor what were its limits and sources. Like all forms of poststructuralist theorizing, it is full of ambiguity and fluidity. For example, is the fluffy pink, exaggerated femininity of Barbara Cartland's presentation in old age an example of resistance to the cultural discourses that suggest that old women should retire into drab, unglamorous, asexual dress? Or is it extreme conformity to the norms of conventional femininity? It is capable of being read as either—and indeed carries elements of both meanings within it. Furman (1999) makes a similar point in her account of a New Jersey beauty shop, where she notes how what counts as resistance and capitulation remains far from clear, as ambiguity is piled on ambiguity.

As with performativity, there are clearly limits to resistance. Dinnerstein and Weitz (1994) explore the ability of women to resist the prevailing cultural discourses that equate femininity with youthful appearance through an analysis of the contrasting responses of two culturally powerful women, Jane Fonda and Barbara Bush, the former through extreme disciplinary interventions and the latter through self-depreciation allied to careful self-presentation. Their analysis, however, reiterates the limits that even such powerful women experience in successfully resisting the dominant models of femininity.

In relation to clothing and dress, resistance can clearly take a number of forms. I noted earlier the radical refusal to retreat from fashion and display evidenced in the New York Web site. In Chapter 4, we will hear from one respondent in the study determined to retain her involvement in transgressive style living as a Goth and who berated the 'vanillas' who gave up and, in her view, sank into asexuality with age. For another respondent, it took the form of wearing loud bright colours, extending at times to a shocking pink wig. As powerful as these forms of active resistance, however, can be quieter, less visible ones, such as the retreat from all active engagement by refusing to buy any new clothes, by treating dress as an entirely practical matter, by sourcing garments from cheap work-related, sometimes masculine, sources, or drab items from charity shops. Resistance to the connection between femininity and youth can also be pursued through attempts to radically embrace age, for example through consciously adopting the status of Crone in pagan circles (Manning 2012). Greer (1991) has argued that the invisibility imposed on older women should be regarded positively, as offering them new space within which to develop aspects of themselves, freed from the demands of normative femininity. Biggs (1997) makes a related point in his suggestion that the performance of old age can offer a mask behind which the self can shelter and hide and where dimensions of the self that sustain the individual and that protect his or her sense of continuity can be nurtured. But these forms of refusal or retreat always come at a cost, that of a more conscious exclusion from normative femininity. As Hurd Clarke records in relation to appearance: 'The apparent throwing off of the burden of beauty ideology was ultimately a call for individuals to resign themselves to exclusion, invisibility and social devaluation' (2011: 67).

Conclusion

In this chapter I explored the ways ageing needs to be understood as both a bodily and a cultural phenomenon. I have observed how these are differentially gendered and how this affects the ways age is presented and experienced. I have also noted arguments suggesting that the nature of later years is itself changing. I can now review how these themes play out in relation to dress. I can note this first through the growing requirements on older women that they engage with the norms of fashion. The last two decades have witnessed a major expansion of the concept of fashionability, extending it to progressively older age groups. This is largely interpreted positively, as a mode of empowerment, a throwing off of the limitations and cultural constraints associated with age. But it also contains elements of ambiguity in relation to the new governmentality of the body. With new pleasures have come new disciplinary requirements. As women are drawn more and more into the culture of consumption and age resistance, so they are required to impose new forms of self-surveillance, monitoring their dress to avoid out-of-date, unfashionable or ageing looks that signal moral failure in this new culture of positive ageing. Just as men according to Katz and Marshall (2003) are required to be 'forever functional', women are increasingly required to be 'forever fashionable'.

Being fashionable often also entails 'moving younger', adopting the styles and looks associated with younger women—certainly avoiding those associated with older. I explore these themes further in Chapters 6 and 7 when I analyse the ways magazines and retailers consistently present a younger look to their customers. But as I noted in Chapter 2, this process of moving younger overlaps with the diffusion of fashion itself, as styles move from younger to older age groups, progressively abandoned by the former as they spread to the latter. This is a continuing movement that itself affects the ways styles are interpreted and evaluated. 'Moving younger' is thus a complex set of cultural processes in which clothes are passed down the age/status hierarchy from young to old, and in which older people attempt to improve their cultural status by adopting younger styles. The degree to which they have been successful in this relates to the question of how far later years have indeed become more integrated with the cultural mainstream.

There are, however, constraints on this process of moving younger. As Featherstone and Hepworth (1991) argued in their account of the Mask of Ageing, there are limitations to the plasticity of the body and its capacity to perform youthfulness. Adopting extremely youthful styles does not always create a youthful appearance, often the reverse, with the contrast between youthful style and the ageing body that wears it pointing up and accentuating age. Magazine journalists see a central part of their work as assisting women to avoid the dangers of overly youthful looks, while still responding to opportunities presented by new fashions. Behind this lurks the familiar cultural trope of 'mutton dressed as lamb'. I noted how this condemnation applies only to women and how it focusses in particular on the element of overt sexuality. Women who dress in inappropriately youthful styles, particularly involving an overt display of sexuality, come under special moral condemnation. This critique is part of a wider moral policing of the bodies and behaviour of women, but it relates also to dangers of failed performance. In this context ideas of resistance are often presented as an analytic way forward. But resistance is a concept fraught with ambiguity. Does it, for example, mean asserting female sexuality in age as against a dominant cultural narrative of asexuality, exclusion and invisibility? Or does it mean resisting the demands of normative femininity that associates it with direct expression of sexuality in dress? There are clearly many modes of resistance and many discursive structures against which it can be asserted. Indeed by one interpretation, resistance needs to be understood as pursued through a continuing set of such reactions and counteractions to discursive power in all its protean forms.

Lastly, it is worth noting how though clothes share themes with appearance-related areas like hair, cosmetics, anti-wrinkle practices and their commercialized promoters in the related beauty ideology, they are also different. They are clearly involved in the expression of normative femininity and related aspects of heterosexuality, but they are not wholly bound up in these, but part of a wider set of symbolic structures expressive of identity and meaning. They are also functional in ways that make-up and anti-wrinkle creams are not. As such they are inescapable. Everyone needs clothes and is required to make decisions about them. This reinforces the point made in Chapter 2 that the focus of this study is dress, not fashion. It is the reach of the former that is ubiquitous and that extends fully to the aged. Clothes are also—potentially at least—aesthetic. They offer opportunities for sensory delight in texture, colour, pattern and cut that can be separate from their role in signalling identity or fashionability. They thus operate differently from other elements in the debate on appearance and age. Though indeed implicated in the culture of anti-ageing and of 'moving younger', they are also wider in the scope of their meanings.

—4—

The Voices of Older Women

In this chapter I turn to the voices of older women as they narrate the significance of age in their experiences of clothing and dress. The comments derive from an empirical study based on interviews with older women, representatives of the media and representatives of branded clothing retailers. The second two groups provide the basis for Chapters 6 and 7. In this and the next chapter, I focus on the views and experiences of older women. Respondents in the study were selected to represent a range of ages from fifty-five and over, of social class backgrounds and of relationship and employment circumstances. A fuller account of the study is found in the appendix.

I use these narratives to address questions raised in earlier chapters, exploring the ways age ordering does or does not still operate in relation to expectations about women's dress and the feelings of older women about this. I look at the role of the body and the changes that occur in relation to age in shaping women's clothing choices. I will address the potential role of consumption in the negotiation of age, and in doing so ask how far older women represent frustrated shoppers unable to find their wishes reflected in clothes on offer. But before doing so I need to explore the links between clothing and identity and the ways these are expressed in the context of age.

Age, Identity and Dress

As part of the interviews, respondents were asked to wear a set of clothes they liked and to reflect on what their clothing conveyed about themselves. The responses to this tended to be somewhat uncertain, even equivocal. The idea that their clothes expressed their identity was certainly not endorsed in a wholehearted manner. Age was not, however, always the key factor in this. Some of the responses were ironic and self-depreciatory in a manner familiar in wider British culture. As Clare, when asked what her dress said about her, commented:

> I don't think like that, to be honest. I mean, I know people do. It's how people talk about cars...Well, I guess I am a Ford Fiesta kind of person. [laughs] And that's probably what my clothes say too...I mean I don't buy clothes for that purpose. I buy clothes to be comfortable.

Many found it difficult to elaborate the link. Partly this reflected a general sense that the values their clothes expressed were so embedded that they could not articulate them and they felt uneasy when asked to do so. But it also reflected their low level of aspiration in relation to expressivity. The overall tone was one of wishing to be acceptable, of 'looking nice', of 'passing muster', as Dot, a widow in her eighties, described it; and this was reflected in the cautious, conservative style many adopted. This in itself says something about age and its cultural status, but it also testifies to the ways expressivity in dress is something the British population pursues only to a limited extent. Accounts presented in cultural studies of the role of clothes in the performance of identity draw heavily, as I noted in Chapter 2, on the analysis of radical, transgressive groups, and they often fail to engage with the day-to-day experiences of the ordinary, mainstream population for whom the principle of conformity, of fitting in and of being acceptable as opposed to standing out, is the dominant one. The idea that dress might be used to express or perform one's identity in a strong sense was foreign to most of the individuals in the study (though there were some striking exceptions).

For some, however, the uncertainty did seem to express something about the experience of age, reflecting a degree of alienation from the person their clothes now suggested. Olive, for example, a woman in her seventies who had worked in fashion retail and been very interested in clothes, articulated a pervasive discontent with what she now wore, which she did not feel expressed who she was, or rather, expressed someone she did not really want to be. These themes of regret and alienation were found in a number of the interviews. Other interviewees, however, did embrace an identity as an older woman more positively.

In the next chapter I explore in greater detail the lives of three women in the study for whom dress and the expression of identity were clearly and strongly linked. Each had adopted a distinctive or alternative style: Helena had created a poetic, romantic look expressive of her inner self; Angela had adopted brightly coloured ethnic-influenced garments as part of a new feminist confidence; Joanne dressed in Goth style. In each case, their dress had evolved in the context of their lives and relationships, though now also increasingly in interaction with age, reinforcing the point that dress and identity are linked in a complex long-term interplay in which ageing and the arrival of the signs of ageing is only one element. It also reminds us of the important analytic principle of not cutting later years off from earlier experiences of life. As we shall see, continuity can be as significant as change.

Age Ordering in Dress

I noted in Chapter 2 there is a long history of age ordering in dress whereby certain forms of clothes are deemed appropriate—or, more significant, inappropriate—for people as they age. I reflected on the often harsh condemnation of women in particular who failed to modify their dress as they grew older. In recent years, however, a new belief has grown up that age ordering in dress is no longer significant, and that cultural expectations in relation to age have shifted under the influence of the wider reconstitution of age and the impact of consumption culture. How far were these views supported in the responses of older women themselves?

In general, their narratives rejected the idea that age ordering had gone; respondents were fully aware of pressures on them to modify their dress according to that traditional regulatory regime. Though there was variation in how they regarded such pressure—with regret, sadness, indifference, acceptance—all recognized its power. As a result the predominant tone in the interviews was one of guarded caution and constraint. Carol, for example, the widow of a bank manager in her seventies who had always been interested in fashion, explained how older women had to be 'careful':

> You have to be careful when you get to my age. I always have to have something with long sleeves. I think one or two of the things are perhaps a bit too young for me. I always wear very long skirts. I don't like showing my legs.

The need to be 'careful' was a sentiment that recurred in the interviews.

Such changes in regard to age, however, came on slowly, so that the women adjusting what they wore was not something that happened at a particular moment so much as gradually and over time. As Celia, a divorced middle-class woman in her seventies, explained:

> I suppose that just happens really. I don't think perhaps you're completely conscious of changing it. It's just something that happens.

The pressure to adjust dress had often set in earlier. Dot, for example, a widow in her eighties, began to tone down

> not long after I married. I began to think, oh well I'd better begin to look more like a matron. [she was twenty-nine]

As she explained:

> I suppose in some ways you've got to think about the hierarchy of—when you're young you're free and easy with no problems, but as you get older you're expected to behave that little bit more soberly.

Cultural ageing is, thus, something that comes upon the individual gradually, operating throughout the life course, and is not confined to later years. As I noted in Chapter 3, the processes of ageing are themselves culturally contingent, affected by the particular cultural field in which they are expressed. In the case of fashion, these can set in early, so that questions of age-appropriate dress can arise from the late twenties onwards. They also operate in interplay with other structural factors shaping social identity: in Dot's case, her roles as a wife and mother had led her to adopt more sober, older dress while she was still only in her thirties. Where individuals place themselves in terms of sartorial age thus varies in line with other aspects of their identity. It reflects the ways structural dimensions such as gender and class intersect with age in distinctive ways. It also reflects personal attitudes particular to the individual. How the ascription of age ordering operates is thus complex, variable and culturally contingent. What is significant here, however, is the way the overall concept is still widely understood and applied.

The persistence of age ordering was also evidenced in the dress adopted by the respondents in the interviews. An analysis of the photographs taken as part of the study showed that their dress retained strong age connotations. They were, in Krekula's (2009) term, *age coded*. None of the respondents, for example, wore clothes that could plausibly have been adopted by an eighteen-year-old. However, six of them wore clothes that could have been worn by a forty-year-old, though the majority of these individuals fell in the younger old age band. The feature that particularly marked out the dress of this group as older was length of skirt. Their clothes, however, did also show considerable continuity with styles worn by young middle-aged women, supporting the idea of broader cultural integration with these age groups. However, I should also note that their dress did intersect with the cautious conservative style that forms the bulk of UK dress across a range of ages.

It is important to note at this point how identity in old age is marked as much by continuity as by change. As Andrews (1999) comments, we are who we are by virtue of the lives we have lived. This means that our identities are formed through time, reflecting elements of both continuity and change, so that although the overt subject of the interviews was age and its role in relation to dress, many of the respondents gave accounts in which age was not the only, or indeed prime, factor in their responses. They did not see themselves as greatly different from the person they had been earlier, and in their eyes still were; this was reflected in the way they talked about dress. Much of what they said was general to themselves and their lives—the kinds of clothes they had liked in the past and now. As Olive, a middle-class woman in her late seventies, explained:

> My tastes really haven't changed, they've always been quite simple. I don't like anything too fancy.

Patricia's classic style had similarly been established earlier as part of office life. As she explained in the interview, what she was wearing was

> what I've worn since I started work really. It hasn't, you know, a pencil skirt perhaps is what I started work in at fifteen...So a pencil skirt and a top, and really I suppose that's seen me through forty years.

Even bodily preoccupations in relation to dress were often less about age than enduring features of their figures, such as a large bust in the case of Anja or short stature in the case of Gillian. These, rather than age, shaped their dress choices. I will explore these themes of continuity more fully in the next chapter when I address the role of clothing in the unfolding narrative of life.

What Not to Wear: Too Young

There was a clear consensus across the interviews about what the 'rules' governing dress and age were, and these followed a pattern familiar from other work (Fairhurst 1998; Klepp and Storm-Mathisen 2005; Hurd Clark et al. 2009). They were largely expressed negatively, in terms of the sorts of dress that should be avoided—typically short skirts, low necks, sleeveless dresses—anything that exposed the body and its decline. As Chris, a former psychiatric nurse, explained:

> I wouldn't show my knees, because you don't show your knees after you're fifty. Some people do and they look awful.

Carol, a smartly dressed woman in her seventies, commented, pointing to her neckline:

> You get a bit wrinkly round there. I think anything to cover up wrinkly bits is good…If it's not top notch, then keep it covered, I think.

The prohibitions particularly centred on clothes that exposed the ageing body in a sexual way or that made claims to sexual allure. I explore the significance of this more fully later in this chapter when I look at the interaction between the body and dress.

Other styles best avoided were more culturally defined. There was a clear consensus across the interviews that frilly or girly styles were particularly unsuitable and unflattering. As Chris commented:

> I wouldn't wear a frilly dress…It would make me look silly. I'm too old. I would look really silly.

Kathie, a woman in her late fifties, concurred:

> I bought a couple of tops, and when I wear them I feel too girly. And I'm not a girl any more, so I don't feel comfortable wearing them.

Such styles exposed the discrepancy between their youthful associations and the ageing face or body of the wearer. Janet was critical of a friend:

> She does wear what I call girly clothes. It doesn't suit you when you've got dyed hair and have your face lifted, and one thing and another. It's pathetic.

Olive particularly abhorred puff sleeves:

> Little puff sleeves! And they're quite pretty, the tops are quite pretty but they have these silly little sleeves that stick up. Well, I couldn't wear anything like that, you know, your skin, crinkly skin. You can't. I mean you have got to hide yourself a little bit when you get older, otherwise you look yuck.

Some of the meaning of girly dress is ultra feminine. Behind the prohibition of such styles lie the normative associations of femininity with youthfulness, so that ultra-feminine clothing comes to be seen as culturally discordant. The conventional version of successful dress for older women is plainer and more neutral than is the case for younger age groups. Indeed some of the meaning of classic dress, which has strong age associations for the fashion industry, relates to this neutral, toned-down style which has removed showy associations of either femininity or sexuality.

What Not to Wear: Too Old

Respondents in the study were also concerned to avoid dress they deemed too old. As Banister and Hogg (2007) suggest in their account of the power of negative selves, as significant as our likes in the articulation of identity can be our dislikes, the versions of ourselves we want to repudiate. It was certainly the case that respondents in the interviews often found it easier to say what they disliked in clothing than what they liked. Many were clear about the sorts of dress they wanted to avoid, and indeed positively refused to wear. These were garments that they felt were ageing, and in an ugly, frumpy way. Elastic waists, pleated skirts and old-fashioned jumpers were singled out for particular vilification. Chris, a former psychiatric nurse in her sixties who wore smart, minimal dress, was clear about the sorts of shops she kept out of, ones that 'do a lot of pleated skirts, and that type of thing, and woollies that have got round necks'. She summed up what she hated with energy:

> I would avoid pleated skirts. I would avoid Crimplene trousers. I'd avoid check trousers of any description. I would avoid dresses that come down here. [pointing to her mid calf]

She was determined to resist this version of old age. Evie, a working-class widow in her seventies with a neat, trim figure and dress style, was also clear that she was 'not going to wear baggy or elasticated stuff'. For Gillian, a retired schoolteacher in her late sixties, 'pleated skirts' represented shorthand for all she was determined to avoid. Patricia broadly concurred in her list of clothes she disliked: 'I don't like elasticated waists they make for older ladies... comfort trousers, Crimplene!' It was striking how often Crimplene featured in this context. Crimplene has come to be the fibre to dread. Occupying a distinctive place in the public folk memory, it is uniquely associated with old age, drabness and lack of style. For this generation in particular it is now inextricably linked with care homes and abject versions of old age and to be avoided at all costs.

The forms of dress that were vilified were so, not just because they were age coded—though they were—but also because they represented versions of ageing respondents disliked, rejected and were determined to resist. They were seen as far too old for them, more suitable for women in their eighties and nineties (and some indeed in the study of that age did wear these sorts of clothes, reminding us of the significant differences contained in the category 'older'). Rejecting them was part of pushing away an undesired future, asserting that one was 'not that old' yet, indeed was still part of the mainstream. But it was also rejecting a version of being older that was inherently repellent and that respondents could not conceive ever wanting to adopt. As Chris asked rhetorically:

> What day do I wake up and I really just want a Crimplene skirt? What day do I wake up and do that?

For Kathie the issue was exemplified in the Classic range in M&S.

> I would hope that I never have to go into the Classic range...By the time I get to that age, I don't think there'll be that department. Well, I would hope there isn't that department still going.

It was clear that many respondents felt they were indeed a different generation; for them, things had changed. They were the cohort who had worn jeans and hippie dress, had shopped at Biba and aspired to Mary Quant. They felt they were not willing to move into age-labelled clothes as their mothers had. Indeed, looking back on their mothers, and especially grandmothers, they reflected on how old they had seemed. Chris explained:

> When my grandmother was older, she wore a pinny and her hair up in braids. And she was the same age as me! I'm sixty-two. And when she was sixty-two, she was walking round in this paisley pinny and her hair up.

Kathie, a divorced woman in her late fifties, similarly remembered, with slight shock, her grandmother at the age she was now:

> when I look back and think, gosh, she seemed so old at the time. She was a proper granny, and yet she was only in her sixties. And I don't feel that I'm as old as she was.

But as Ada, a working-class former cleaner in her eighties, pointed out, women of the previous generation had often lived hard lives. In the past, 'grannies were grannies once they got into their sixties.' They wore different clothes:

Most of them, there again, would wear black. And they always had the old overall, but
I'm talking about the working classes, you see.

This was not just a matter of style. As she pointed out, life for these working-class
women had been hard. Housework was arduous: lighting fires, blacking stoves,
scrubbing brick floors. As a result, they aged physically:

> It was hard work, I mean that's what wore the women out. There weren't shop jobs.
> There weren't easygoing jobs like there is today. So that a sixty year old is, well isn't
> sixty really. They've got to reach until they're about seventy.

To this degree Ada provides evidence to support the popular view found in the media
that older people are actually younger than in the past, though in her case she roots
this not in cultural factors but in the material facts of the previous generation's lives.

Chris believed that though clothes were still ordered in terms of age, this was not
to the degree they were in the past:

> I think the young people still wear the young things. There are some things older people
> would not wear, or should not wear that younger people wear. They shouldn't be seen
> in them, no. And some younger people wouldn't be seen dead in some things that older
> people wear I'm sure.

But she still saw her generation as different; and she certainly did not intend to go
into old lady shops:

> I don't know if you know Jacques Vert, but you'd expect someone of my age to be in that.
> But we're not, we're in jeans. We're still in jeans. And I'll be in jeans when I'm seventy.

She was very conscious that she did not want to adopt old-labelled clothes.

> I say, 'What day do I wake up and I really just want a Crimplene skirt?' 'What day do I
> wake up and do that?' I don't think I'm ever gonna wake up and do that...I don't think
> our generation ever is. I think that generation's gone...We won't change a lot. We'll still
> be in our jeans, and we'll still be in our tops.

Jeans and Crimplene here stand as symbolic polar opposites for this generation,
exemplifying the changes that have taken place or are in the process of taking place.

Chris certainly saw herself as still part of the mainstream of fashion. She recognized that the young wore clothes distinctive to them, and she avoided styles she felt
would make her look 'silly' or 'pathetic', but she noted and remarked on trends and
was dressed in a mainstream, age-neutral way. Kathie similarly felt that there was a
generational change and she pointed in particular to the role of work: 'My mother's
generation didn't go out to work. They did become invisible.' She worked in a payroll

office alongside young people and felt this kept her in the swim. But at the same time, it made her very conscious of issues around age and suitability. She had internalized the gaze of youth:

> I'm very conscious of what I'm wearing, because I know that I can't wear what they're going to be wearing. And they do look lovely, you know, when they come out. But I know I'm not their shape or their age, to be able to—and I couldn't, I'd look ridiculous in their sort of clothes. So yes, I do think about it—I don't want to look too grannyish when I go to work.

Clare recognized that like it or not, age ordering still happens, and a significant part of this arose from changes in the body that meant that she could not wear younger forms of dress.

> Age ordering happens by default because you simply can't find the kind of clothes you want to wear, because they're all too young. You feel that they're too young, unless I imagine you're stick thin, and Botoxed perhaps. [laughs] And have no arthritis.

The Body Changes

Many of the comments concerning unsuitable dress were rooted in perceptions of the way the body changes with age. The interviews revealed a widespread sense that old bodies were unattractive and best kept covered up; and it was clear that respondents used clothes to 'mask or compensate for bodily transgressions' and to hide how their bodies fell short of the cultural ideal in the ways suggested by Hurd Clarke and colleagues (2009: 709). Some of the comments on age had a preemptive, defensive quality to them—internalizing the judgement of wider culture while attempting to deflect its attack. Many reflected quite considerable degrees of self-dislike. Olive used the word *yuck* to describe how her body might look if on view. Clare reported that she concealed the bits of her body she did not like, so she could remain 'part of the human race basically and not too rough and horrible'. Respondents thus reflected the wider ageist and sexist culture that Hurd Clarke (2011) has analysed in relation to appearance generally. As she notes, the overwhelming impression from this literature is one of internalized ageism in which older women have learnt to evaluate their bodies and their appearance in highly negative ways. This response was clearly reflected in the study. It was notable that no one asserted that it was acceptable for old bodies to be on display, nor did anyone articulate direct anger at these negative evaluations.

Changes in the body present problems not only in terms of appearance but also fit. Olive, who was seventy-nine and had always been fashionably dressed, bemoaned the problem of finding elegant clothes that could fit the way her body had changed.

> I find it difficult, when you're older, you know to get things to fit you properly...you've always got a big tummy when you get older and there's nothing you can do about it, nothing at all. Unfortunately I've lost a lot of weight in the last five weeks. I've lost over a stone in weight for some unknown reason. But I've never, ever lost it round my tummy.

With her professionally trained eye—she had worked in department stores—she could see that elegant clothes aimed at older women could be found in smart towns in Kent or Suffolk, but these were really targeted to those in their fifties whose bodies had not changed greatly.

> The clothes are extremely expensive there, but they're not for me. They're for the thirty-five up to fifties. Very, very elegant clothes they are in their own way, but they're just not for me because they're cut on the bias...which makes my tummy look much too big. So you have to take that into consideration. You don't want all your bulges showing, do you?

As a result, the clothes she wore were a disappointment to her and fell short of the stylishness she had earlier displayed.

Clare, in her late seventies, similarly found fit was the problem. Her body had changed so 'I can no longer buy clothes that fit, or that suit me'. She felt that everything is 'cut so tightly into the body'. She blamed the UK TV fashion makeover duo, Trinny and Susannah, for this emphasis on close fit and showing curves.

> They always seemed to be saying, 'Wear everything that emphasizes your curves.' Well, I don't want to emphasize my curves. I want to hide them...because my curves are not nice curves.

It is certainly the case that one of the ways makeover experts like Trinny and Susannah, Gok Wan and others achieve a stylish and younger look among the older women they dress is by using controlling underwear and tight cut that has the effect of imposing a younger feminine figure. In this way they reconstitute older bodies nearer the ideal, that of the premenopausal body, reinforcing the association of femininity with youth.

Some, particularly younger older women, disliked loose dress and saw it as frumpy and ageing. Gillian, a retired schoolteacher in her late sixties, was pleased that she still had some shape and was critical of women who hid their figures with age:

> I like to think I've still got a bit of shape, I'm quite pleased. I'm not showing off, but I've still got a bit of shape. Clothes should follow the shape line.

That view was most strongly expressed by Joanne, a woman in her late fifties who dressed as a Goth. She always wore corsets and railed against mainstream 'vanilla' older women who retreated into shapelessness, abandoning any attempt at a figure:

> They don't show off whatever figure they've got. They mask it with tops and skirts that blend into each other, so that you're a rectangle. I'm not going to do that. Even if my belly gets bigger and my waist gets bigger, I'm still going to have a figure when I go out. I'm not going to be a box or a rectangle.

Many women put on weight as they get older. Many respondents saw this as ageing. I noted in Chapter 3 how slimming is widely adopted as an anti-ageing technique to counteract this association. Patricia commented: 'If somebody is rather large, ... you tend to put years on them.' Size also affected the kinds of clothes women are able to wear. As Janet commented:

> I think you're really governed by your size ... You do get bigger as you get older, and you get dissatisfied, and you feel uncomfortable in a lot of things you wear.

Putting on weight with age thus restricted choice and undermined pleasure in dress. It also acted to push women towards shapeless clothes, or ones with 'give' that were more comfortable, but that lacked the style that cut could provide. Olive agreed that modern clothes required women be slim. Nina, who was very slim and elegant, remarked rather tartly of a friend:

> It does depend on your figure. I mean you know I've got a friend who spends quite a lot on clothes, and whatever she did, she's not going to look elegant, because she's plump.

For her, plumpness and elegance were incompatible. It was notable that the two most elegantly presented women in the study (Nina and Chris) were both very slim, with bodies nearer the youthful ideal of modern fashion, so that they would have had little difficulty in fitting into clothes designed for young women. There was no problematic flesh to get in the way of their elegance. As I noted earlier, curves that at a younger age are womanly and feminine become problematic with age, undermining claims to elegance and femininity. Nina noted, in a somewhat self-satisfied way, that her figure did not pose such difficulties. Unlike other older women, she did not have to hide her body:

> I think as they get older they hide their bodies because their bodies have changed some-times. I mean I've been lucky that this hasn't happened. But a lot of people have got sort of funny shapes and funny bits and pieces, so they sort of just cover it up.

But such judgements mean that most older women, if they are to remain fashionable, have to impose rigorous discipline over their bodies and their lives, and even that may not achieve the desired look of youthful femininity.

Loss and Regret, or the Sadness of Exile

A number of the interviews were permeated by a sense of sadness and regret. Many of the women had enjoyed dress earlier in their lives, but felt they no longer could. For them this represented a form of cultural exile from femininity and the cultural practices associated with its display. These form a significant aesthetic element in the lives of many women, and the loss of such was a source of sadness. Many of them had faced the 'changing room moment' when garments that had once looked attractive no longer did. As Patricia explained, older women go into the changing room and

> look in the mirror and think, No . . . That isn't me, how I am now.

The editor of *Vogue* expressed this sadness at the loss of a particular personal aesthetic:

> I've always loved those kind of vintage tea dresses and things, and suddenly I look really tragic in them now. But they're still in my wardrobe because I like the dresses. I won't get rid of them, because they're part of my identity as the person that always wore them. And it's hard really to confront those things that you can't wear.

For Sarah, a self-confessed 'arty type' with a slightly romantic, bohemian style, ageing was permeated by a sense of loss. She too had faced the changing room moment.

> I'm very sad, I'm very upset. I mean some of the styles are quite gorgeous and I'd love to be able to wear them . . . When you're in the changing room and you see, oh goodness! Is that me? [laughter] And I just think, no no, I can't wear it any more. It's a lovely style, and I just can't wear it. I just feel very sad. And then I've got to look for something that's more appropriate for my age.

Kathie, a divorced woman in her late fifties who worked in a large office full of younger people, was similarly sad that she could no longer wear the sorts of clothes she liked. The youthful styles worn by her young colleagues were now beyond her. For her, this carried a clear sense of loss, not just of youth, but of femininity. One of the ways she tried to counteract this and sustain a continued sense of femininity was by wearing deliberately pretty, feminine underwear. She had an extensive collection of matching sets, and made a point of coordinating or contrasting the colours of these with what she was wearing on top. For her it did not matter that she was the only person who would see this. It was a private pleasure and a form of compensation: 'It makes me feel good underneath . . . It's making up for what I can't wear.'

Becoming Invisible

For many respondents, toning down was part of a wider cultural process of becoming invisible as older women. I noted in Chapter 3 the systematic exclusion of older women from visual culture and the social evaluations that underlie becoming culturally absent. For some respondents this process took on a defensive quality, designed to protect the self from slights. Biggs (1997) has explored what he terms the Masquerade of Age whereby older people engage in a form of masquerading to hide and protect their true selves behind a defensive front, learning to perform age in a way that protects the inner self from wider cultural slights. Some of the negative comments expressed in the interviews about the body and appearance, with their preemptive quality, reflected such a response. Adopting toned-down, dull forms of dress could be a means of hiding, of not drawing attention to the self. Strong colours, bold patterns and fashionable styles threatened the reverse, consciously drawing the eye and making a claim to attention. Kathie explained that she had moved into darker shades as she had become older because, 'I don't want to be in the forefront any more.' She preferred 'to cover up and fade in, disappear into the background rather than being in the foreground'. Dot similarly explained:

> Strong colours draw attention to you. It's all very well if you're young and beautiful, but when you're getting a bit older and past it... [her comments trailed off at this point]

She then added:

> I don't want to dress in a way that causes too much attention to me. I don't want to be outstanding.

Some of this is reflected in the use of colour, particularly the adoption of low dark tones traditionally associated with age. I explore the role of colour more fully in Chapter 7, but simply note here that, although a number of women did express traditional ideas around toning down and adopting more self-effacing, neutral shades, a number embraced colour with positive relish. As Anja said:

> If I saw something in a colour that I liked, I would buy it, and I would wear it. It wouldn't worry me at all. I've got some outrageous colours in my wardrobe.

Indeed in the interview she wore a bright blue and lime green overshirt. Gillian similarly chose a salmon and cream blouse; and Jessie, a violet jersey with contrasting green necklace. Clearer colours are now a prominent feature of the older market, endorsing ideas that older women are no longer as self-effacing as in the past and evidencing a cultural trend towards older women presenting themselves in a brighter, more visible way.

For Clare, however, the cultural invisibility of age was not necessarily a bad thing. A quiet, watchful person, she was happy to fade into the background.

Clare:	I like to listen to what's going on. I do try to write stories and novels and things, and I'm quite interested in just being there, hearing.
Interviewer:	Was that always something about you?
Clare:	I don't know. I'll tell you what I really think it is. I think it's total relaxation, because I just don't care anymore. And I think when you're younger you're trying to make some kind of an impression and you're very anxious about what you're wearing, or at least I was—is this the right thing? And so you make very bad choices sometimes I think. And when you're older you just think, Well, I'm me, I know who I am and this is what I wear. That's it.
Interviewer:	That's very interesting. So you're saying that in a way you're freed?
Clare:	I think so, yes.
Interviewer:	Because sometimes people say as we get older that you become invisible as a woman.
Clare:	Oh, you do. Yes, you do. Which is in some ways quite nice.

For her there was something positive about invisibility that echoed the argument of Greer (1991) that older women should embrace invisibility, seeing it as a form of freedom from the hypervisibility imposed on young women and their bodies. Clare felt that she did not have to bother anymore, presenting herself in a particular way. She could just be herself. She felt this contributed to the confidence that had come to her with age. She was happy to be quiet: it suited who she felt she now was. This was reflected in her modest style of dress: in the interview she wore black trousers and a denim overshirt. She was not interested in consumption, on keeping up to date or looking younger. She had lost her husband and still missed him greatly. Her world now centred on books and writing and on the wildlife in her beautiful, overgrown garden. Her narrative stands in clear opposition to those who argue that positive involvement in consumption and the extension of fashionability to older age groups is a form of empowerment.

Resisting Dereliction

The body in age is subject to distinctive forms of surveillance in which signs of dereliction—stains, drooping hems, down-at-heel shoes—signal moral collapse and threaten exclusion from the mainstream in a way that is not the case for younger people. Keeping up a good appearance is thus an important part of maintaining one's status and acceptability in this harsher moral climate.

For many of the older working-class women in the study, however, the values of neatness and cleanliness in dress were long-established ones. These, rather than any idea of smartness or fashionability, were the prime virtues. Ada, a working-class woman in her eighties who had worked all her life as a cleaner, had never been interested in clothes. She regarded such things as flighty. What mattered to her was to be neat and comfortable and able to do her work.

> I have never followed fashion. The way I looked at it you'd got to look clean, tidy and dress nicely. And that has been the way I've looked. I've never followed fashion in any way whatsoever...Cheerful and clean, and that suited me.

This reflected the virtues of her upbringing:

> I was brought up to be, as a kid, and I was always neat, very, very poor, but my aunt made sure I was always neat...I think if you're neat, you can go anywhere.

Evie, another working-class widow, also articulated these traditional values and the significance of maintaining them into later years. She disliked the modern fashion for what she saw as crumpled fabrics, 'screwed up stuff'. 'I'd just feel scruffy in it.' She explained how her generation

> were used to having everything ironed, and everything had to be nice and smooth...My husband wouldn't go out without his shoes polished highly. The same as when my daughters were young, they wore Startrites, and then they wore highly polished shoes for school...They looked like chestnuts—lovely.

When asked to describe her style, she replied: 'I would say it was neat and acceptable.' The word *acceptable* is significant here, and points both to the importance of keeping up standards and to the relatively limited level of aspiration in regard to fashion many respondents entertained. She explained the important of keeping up a certain standard to send a message that she was not an old woman to be pitied:

> I don't want to walk along and somebody think, 'Oh we've got to move out of the way for the old dear.' I mean I'm dressed, as far as I'm concerned, presentable. Not to be thought, 'Oh dear, she's old.' So I'm just carrying on wearing what I've always worn.

For her, wearing neat, clean, modern clothes was part of resisting exclusion, showing she was still acceptable and not a pitiable old woman.

For Gillian, a retired teacher in her sixties, maintaining a good appearance was similarly important in signalling to the outside world her standing as an older woman who was not 'past it', sidelined or, even worse, derelict or shameful. It was also a means of reinforcing such feelings in her own eyes. In the interview there was a sense that she had passed through a period of depression after her retirement. She had moved house and was starting a new life in a new town. Dressing well was going to be part of this. Living alone, she gave an impression of someone for whom dress was a consciously adopted form of support in the business of not allowing herself to get low:

> Well I got into a rut, and I think when you're on your own, the only person who can get you out of a rut is yourself. Well that's my philosophy. And that's what I decided to do.

She was critical of the way many women let themselves go and did not make the best of themselves.

> It's important to be part of life you know. [Dressing] in the best way that you can say, not exactly look at me, but here I am. I'm whatever age I am, whether you're thirty, forties or fifties. I think it helps psychologically to say: This is me. I feel good about life. Life is for living, let's live it. It's psychologically important.

She felt that if she wore sloppy clothes, it would say she was

> definitely of an older age group, and definitely not interested in life so much, and in the last third of my life. Whereas hopefully I like to think that, although I may be in the last third of my life, that I'm still with it, still interested in life.

Her narrative expressed a clear sense that older women need to resist the pressures to retreat and become invisible. Still being seen, still being part of things, was important to her in terms of how others saw her—her standing in the public world—and in terms of the effect of this on her own sense of self.

Engaging with Consumption: Frustrated Shoppers?

As discussed in Chapter 3, the reconstitution of ageing thesis rests in part on arguments about the growing significance of consumption in the negotiation of identity. Under conditions of postmodernity the location of identity shifts from production to consumption, and there is a new focus on lifestyle as the definer and expresser of the self. The world of goods, preeminently consumption goods, becomes increasingly significant. Gilleard and Higgs (2000), Ian Rees Jones and colleagues (2008, 2009), Phillipson (1998) and others suggest that these shifts have profoundly affected the nature of later years, contributing to a wider reconstitution of the experience of ageing, which is now marked by integration and continuity—at least for those with the income and health to enjoy these possibilities.

The study sample was selected to cover a range of financial circumstances, from the prosperous middle-class retired to those living on state benefits (though no one in the study was in visible material poverty). It was notable, however, that money was less of a barrier to engagement with fashion than might be expected. Partly this was because a number of women—at least at a psychological level—felt relatively prosperous. They looked back to earlier stages of their lives with young families, when money was short and when children, rather than themselves, were the spending priority. As a result, later years for them seemed a time of relative ease, even self-indulgence, in spending terms. In addition, some of the women had had very hard childhoods or adult lives with little money. For them the state pension was good by contrast. Ada was a working-class widow in her eighties who had worked as a cleaner all her life, but she still had a variety of neatly pressed skirts and tops that she showed me. Evie, seventy-seven, who was similarly on a low income as a widow of a casual worker, could still afford to buy clothes relatively regularly. Having lost her husband, she was lonely, and going into town to shop was a pleasant way to pass the time and get out of house. She explained how, far from buying *fewer* clothes, she now bought more than in the past:

> I buy more, yes...I think it's because I've got nothing better to do really. That's why I've got all the colours...Years ago people had about two or three T-shirts and that was their lot, whereas now you think, oh that's a nice colour, I'll think I'll have that.

She showed me a considerable range of clothes, neatly arranged on shelves and hangers. Dot, a widow in her eighties living on pensioner credit in an almshouse, also felt relatively unconfined by income. 'I'm not sort of clothes mad. If I happen to see something that I fancy, I'll have it.' So even among those with low incomes, there was a clear sense that they could buy clothes if and when they wanted. Income was not the barrier to engagement that might have been expected. A key factor here is that clothes have become so much cheaper. The real cost of clothes in the United Kingdom declined from 1961 to 2001 by 70 per cent (this compares with a 20 per cent decline in the real cost of food). As a result the fashion cycle has intensified: by the 2000s women in their seventies were shopping for clothes as frequently as those in their teens and twenties were in the 1960s (Majima 2006; Twigg and Majima 2013). This has had a marked effect at the lower end of the market, where the introduction of mass-produced value ranges, especially by the supermarkets, has transformed the availability of clothing for those on low income. Having the tee-shirt in all the colours is now something even women on the state pension could consider. Among the better off there was an even stronger sense that they could buy most things they wanted: the limit was that they were no longer interested in fashion or found little to tempt them.

The theme of the frustrated older shopper has emerged strongly in recent marketing literature, and I will outline in Chapter 6 how it is reflected also in the media. Were these frustrated shoppers? A number of the respondents certainly articulated a sense that the high street had little for them. They felt alienated from it because fashion was so centred on the young (and thin). As Clare explained:

> I've found modern fashion is for children basically. I mean little short things and puff sleeves and very exposed bosoms and all this, I just can't cope with any of that, because it doesn't fit me.

She felt fashion bordered in the 'paedophilic', with 'all these little girls with their toes turned...in.' Older women were ignored:

> English clothes are so dominated by street fashion for the young, it seems to me, so we're left out. I mean all my friends say the same. All my friends of my age say there's nothing for us anymore.

As a result some retreated from shopping, even though they had money to spend. Olive had loved fashion earlier in life and she used to be dressed in 'the latest, the latest fashions...I've always spent a lot of money on clothes.' But now she found little to tempt her, and she spent much less:

> Oh much less...Oh gosh yes, almost nonexistent really, my money doesn't go on clothes very often [because I] can't find any, can't find anything...I'd love to spend a fortune if I could find the right clothes, I would really.

As a result there was a discrepancy between the person she had been—always smart and fashionable—and the appearance she now presented. It was not that she was badly dressed, just that her clothes were ordinary. There was little of the sense of distinction that must have marked them earlier.

Not everyone experienced this sense of alienation. Anja, who wore a bright, casual dress, felt there were lots of attractive clothes for older women; shoppers just had to look for them. The key was to avoid focussing on age itself:

> I think it should be up to us to adapt what there is for us. And, you know—what do I mean? I think there are lots and lots and lots of lovely clothes about, and much of it is suitable for any woman, any age.

Her shift into casual dress after retirement had allowed her to access a range of clothes that, by virtue of their relaxed character, were not strongly age coded. The rise of casual dress as the predominant form for all ages noted in Chapter 2 has had the effect of opening a new range of dress for older people that can be sourced in the mainstream high street. Chris similarly thought that women should avoid age-related shops, and she believed that there were ageless styles to be found in mainstream high street. Citing the Danish chain Noa Noa, she explained:

> They're not age conscious clothes...They're not for young people, they're not for middle people and they're not for old people. They're for anybody, anybody.

The lack of enthusiasm for shopping, however, also reflected a sense by many that they already had wardrobes of clothes. This is the common experience of people in rich Western countries today. It is the function of the Fashion System to stimulate demand for goods in a saturated market through the promotion of new styles. The fact that some of these women felt no need for more clothes could, therefore, be interpreted as a failure of that system to reach all sectors of the population; in other words a failure to address the older market adequately. But it could also be interpreted in terms of a movement towards postmaterial values in line with Metz and Underwood's (2005) argument that people in later years shift their discretionary spending away from goods towards experiences. As Patricia explained:

> I think as you get older you just don't need to spend money. You just don't... I think you don't need material things. We're all different I suppose, you don't need material things because, hey, you'll soon be gone. So what is the point, you don't need them. You had them all, why keep buying more to add to what you've got.

The shift away from fashion may also reflect a disengagement from aspects of life that offer less in the way of satisfaction than they did in the past. Why spend energy on something that offers declining satisfaction? We saw how Olive had always loved fashion, but now found less and less to attract her in it. That sense of personal disengagement was reflected in a number of the interviews.

Lastly, it was not always clear how far the frustration expressed was really with what was on offer in the shops and how far it reflected a deeper dissatisfaction with the way the women now looked. As Clare, with characteristic thoughtfulness, commented:

> As you get older this is something that you just don't know. You don't know whether you're grumpy because you're old, or you're grumpy because things really aren't what you want. It's very difficult to know.

Performance

Most of the women in the study did not present their dress in ways that could be interpreted as performative, at least not in the strong sense usually implied by the term. Their aspiration in relation to expressivity and identity was limited; their desire was to be acceptable. In a small number of cases, however, the approach was more directly performative; and three of these are subject to a more extended account in the next chapter. Beyond these, the main respondent for whom dress did play a strongly expressive role was Nina. She was an elegantly dressed doctor's widow in her late seventies or early eighties (she declined to give her age). Her approach to dress was strongly performative, so that getting dressed, being consciously dressed in the public sphere, in relation to others, particularly in the context of a new romantic relationship, was a central part of her embodied life at the lived day-to-day level.

> I do dress. I do take care every day about my dress. I wouldn't go out to breakfast dressed in something I didn't want to wear or feel alright in. And I do dress in relation sometimes to who I'm with. And the way I dress for Ian has layers to it, that you can't necessarily see, which are related to being with him.

This had always been the case:

> The way I dressed and clothes were always very important to me.

In the last few years her dress had changed, but this was not about age but this new relationship. She had previously dressed in bolder, more ethnic styles, but her new partner liked more minimalist, defined lines and colours like black and grey.

> The last five years it's changed, or I've changed the way I dress...I've a new relationship in the last five years and he's somebody who likes more simple lines. He's an artist...and I notice he admired people who were dressed in a sort of more drawn line.

She felt that friends have been critical of these changes, feeling she has abandoned who she was, though she clearly also thought that they were jealous of her new relationship.

> One particular friend is very critical. And she connects it with what she thinks is a change in my attitude to things as well. So she says you know that I haven't got the sort of political views that I had. Actually I have the same political views, so it hasn't actually changed that...She gets very cross because I'm dressed smart and sexy sometimes, when I'm supposed to look, God knows what.

She clearly articulated a sense that what she wore was important to her and would be noticed.

> I want to present smart and sexy because I'm with Ian, or I'm going with him where there is going to be a sexy girl, quite often younger. Then I'm going to compete. So I'll bring my top up or I'll wear a dress which is lower.

Clothes for her were not just strongly performative, but linked to the conscious expression of sexuality and the repudiation of the sexual invisibility that is the common experience of older women.

For Kathie, it was not so much that her dress was performative, as that she would have liked it to have been more so. This was a feeling that she had had for many years, and it was not confined to the experience of age, though it intersected with it. She did not feel that her clothes expressed who she was, and when asked if she would like to dress differently, warming to the subject, she explained how she had always longed to dress in a much more flamboyant manner. Her dream of herself was as Cruella de Vil, the cartoon figure from *101 Dalmatians*, an ultra-glamorous, self-possessed, witch-like woman. This was a long-established fantasy, but now that she was getting older, the prospect of ever achieving it was receding, so that ageing for her was a process of moving away from such dreams, a closing down of those possibilities. She reported that she was shortly going to have a sixtieth birthday party where she did indeed plan to go as Cruela. This represented her last chance to express this hidden, denied part of her personality: 'It's my last stab at really sort of being outrageous.' She could see age coming towards her:

> I think there's always that little bit of devilment I've got in me, I've always had that, but it's there in the background waiting to come out. But I just think that when I get to sixty, I mean seventy, I can't see me doing the same things that I'm doing when I'm sixty even…It is a last chance. Who knows what's round the corner?

There was regret and sadness in her interview. She clearly felt caught between the lives of her younger colleagues with their access to pretty, feminine and sexy clothes and the darker future that lay before her. She recognized the passage of time and the way opportunities were slipping away from her and she was determined to have one last clothing fling.

Conservative, Classic and Comfortable

We now turn briefly to the interplay between particular styles of dress and age. Across the interviews accounts of conservative dress were common. Patricia described her dress as: 'classic conservative, although not conservative dull.' Janet reported her style as: 'Well fairly conservative, or old-fashioned, if you like to say that.' And this was reflected in the look of most of the interviewees, which was indeed fairly neutral and conservative. Such forms of dress are fairly common across the UK population. But they can have additional aspects as forms of age-related dress, both in the sense that they are often slightly backward-looking, and that they express the values of caution, carefulness and a slight formality thought appropriate for age. This is neutral, sober, cautious dress with relatively low fashion aspiration. Within the fashion industry, 'classic dress' is often used as a code for older person, as seen in the account of M&S's ranges.

Classic dress is slightly formal, and many of the respondents had increasingly moved towards more casual modes. For some, this was the result of changes in their day-to-day lives. They had fewer formal engagements. Widows went out less often;

and with retirement, office dress was no longer needed. Anja, who had been a senior probation officer, had got rid of a wardrobe of suits on her retirement in favour of the relaxed casual dress she now wore. These shifts into casual dress also reflected the general movement in the clothing lexicon towards casual dress noted in Chapter 2, into which older women have also been drawn. The shift is also linked to the pursuit of greater comfort, associated in the minds of many respondents with getting older. Some clearly prioritized comfortable clothes and were pleased to be able to do so. Later years made fewer demands. As Celia commented:

> It's a much more relaxed type of life that I lead…We relax as we retire and perhaps neglect ourselves a little, perhaps…I'm quite happy in old trousers and my wellies and my hands in the garden.

Janet similarly reported: 'I do like easy clothes…I don't like anything tight. I like casual clothes really.' It is important to recognize, however, that comfort is a complex category that is as much social as bodily, as demonstrated by the quotation in Chapter 2 from the older woman who felt that formal dress was as comfortable for her as loose casual clothes.

As part of the move to casual dress, many of the women wore trousers. Again this reflected a general shift over the last twenty years, whereby trousers have become mainstream for women of all ages. Most respondents belonged to a generation who had not worn them earlier in life, but had taken them up in their fifties and sixties. Their adoption thus reflected universal spread rather than the maturation of a cohort. Their views on trousers contained a mixture of meanings and evaluations. Though they were happy to wear them, and had absorbed them into their standard dress, a number still felt they were slightly mannish. Celia wore them happily (her domineering ex-husband had disapproved of them as unfeminine), but she would not wear them for church. Trousers thus still carried some of their traditional meanings for this group, linked to ideas about femininity, including of subordinated kinds. Their widespread adoption, however, had additional aspects that did relate to age. Trousers conceal legs that are no longer smooth and vein free. They also, unlike skirts, work well with flat or laced-up shoes. One of the problems with difficulties over balance or arthritis is that light, high-heeled shoes become difficult to wear, and this in turn makes skirts look heavy and less attractive. Clare said with regret:

> I am most comfortable in very supportive shoes, which means lace ups. I mean, I have slip-on shoes, but even those look clumsy with skirts.

She felt this was a barrier to looking more elegant. Similar regrets about no longer being able to wear pretty or sexy shoes were expressed in Hockey and colleagues' (2012) shoe project.

Conclusion

Responses of the women in the study were mixed. All, however, recognized the continuing power of age-related norms in relation to dress. No one asserted that these had gone, and their broad character was recognized by all. They might regret their nature, but most had simply internalized them, so that they were a species of common sense, something you had to recognize as you looked in the changing room mirror. This naturalization of cultural norms was particularly strong in relation to aspects that applied directly to the body and its visible appearance. Here respondents had internalized the largely negative evaluations of the wider ageist culture. No one questioned why, or indeed whether, older bodies should be covered up and hidden. These 'facts' were accepted and absorbed into their clothing choices.

At the same time a number of the respondents were clear that things were different from how they had been in the past. The situations of older women had changed, so that they could now dress more freely and wear younger styles. They were not confined in the way they were previously, nor did they intend to be so. Many were determined to avoid forms of dress associated with age, retaining their allegiance to jeans and tops and avoiding pleats and Crimplene. In particular they contrasted their dress with that of their mothers and grandmothers. They did not assert that age ordering had gone, but they did believe that it had weakened. Many believed there were still attractive clothes to be bought: if you looked carefully you could find mainstream garments that suited. And some identified forms of dress that transcended age coding and enabled women of all ages to look good. Others, however, did conform to the frustrated shopper image. They found little that was attractive aimed at them in the shops. What there was, was difficult to fit. A number of better-off respondents had money to spend, but little enthusiasm for what was on offer. Despite this, most respondents did still find some enjoyment in dress, though at a muted level. Their aspirations to be fashionable or smart or noticeable were not high. Partly this did indeed reflect the processes of age and the retreat from social visibility associated with it; but it also reflected more enduring features of the dress of the mainstream population expressed in the conventional, cautious modes that dominate the high street.

−5−

Dress and the Narration of Life

In this chapter I address the role of dress in the narration of life, exploring the intersections between clothing, embodiment, identity and age. Dress and the self are intimately linked, and this remains true throughout the life course. They thus offer a fruitful field through which we can explore the narratives of peoples' lives; the ways the experience of body and self change and develop through the life course; and the interplay between these processes and sociocultural expectations in regard to age.

Narrating Lives

Narrative draws on the deep cultural trope of life as a journey, in which we are presented with a story, a personal narrative of the self. At a profound level, humans are storytellers and story listeners—biographical beings as much as biological ones (Bruner 1999; Kenyon and Randall 1999). In recent years, across the arts and social sciences there has been a revival of interest in such narrative. Part of the wider cultural turn, it has enabled age studies to incorporate insights from literature, from oral history and from the arts and humanities more widely. A parallel revival of interest in biographical work has occurred within sociology and social history, some of which directly addresses the processes of ageing (Thompson et al. 1990; Chamberlayne et al. 2000; Ray 2000; Bornat 2002; Andrews 2009). From a different direction, literary scholars are also increasingly interested in later years. Gullette (1988) and Kathy Woodward (1991) both developed their pioneering accounts of age in relation to its literary treatment; and there is a growing body of work exploring the experience of age as expressed through novels, poetry and other literary forms (Basting 1998; Waxman 2010; Worsfold 2011).

Change lies at the heart of narrative. Centring the account on narrative thus helps to undermine a static concept of age as a fixed state, allowing me to emphasize instead the dynamic element that sees ageing—and life itself—as a passage, a development, an unfolding that encompasses both continuity and change as part of the continuing process of becoming older. As Andrews (1999) has emphasized, we are who we are in age as a result of the long lives we have lived. As we reflect on our lives, our lives' meaning emerges. Though such processes occur across the life course, there is—many have argued—something about later years that provokes life review (Bruner 1999; Coleman 2011). Indeed identity itself can be seen as a form of life story, a sense of the self created and caught in a web of changing narrative. In Kierkegaard's celebrated dictum, we live life forwards, but understand it backwards. This is especially significant in light of the ways our lives unfold in unexpected directions, or ones that reveal aspects of truth not previously understood. Narrative thus provides a lens through which we can view the ageing process, a unique way of seeing what becoming older involves (Kenyon and Randall 1999). It also has the merit of emphasizing subjectivity and lived experience, helping to counteract the 'othering' of age characteristic of much work that addresses age, even in social gerontology.

In this process of narrative, clothes can play a significant and distinctive part. Clothes are intimately linked with identity at both a personal and a social level. It is unsurprising that novelists have found them a potent field in which to explore the interplay of incident and character (Hughes 2006; McNeil et al. 2009). There is moreover something about the directly embodied nature of clothes that endows them with an emotional charge. They are powerful memory objects entangling the events of a person's life and can thus be used as a vehicle for selfhood (Hoskins 1998: 2; Ash 1996). Clothes thus capture the dynamic of life and the intersection between historical and personal pasts. They are not alone in this. Food offers a parallel sphere in which concrete, bodily based memoirs can be particularly evocative, as Proust famously showed in his account of the madeleine, and as Slater (2003)—in a different register—illustrates in his slightly oblique narrative of his childhood and adolescence through the medium of food and, in particular, food products of the period (Smash, Angel Delight). The power comes from the embodied concreteness of the subject that reaches directly to memory and emotion. The same is true of clothes. Women frequently describe their lives in terms of the clothes they wore. As Sophie Woodward notes, the temporal specificity of clothes means they can fix and define a moment: 'The dress I wore when…' (2007: 120). Telling life through the chronology of styles is indeed part of how life stories, particularly for women, are told. Clothes anchor people's understandings of the past and measure the passage of time. In the interviews reported in the previous chapter, respondents frequently described being young in terms of what they wore, using the concrete particularity of dress to catch the historical moment, recalling with warmth the excitements of the New Look, the trailing skirts of a Laura Ashley dress, the freedom of hippie style, as well as the neat smartness of a Gor Ray skirt.

Clothes indeed embody time itself. Dress reveals the historical moment in a particularly vivid and concrete way. Viewers can, for example, date photographs clearly from the styles of dress displayed in them. They bring before our eyes the exact historical moment. There is an inescapable quality to the way the context is stamped on the individual. This is present even in the lives of individuals who have no interest in fashion. Such processes can be applied to earlier periods also; indeed dress studies as a discipline developed out of art history's attempts to date paintings where styles of dress often offered one of the few concrete clues as to period (Newton 1980; Ribeiro 1995, 2002; Taylor 2002, 2004).

Clothes also make the passage of time visible, as styles pass into history, moving from being cutting edge to out of date and dowdy, to quaint and odd and—possibly—to intriguing and beautiful. In reflecting on personal images or memories, respondents are thus not just reflecting on themselves, but also on themselves in a particular historical moment. Images and memories allow them to link their narrative to the larger historical context within which their lives occurred, so that dress, although in some senses a matter of surface, brings to mind the intersection between personal and historical time. The person in the photograph is not just that individual at the age of twenty or forty, but that individual in a particular and distinctive historical context; and the clothes make this visibly manifest.

As noted in Chapter 2, Weber and Mitchell argue for the methodological benefits of such 'dress stories' in which garments and memories about them are the basis of critical reflective memory work that aims to make the past usable in the form of memoirs, poems or art installations. For them, dress is significant because it offers 'a method of inquiry into identity processes and embodiment', so that talking about clothes 'forces us to speak, directly or indirectly, about our bodies' (2004: 5). Clothing, they suggest,

> can act both as entry points for personal (and private) autobiography in relation to questions of identity, as well as entry points for understanding of the social components of identity as read through individual and collective responses to a particular clothing artefact. (2004: 4)

Discarding dress can also be part of these processes of reflection and memory. In modern wealthy societies, dress is constantly put aside because it has moved out of fashion, so that it becomes dated and unattractive rather than worn out. That is written into the nature of the fashion cycle, with its constant drive for obsolescence. But clothes are not always discarded. Many women retain wardrobes of clothing they no longer wear, as Guy and Banim (2000) analysed in their study of retained dress. Sophie Woodward (2007) also found that women kept items of dress significant to them, often because they represented past selves or stages of their lives. Some garments are kept because they are much loved, but are now out of date (a special party dress), or because they have significant meaning (classically a wedding dress (Friese 2001)). Gullette (1999) recounts how she has a bottom drawer of such memories in the form of fabric and dresses that she is reluctant to discard because of the memories they enshrine, in particular of her fashion-loving mother who helped select her clothes.

Sometimes clothes are put aside or discarded because the person has become older. It is the individual who has changed, not the garment, so that the style no longer 'suits', does not flatter or may even look inappropriate because the wearer has aged. Sometimes the garment no longer fits because the body has changed. Reviewing one's wardrobe can thus be part of a process of acknowledging one has become older. In this way the classic 'wardrobe sort' that is part of the biannual experience of many women in Western cultures takes on an additional meaning, as a point at which one faces up to the changes wrought by age. Gullette (1999) has drawn a parallel here between the fashion cycle and the cultural imposition of age. She traces the movement of garments from initial desire and pleasure in wearing to disenchantment and discarding, seeing this as a metaphor for the wider discourse of decline through which women learn to internalize at a deep psychic level their own sense of themselves as beings that are discarded, passed over, in what she terms the 'other end of the fashion cycle'.

Three Trajectories of Time and Change

I want to explore these themes in terms of the interplay of three trajectories. The first is the trajectory of ageing. Becoming old is a sociocultural process in which individuals move from youth through middle age to old age. This movement finds expression in a variety of social and cultural forms, of which clothing is one. One of the clearest ways we can see this is through the process of age ordering, discussed in Chapter 2, through which we learn gradually to don the mantle of age. The narration of life is, in part, an account of this movement into age, shaped by sociocultural expectations, prompts, requirements, impositions, external readings of the self and reflections on them by the individual. Together these make up the ways we are, in Gullette's (1997) words, 'aged by culture'.

The second trajectory is that of historical time. We are not just young or old, but young and old in a particular historical moment. Narrations of life, as demonstrated in the case studies presented in this chapter, are clearly located in distinctive historical eras. The choices these women faced were shaped by historical contingencies that operated at different times; and the lives they led display the social and cultural currents of the period. In terms of dress, this is clearly reflected in changing styles and fashions. Indeed the dominance of these means that memories and images can be easily dated. A significant part of our experience of the past is through the material artefacts that shaped its form and that survive into the present as objects, images and memories. Dress is part of this.

The third trajectory represents the ways individual lives and identities change, not just as a result of ageing or historical change, but as part of the unfolding of an individual's life. The trajectory of ageing should not be presented as a unitary or fixed one, as earlier work on the life course, particularly within the framework of psychology, did. Rather it should be understood as socially and culturally variable, the product of a complex interplay of forces in which self-conscious reflection and deliberate agency can play a part. This is a theme of one of the narratives in particular.

Three Lives

The chapter focusses on the life stories of three women in the main study, each of whom has adopted a distinctive mode of dress. The narrations centre on tensions in relation to continuity and change, particularly in relation to age; the interplay between relationships and dress; and ways styles of dress intersect with the trajectory of an individual's life.

The three were selected for additional interview and analysis because each had adopted a distinctive mode of dress that was situated very clearly in circumstances of their lives, in which there was a complex interplay between their distinctive modes of dress and the process of becoming older. Their clothes were not as clearly oppositional as those in Holland's (2004) study, but they were distinctive and self-consciously chosen. However, in selecting such women for special attention, I do not want to suggest that their dress was in any sense more agentic or significant than that of other women in the study. Choosing conventional dress can be just as much a product of agency, as was clear from the main interviews, where the careful ways in which respondents spoke of their dress clearly displayed this, even though the clothes they wore would appear to many observers to be unremarkable and conventional. Had time permitted, I would have undertaken biographically based interviews with all the women in the study.

Presenting these three lives also allows me to give a fuller, more individually focussed account. Researchers often have the experience that while each respondent in a study remains fully present to them—before their eyes, in their surroundings, with the whole narrative in mind—this is not the case for readers, who inevitably experience respondents disjointedly, dispersed into fragments by the demands of an analytic account. This chapter, by contrast, gives an opportunity to present respondents more holistically in terms of their individuality and to explore the intersection of that individuality with dress. It also acts as a reminder that questions of change and continuity surface throughout the life course and are not confined to later years.

As in the book as a whole, the names of respondents have been changed, though permission has been gained to use their images.

Angela

The central theme of Angela's narrative was her journey from secretarial college in South Kensington in the 1960s, through an unhappy marriage to a doctor, to independence via education and the influence of feminism, to life on the alternative music scene on the north Kent coast. At each stage of her life, the clothes she wore changed radically.

I interviewed Angela when she was living in a decayed seaside resort with high levels of deprivation. Though it has long-established working- and lower-middle-class communities, it is a fractured social landscape used to house asylum seekers and recipients of community care. Angela had had financial ups and downs with problems of debt, and was currently living on pensioner credit. She was, however, brought up in middle-class circumstances in Berkhempstead, where her father was a teacher. The options facing girls in the 1960s, even those who, like Angela, had gone to grammar school, were limited: nursing, teaching or secretarial; and she was sent to a private college in South Kensington to train as a secretary. This was a year-long process whereby young women learnt not just secretarial and office skills, but also social manners and comportment. At the end of their training they would expect to be placed in a company at the directorial level; and part of the implicit expectation was that this would provide opportunities to meet a suitable husband. Knowing how to dress and present oneself was part of the training. The picture shows Angela in a fresh cotton dress with the bouffant skirt of the period and elegantly crossed secretarial legs. But she never felt at ease at secretarial college: the other girls were 'smart, well off and self assured', and she was not. When we look at the picture, however, none of this is apparent: she seems elegant and self-possessed, though her description of how she felt at a bodily level is quite the reverse:

> I've always found it difficult to dress. I've always felt a bit of a lump...I just felt a lump. I didn't feel comfortable in fashionable, elegant clothes. They just weren't me...I did lots of sports at school. I was good academically...but I was also very physical. I wasn't this sort of feminine, little girly sort, I never have been...I'm a bit of a clumper. I stride and I don't sort of totter.

In her early jobs as an executive secretary she had to dress smartly, but again she never felt at ease. She did not have a great deal of money; and there was not the range of inexpensive clothing there is now: she mostly shopped at C&A. The unease

Figure 5.1   Angela (seated third from the left) at secretarial college in South Kensington in the 1960s

over dress was paralleled by unease in her role. She did not enjoy being a secretary, particularly working in strongly commercial fields which she found disillusioning.

Angela married and had two children. Her husband was a doctor, and they married when he was still training. He came from a conventional family of higher social class than hers, but had a somewhat uncertain career marked by educational starts and stops with frequent changes of job. In analysing the interviews I was struck by the underlying theme of status anxiety. I had originally seen Angela in the first interview as coming from the secure middle class, but later comments and analysis suggested a slightly different picture; less secure, more anxious. Her father, though a schoolteacher, left school early and did not have a degree; home life was economically constrained and unhappy; the other girls in South Kensington came from better-off backgrounds. A central theme of the interviews was feeling uncomfortable— uncomfortable in clothes and in social roles, and this sense of unease was shared by her husband. Once established as a doctor, he wanted her to dress differently:

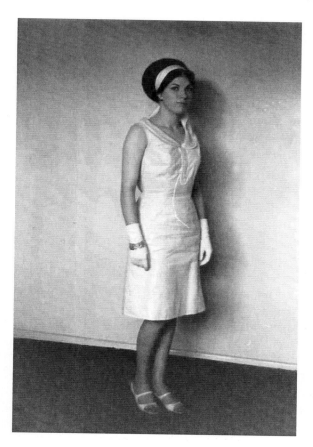

Figure 5.2   Angela dressed for a party when in South Kensington

Angela: And he started saying, 'I think you should dress up a bit more.' [laughs] And we lived in a very middle-class dormitory, London dormitory town, where everybody shot off, all the husbands shot off at the station in the morning, and their little wives went down in their housecoats and drove home to the kiddies and ohh!

Interviewer: What did he mean by dressing up?

Angela: [laughs] What did he mean? He wanted me to wear something that looked a bit more as though we had lots of money. And we didn't, because then I wasn't working.

He even took her out to buy things he thought would be appropriate for her to wear:

Angela: I remember one point where he'd just got some kind of salary increase that was quite substantial, and he said, 'Look, I think we ought to go and buy you some clothes.' So we went down to the smart shop, and he chose—I mean obviously it was a joint thing, but he chose the things that he wanted me to finally buy, out of the things that I thought [were] reasonably acceptable. And do you know, I never wore them. They went in the cupboard. And I just never felt comfortable wearing them.

Interviewer: What kind of clothes were they?

Angela: Well, one was sort of a knitted skirt suit. I mean it was very swirly—I'm trying to remember what the top was. Very, very fine knit. Beige [laughter]. Oh God, beige, navy blue.

Interviewer: Right, so those kind of colours.

Angela: Those kinds of things. There wasn't a lot of choice to be honest. It was a very respectable town, and they sold respectable classic clothes.

She felt trapped because she had no money: 'I didn't have any money you see…And this clothes issue was one of the things that came up between us.' He was able to exert control through his role as the sole source of income for the family, and with it authority over her appearance in ways that reflect Pahl's (1989) findings on money and marriage more generally.

After they separated, she realized how constrained she had been. Her clothes had been a focus of conflict in the marriage, taking on a symbolic significance: 'My ex-husband used to call my clothes outlandish, and that was before I got outlandish!' She moved to Cambridge, which she found a much freer place. Living on benefits, she moved into bohemian circles, took Open University courses, went to college and came under the influence of feminism. The way she dressed changed radically. She began to experiment with alternative dress, with bright colours and countercultural modes that she found in the Cambridge market: her favourite stall there was called 'Loud'. This set the style of dress she now wears. Her life thus intersected with a

Figure 5.3   Angela in radical dress

number of the themes of classic second-wave feminism: the limited gender roles available; the restrictive marriage; the escape though education; and the adoption of countercultural values and styles.

On the day we first met, she was dressed in loose trousers and a jacket in finely woven stripes and patches, of somewhat Tibetan feel, in shades of purple, and a bright pink nylon wig (Figure 5.4). She made a point of wearing boldly coloured clothes and showed me a number of jumpers and outfits in strong colours. The most dramatic part of her look was the wig, which she had put on specially to meet me. She had earlier coloured her hair with vegetable dyes; as her hair became grey this did not work so well, but she liked the effect of pinks and purples. She wore the wig when she met her current partner, after they had become friends on the Internet: 'When I came down to meet Mike for the first time, I bought this just to say, Watch it! I'm not ordinary.' Mike, whom she describes warmly as the 'black sheep of his

Figure 5.4   Angela today in her pink wig

family', is a musician and DJ on the alternative scene. However, she found it hard to wear the wig locally. Cambridge had been a more tolerant, laid back environment, but Thanet was much more on the edge—a place where if you wore unusual dress you might get shouted at.

She believed men found her clothes threatening: 'If I wear things like this, men feel threatened, particularly men of my age group.' This perception relates back to her youth, when being clever was something girls had to hide:

> I've always been alarming to men 'cos I'm very bright and that terrifies them. So I mean, maybe that's why I needed to dress in a more conventional way when I was younger. I mean I do remember my mother saying to me, 'Well, men don't like intelligent women.'

Angela was in her sixties, but her commentary on dress was not greatly concerned with age. She had come to her current style as a result of her life's journey, and it reflected who she felt she was now. She was aware of the ways older women feel that they have to tone down their dress or move out of the limelight, but she had found a form of dress that did neither and felt no need to adjust in light of getting older. She was not going to give up the gains she had made. Indeed one of the things she discovered about herself was that, despite her earlier lack of confidence, she in fact liked to stand out, to be noticed. She did not want to become invisible or disappear into the background:

> I suddenly realized one day, it was quite some while ago, I was thinking about what I wear, and I was thinking: mostly I don't want to stand out, but I wear clothes that say, 'Look at me.' And it was a bit of a shaker to realize that. I don't want to disappear into the background, I really do not want to disappear into the background. I like to be noticed.

As a result she consciously avoided any pressure to tone down. When asked if certain colours were associated with older women, she agreed, citing 'less bright colours, browns, greys, the burgundy type colours, navy blue.' When asked why, she said:

> Cos they don't shout sexy...I think the social perception is that older women are not sexy or are not desirable in some form or other. But that is dictated by young people. I mean those of us who are our age know damn well we're bloomin' sexy. It doesn't stop us being sexy. In fact I, you know, if we're talking about sex, my sex life is better now than it's probably ever been.

Her current dress is not sexy or alluring in a conventional sense, but this did not stop her asserting the reality of sexuality in older women. In many ways alternative dress does not conform to dominant ideas of sexiness, which is an implicitly young style centred around erotic display through which the cultural linkage of femininity and youthfulness is reinforced. Her avoidance of conventional sexy dress meant that the shift towards being older was not experienced as undermining sexuality in the way that it might—and does—for more conventionally dressed women.

Helena

The central theme of this interview was continuity. Helena developed a distinctive style of dress in her twenties that is closely related to her sense of self. It was a romantic and poetic look that linked to the realm of imagination; and she continued to dress in this style despite the changes of age.

Helena was brought up in a town near Canterbury where her father was a government scientist and her mother full time at home. It was not an easy childhood, and her relationship with her mother was full of tension and difficulty, including over clothes. She did not initially go to university, but settled down with her future husband who had dropped out of university and later developed a successful joinery business. She got a job as a clerk at the Department of Health and Social Security (DHSS). This worked well, as it offered her a stable environment:

I needed to be grounded because I was very, very fucked up. And sort of having lots of forms to fill in and getting people their Giros on time was remarkably grounding...It was very good, you know it was steady, it was calm and it stopped me going bonkers.

One of the good things about the office was that her employer let staff wear what they wanted, and Helena began to develop her characteristic style. The look she favoured—and still favours—is a romantic, poetic one that draws on a mixture of Edwardian and 1920s style:

I kind of fell in love with the Edwardian period, and I have worn black stockings, thick—and I didn't have good legs anyway—and I've worn thick black stockings since I was fourteen or fifteen. And in those days you couldn't get them. You could only get American Tan, if you remember, ghastly...I used to buy great job lots of these in Debenhams and dye them black. And I'm probably the only woman who went through the summer of 1976 in thick black tights.

Her style is based around leggings, hats, scarves and baggy smocks with something of the look of the Edwardian child. She was a pioneer of the charity shop, vintage look.

I just kind of made stuff up...I had a thing about granny dresses. I called them granny dresses, and sadly they've all gone, but they were kind of big dresses that had fitted big grannies, but what you could do, what I used to do, was roll them, sort of hitch them up with a belt or something, and then you were left with a kind of 1920s Bloomsbury type dress. And then if you wore a cloche hat, thick black stockings...I mean I used to put rags in my hair,...So again it kind of always went back to the Edwardian idyll and James Joyce.

This way of dressing was linked to her love of literature: she was finishing a doctorate on Joyce.

Her look coincided with the early days of Laura Ashley in the 1960s and early 1970s, when it was small scale and different, before it became corporate and conventional.

In South Kensington they had their original store...All they had was a kind of warehouse upstairs with racks and racks of clothes, and then downstairs a big changing room. And you could get beautiful clothes for about seven or eight quid. And in those days I wore long dresses, before they were very fashionable, and you could get long dresses there, beautiful long clothes. And they were very cheap, but everybody equated them with drugs and degeneracy. And I was, at the time certainly very anti drugs but, you know. I liked floating down the street, and people thought it was odd. But then it was adopted by the middle classes and the prices went through the roof. And that, of course, is what destroyed them.

She works on items of dress, adapting, altering or dyeing them:

> I buy most of my stuff from charity shops, originally for financial reasons, but also because you can get really good interesting stuff. But I tend to dye most of it. I do masses and masses of dyeing.

Her clothes were always beautifully coloured, never bright or garish, but subtle and creative in their colouring, using contrasting necklaces and mixing different textures and colours. Her hair, drawing on the pre-Raphaelite ideal, was hennaed and flowed freely, and she often wore plum tones that vibrated with the henna. The love of colour was evident also in the interior of her house. The room where the interview took place was painted apple green, with dark toning and contrasting colours of blues and greens for the painted furniture and textiles, presenting a complex, elaborate interior much like her clothes.

Clothes for her were part of a romantic interior life. She described herself as someone who has always lived in the imagination: 'The way I dress, a lot of it, was really just being creative with myself, as a way of escape I think, and a way of mythologizing myself.' After having children, she did a degree in English literature, followed by postgraduate research. For her, dress was a form of self-expression, but also an escape from the mundanity of the world: 'The work I do at the university is essentially exploration of self...So I think I have a lot more self-understanding, and I think I now realize that I was dressing the way I did to try and circumvent reality.'

This links to her literary interests:

> A lot of the stuff I'm trying to express in Joyce is about romantic irony, which, in a way, is the same thing, because it's about self-parody. And in a way that's what you're doing. And it's about mythologizing the actual...it's connecting spirit and the material, and it's a way of detaching yourself from yourself...[Joyce] mythologized himself as Steven Daedelus. But it took me ages—I mean it's taken me many, many years to make this connection and to see what I was doing with my clothes. But still, it's all a part of the same thing. And it's about— but it is expressing yourself creatively, but it's also becoming part of something bigger.

Despite the fact that the general theme of the interview was continuity and her wish to retain a sense of self above and separate from ordinary fashion changes or conventional ideas about what should be worn, she acknowledged that as she has grown older she has begun to adjust in some measure:

> I'm not as adventurous as I was, and I no longer look as good in romantic stuff because I'm too old. But it's kind of evolved into a—you know, I think you can wear what you like as you get older, if you don't mind looking slightly ridiculous. And that works, that works, because when you're young, you don't want to look too ridiculous because—well you're a young girl and young girls should be beautiful if they can be or whatever. But you can—well

> I guess I always did look a bit ridiculous, but I didn't care. But as I've got older you grow into that.

When I responded by saying that some women feared looking ridiculous, she replied: 'Oh no, you have to embrace it.'

She felt that as she had become older she had acquired new qualities that replaced those of prettiness: 'You have to say, ok I'm not young anymore and I'm not pretty as I used to be, but on the other hand I've got other strengths now.' This related to a sense that she had an interior life, a clear authentic self that had come as result of the life she had lived and the interior life she had developed. Some of the styles she used to love look less good on her now, for example the Alice in Wonderland look: 'It's lovely but I don't think my face is quite right for it anymore.' Faces change, and

> you get a kind of gravitas that you didn't have when you were younger, you know your face is more—I hesitate to say grim, but it's not as childish.

Clothes for her were an expression of inner truth and authenticity; and she did not care what others thought if they were true to her:

> Provided I'm happy, to be truthful provided I'm happy with it, I don't give a monkey's what anybody else thinks. But it would be different if I wasn't, then I would feel uncomfortable.

In pursuit of this she was willing to risk looking ridiculous, even 'bonkers':

> I've said this about this Alice in Wonderland dress, but it depends you see. If you're trying to have long tousled locks because you want to be sexy then I could see if that is your aim then that might not be appropriate, it mightn't suit your face. But if you want long tousled hair because you want to look bonkers then it doesn't matter.

Her mother was beautiful, very bound up in her appearance; and as she grew older the loss of her looks was a source of vocally expressed anguish. She was very fashionable in the conventional mode of the period:

> a veritable fashion plate, spent a great deal of money on clothes and her appearance. And when she went into middle age, felt the loss of her looks very, very deeply. In fact it destroyed her.

Helena's style of dress was a source of conflict. 'She very much disapproved of my dress.' Clothes became a

> fearful bone of contention. I mean I was very good on the whole. But the clothes were something I could not be good over. And she found the whole Sixties thing anathema.

But then, how much of that, in retrospect...I mean I was very naïve, how much of that was jealousy? I'm not sure.

She saw now how many older women lose confidence:

I guess losing self-confidence is something that does happen to a lot of middle-aged women. But it depends how much your identity is tied up with how you look. And as I say, I had a very cruel example in front of me, with my mother, of somebody whose identity had been wholly tied up with her appearance, and then when that started to go had nothing. And that is very sad. And there must be a lot of women like that.

Her mother's ageing thus became an image of how not to age and of the vulnerabilities and tragedies that could come from this. She related her mother's fate to the current situation of older women, wandering dissatisfied around the local department store. They are stuck because they follow the dictates of fashion, which no longer suit them, rather than expressing their own style:

My mother adored Fenwicks. But if you go to Fenwicks,...you see women of about my age, or older, wandering around with a very dissatisfied look on their faces, sort of holding things up. And they've obviously got pots of money. But you can see that they feel that they've got to wear what they're being told they have to wear.

Like her mother, they are vulnerable because they have no real inner sense of self:

That was what destroyed her basically, she had no other resources.

Joanne

The central theme of this narrative was resistance and the determination not to abandon the erotic in dress. Joanne was fifty-nine and dressed as a Goth, wearing floor-length outfits in black or Goth-related colours like purple; hooped, laced and elaborately decorated skirts; and tight corsets. It is a dramatic, sexy, romantic look, though its femininity is cut by heavy Doc Marten-style boots raised on thick rubber platforms and armoured with silver plates and straps. Joanne was brought up in Lancashire, in a skilled working-class family. She married young, having left school to work as a window dresser in a shop in Southport. Her first husband was an accountant: very conventional and controlling. 'Basically he had the cheque book'; and she wore what he thought suitable for an accountant's wife, which meant 'whatever was in Debenhams'. After twelve years of marriage, they swapped partners with their best friends, and she was happily married to her second husband for over twenty years. Though also an accountant, he was very different; and under his influence she experienced new freedom and confidence. He encouraged her to wear younger, sexier clothes: the ra-ra skirts of the 1980s. He shared her interest in Goth style. Together they developed a taste for dressing up. Initially this related to the clubs and gigs.

> We used to go to clubs in London virtually every Saturday night. Slimelight is the greatest Goth club in the world... We used to travel up at night. It opens at about 10 o'clock, and it finishes at 8 o'clock in the morning. We used to go up there quite a lot in the summer periods, about five or six years ago. We also went to fetish clubs. We got fetish burnout basically. So we've matured, I suppose, in a way.

She still had a wardrobe of rubber wear that dates from that period; but she noted wryly that it was not the sort of thing you could sell in the local boot fair.

She now wore Goth dress all the time, including, in modified form, at work. There was a period, however, when she and her husband felt they had to compromise and wear conventional dress. This was when they sent their sons to boarding school. It was not a happy period for her:

> Our two boys went to boarding school, so we had to dress as boarding school parents. Chintzy prints, Viyella, Jaeger, Country Casuals, and we didn't really like it... For six or

Figure 5.5   Joanne during boarding school days

seven years we were people that we didn't want to be...I was somebody I did not want to be, and I hated it. And it was not relaxing. It was, 'Oh God, there's another function at school. What have I got to wear now!'

Once the boys had left, she could return to dressing in the ways she liked. Holland (2012) in her recent study in which she returned to the women who had adopted alternative 'non traditionally feminine dress' similarly found that children were a major source of pressure to conform.

More recently for Joanne the demands of conventional family life pressed in again when her son was getting married. She sensed her future daughter-in-law was anxious that she 'would show her up' at the wedding by arriving in Goth dress, which in many ways represents a black reversal of bridal dress. So she decided to 'go normal', buying a black and silver knee-length dress at Marks & Spencer which

Figure 5.6   Joanne in Goth dress and corset

Figure 5.7 Joanne at a club

she wore with a pair of high heels dating from the boarding school days. However, she needed to spend the weekend before practicing with these relatively unfamiliar items. Her daughter-in-law was relieved and grateful. Overall Joanne felt she had done the right thing: though she did not like the clothes and did not feel comfortable in them, she had made the effort not to embarrass her daughter-in-law. She did, however, tease her a little. She owned a black lace tablecloth with spiders and coffins on it, and arrived at the reception with this draped over her head.

Eroticism and femininity were at the heart of her narrative. The look she adopted was consciously feminine: corsets, ribbons, lace, albeit with heavy boots and metal flanges. She actively disliked trousers and never wore them. Goth style, she believed, is ageless and flatters all shapes through its ability to create an erotic hourglass figure. Corsets were an important part of the look, and she showed me several that she had had specially made. Her ideal is burlesque artist Dita von

Teese, and she showed me a picture of her in a corset, telling me: 'That's my husband's lusting photograph.' Corsets do, however, require women to breathe differently, more shallowly. Though she said that she never laced her corset so tight as to pass out, as some women do, there was a slight fetish aspect in her comments. She certainly liked the sense of sexiness corsets give, and she described how when she took them off, she got a rush as the blood returned. She said that she did not find them uncomfortable because they were empowering and made her feel good. Throughout the interview, she interpreted comfort in the social sense of feeling at ease with yourself and looking as you want, rather than in terms of easygoing casual styles.

She was very critical of older women who abandon any pretence of looking attractive or erotic, giving up trying to create a figure for themselves and electing for the 'box option'. She called them

the anorak brigade. A lot of older people wear anoraks. Or those like puffy jackets. If you took those off, and put yourself in a decent coat, a fitted coat...There's no shape to them. So there are a lot of people out there that look really old, that don't need to be looking old.

She is determined this is not going to happen to her:

Even if my belly gets bigger and my waist gets bigger, I'm still going to have a figure when I go out. I'm not going to be a box or a rectangle.

Throughout the interviews there was a strong theme of resistance, of not giving up and of the importance of making an effort:

It's a case of just making an effort and being positive about yourself, and not relying on anybody else to dictate what you have to wear or how you have to be...I think a lot of people fade to grey after the age of sixty. They, like, stop trying...And I'm not going to let go.

A year elapsed between the two interviews, and there was a different feel to the second one. There had been changes in her life: most notably, her husband was diagnosed with a serious condition (he has since died). She still emphasized continuity of identity, saying that even if she were to lose him she would retain her style of dress and life; and the theme of defiance and resistance was still there: no twin sets for her. But there were slight signs of moving on in dress. Her husband had proposed a new style for her: leggings and a long top, still in black but more related to current fashion, and crucially I felt, less focussed on the overt sexuality of Goth dress. She was considering this, though as yet she had no desire to give up the long, flattering skirts or voluptuous corsets and shaped bodices of the Goth look.

Conclusion

I have followed the personal narratives of three women who have consciously adopted distinctive dress. I want now to return to the interplay between these narratives and the trajectories of time, change and age. As I noted at the start, each life is distinctive: there is no single or predictable way in which it unfolds or in which individuals age. And that is true of the examples presented here, each displaying patterns of looping back, of change, of new directions, with late entry into university life, new partners, different jobs—or non-jobs—new perceptions of the world, how it works and what matters. This is most striking in the case of Angela, who could hardly have predicted her current life as a pensioner on the alternative music scene of Thanet from the starting point of that South Kensington secretarial college. But it applies to Helena also, with her doctoral work on Joyce, who started out from difficult relations with her mother and the shelter of work in a DHSS office. The unexpected and consciously chosen is also present in Joanne's life. These jumps, starts and changes—and continuities—are reflected in the clothes these three women wore and wear. Their dress makes manifest the individuality of their lives.

At the same time their narratives intersect with the second trajectory, that of historical change. As I noted at the start, we are young and old in particular historical times. Helena's and Angela's lives were clearly affected by the wider cultural context of the feminism of the second wave. Both missed out on university initially, but both looped back into formal education in a way that is characteristic of many women of their cohort.

Helena's and Angela's narratives of dress are imbued with a concrete feeling of the past: Angela's account of the manners and modes of the secretarial college in South Kensington in the 1960s; Helena's memories of Laura Ashley's changing rooms, the decadence as well as the freshness of the long, trailing skirts. In Helena's case, her look, though distinctive and personal to her, reflects a particular historical moment—that of the neo-Romantic, pre-Raphaelite revival of the 1970s. Angela's current style also draws on early alternative, feminist or hippie fashions of the counterculture of the Long Sixties (Marwick 1998), with their brightly coloured ethnic influences and their conscious rejection of the elegant, structured or discreet. Goth dress also is rooted in a particular period: that of the 1980s when it first made an appearance as a street style. Each thus takes into the experience of age, features of dress distinctive to the historical period in which their lives have unfolded.

Lastly the narratives also intersect with the experience of ageing itself and the cultural meanings that attach to this process. Each respondent reacted differently to this. In Angela's narrative of dress there was little directly addressing the issue. She had chosen an alternative style that lay outside the age coding of conventional dress, and as a result required less in the way of special adjustment for age. For her, it was simply a style she liked and felt expressed who she was. In her earlier adoption of this, there had been an element of conscious defiance; it was an act of independence with a clear element of 'look at me'. She was not going to allow ageing to undermine these gains or erode her public assertiveness. The style was slightly asexual with its loose comfortable trousers and baggy overshirts, though she attested strongly in the interviews to the sexuality of age. It was certainly anti-glamorous in conventional terms, but as a result raised questions of age less strongly than would have been the case with styles that directly emphasize the eroticism of youth. By choosing a countercultural style she had managed to sidestep some of the traditional equation of sexuality with youthful femininity. Joanne had taken a very different route. Her style was consciously erotic and glamorous. She railed against the asexuality of older women, the way they abandoned any attempt to look attractive or to maintain a normative female figure. For her, identity was closely bound up with remaining glamorous and desirable, of resisting the erosion of age, as she had earlier resisted the neutrality of the 'vanillas'. Helena presented yet another approach to the issues of ageing and dress. She recognized that some of the looks she had enjoyed were now less successful; and this was particularly so with romantic, kooky styles, but her response was to push past this difficulty, to embrace it even at the risk of looking yet more eccentric. In this way she forged a new look that drew on qualities of romance and poetry more enduring and more interior than just youthful prettiness.

–6–

Magazines, the Media and Mrs Exeter

In this chapter I explore the world of the media and its representation of fashion and age, focussing on the role of women's magazines. The chapter draws on an analysis of four magazines, aimed at different sectors of the market: *Woman & Home,* a classic women's magazine primarily read by middle- and lower-middle-class women in their forties to sixties; *SAGA,* a proponent of Third Age lifestyles read by slightly older and more affluent women (and men); and *Yours,* a mass market magazine read by working-class women in their sixties and seventies. The aim was to understand how fashion operated in magazines aimed at older women. The fourth magazine was *Vogue,* chosen to represent the premier UK fashion magazine. Here the task was slightly different: to understand how age was presented, but also effaced, in a magazine focussed on high fashion. This was achieved primarily through a concept of 'ageless style', and this forms the basis of its current approach. But this was not always the case. Age has been managed differently by *Vogue* in the past, and in the last section of the chapter I explore the lost world of Mrs Exeter.

Magazines and the Constitution of Identity

Since the 1970s women's magazines have been the focus of extensive sociological analysis exploring their role in the constitution of women's identities under late capitalism. Initially such analysis, rooted in the feminism of the second wave, was highly critical, presenting women's magazines as key sites reinforcing women's subordination and entrenching inauthentic and oppressive versions of femininity. In the 1980s and 1990s this analysis gave way to a more nuanced account influenced by postmodernism that acknowledged the polysemic nature of women's magazines: their capacity to reinforce traditional gender identities at the same time as offering critiques of them (Winship 1987; Hermes 1995; Aronson 2000; Gough-Yates 2003). Reception studies, led by Hermes, unpacked the complex ways women consume these cultural products, the distinctive and bounded ways they fit into their lives and the interpretations they bring to their consumption. Gough-Yates (2003), focussing on the phenomenon of the New Women magazines of the late twentieth century, explored how new markets of potential readers were discursively constituted by media professionals through a focus on identity constitution and lifestyles, particularly in relation to the imagined category of the 'new middle class'. More recently McRobbie (2008) has returned to her earlier work on girls' magazines and the intersecting themes of gender and class to attack current work within cultural studies for its complicity with postfeminist values.

We are thus familiar with arguments concerning the role of women's magazines in the constitution of gendered—and to some degree classed—identities. There has, however, been relatively little work that extended these understandings to the constitution of aged identities. Partly this reflects the wider neglect of age noted earlier within sociological theorizing. Cultural studies (the principal arena in which media images are analysed) has been similarly neglectful, focussing heavily on the youthful and transgressive, reflecting the values of its subject matter in its own analyses. But the absence of work also reflects a sense that identities in young women—and most of the work on magazines focusses on young, often teen-aged women—are fluid, capable of being moulded by the cultural productions of capitalism, whereas those of older women may be more fixed, the product of lives already lived, rather than ones in the process of being formed. New work around identity and age, however, suggests this may not be the case, resting as it does on a concept of identity as something formed in youth and carried forward into later life, as opposed to developing over time, unfolding and changing through the life course in interaction with cultural structures, including in relation to age. I have also noted arguments that suggest identities have in general become more optional, less socially entrenched under conditions of postmodernity, and more the product of agency and choice in which patterns of consumption can play a significant role. This, it is suggested, can be true of later years as well as earlier ones.

Magazines, thus, need to be seen as sites of contestation over cultural meanings, primarily of gender, but increasingly of age. The media present encoded messages about cultural values, which individuals must then decode, interpreting them in the context of their own lives. But these coded messages have limited numbers of possible decodings; there are always preferred readings. Given the economic and cultural location of most media these will reinforce the dominant values of a society. In relation to women's magazines, this means the dominant values of femininity and the importance of maintaining these as one ages through practices like beauty regimes and engagement with fashion (Dinnerstein and Weitz 1994).

Women's Magazines, Fashion and Age

Though it is sometimes asserted that there are no magazines for older women, this is not in fact the case. Perusal of UK market data sources such as British Rate and Data (BRAD), which lists all UK magazines with brief information about their characters and readership, throws up a significant number of classic women's magazines aimed at the over fifties. One of the features of the magazine sector since the 1980s has been the way it has pursued finer market segmentation. The days of the 1950s, when mass market magazines like *Woman* reached across all age groups, and to some extent social classes, have gone. Magazines are much more narrowly targeted now, with lifestyles as the key determinant. But underlying lifestyle is nearly always a concept of age; significantly, the two parameters on which BRAD provides readership data are age and socioeconomic status. The magazines do not, of course, market themselves in terms of age, and the journalists working on them deploy a systemic age slippage whereby the magazine is described as reaching—and imagining—a younger reader than is in fact so. It remains the case, however, that magazines are quite closely targeted in terms of age.

The Magazines Aimed at the Older Market

Woman & Home is a classic women's magazine with a typically strong emphasis on beauty and fashion, which occupies about a fifth of the editorial space. The treatment is upbeat and glamorous, with both classic fashion spreads and extensive makeover sections. There is a strong emphasis on being positive, on new beginnings and the potential role of clothes in this. Fashion is seen as a central part of the 'treat' of the magazine. Printed on glossy paper with a spine, it is produced by IPC from its main London office in conjunction with a range of fashion and other titles. The readership centres on those in their late forties to sixties, predominantly middle class. The circulation data is taken from British Rate and Data (BRAD 2008) for the period when the main interviews were undertaken. A value of 100 represents the population norm for the subgroup, and figures above and below display a bias towards or against the category.

Table 6.1 *Woman and Home*: Readership by age and socio-economic status

15–24	25–34	35–44	45–54	55–64	65+
17	47	67	141	207	128
A	**B**	**C1**	**C2**	**D**	**E**
167	132	120	79	46	64

SAGA Magazine is a general lifestyle magazine aimed at the affluent retired, promoting consumption lifestyles. It is an offshoot of the travel and insurance corporation. Fashion only developed significantly in the magazine in the early twenty-first century, and it provided a relatively small and varying part of the offer, partly because the magazine is aimed at both men and women. It has relatively high production values with glossy paper and a spine, and at the time of the fieldwork it included fashion shoots mirroring those in mainstream fashion magazines. In general the coverage reflected that of newspaper colour supplements and other lifestyle magazines.

Table 6.2 *SAGA Magazine*: Readership by age and socio-economic status.

15–24	25–34	35–44	45–54	55–64	65+
2	4	8	47	206	308
A	**B**	**C1**	**C2**	**D**	**E**
225	145	113	67	44	60

Its readership is older and more affluent than that of *Woman & Home*. The interview was with the freelance fashion editor. Since the interview, fashion has been downgraded in the magazine.

Yours is a mass market publication aimed at older and less affluent women. It is a fortnightly, printed on cheaper, nonglossy paper and stapled. It is published by Bauer, who own *Heat* and *Grazia,* but significantly it is edited from its Peterborough office in conjunction with other special interest magazines, not from London where the more directly fashion-oriented magazines are produced. The magazine is less glamorous and aspirational than *Woman & Home*. It does not do fashion spreads as such, but covers fashion mostly through showing readers what is currently available and stylish, and how it might be worn. It does do makeovers, though of a more modest sort than those found in *Woman & Home,* for whom glamorous restyling is a central part of the magazine. Clothes tend to be cheaper, concentrated on high street staples like M&S and the value retailers. There is a warm, homely tone, and the magazine has a particularly close relationship with its readers who regard it as a 'friend': the editor receives over 750 letters and e-mails per issue. Circulation data confirms that it is heavily read by women over sixty-five, and that it has a socioeconomic profile weighted towards lower-middle- and working-class readers.

Table 6.3 *Yours*: Readership by age and socio-economic data.

15–24	25–34	35–44	45–54	55–64	65+
7	10	24	48	125	342
A	**B**	**C1**	**C2**	**D**	**E**
31	58	110	128	94	153

Magazines need to be seen both as commodities, products of the print industry, sites for selling consumer goods; and as cultural products, circulating in a cultural economy of collective meanings, producing patterns, narratives and models of and for the reader (Moeran 2004: 260). In this journalists have a specific role to play as cultural mediators shaping the ways later years are presented, imagined and performed within a commercial culture. In doing this, they often draw on their own life experience. All four of the editors in the study were themselves over fifty, and three of them had graduated to older magazines after working on younger ones earlier in their lives. Personal experience thus affects the way they present the issues, making them sympathetic to the situations of older women, though at the same time retaining strongly 'realistic' views that implicitly endorse the ageist valuations of wider culture.

Tensions in Visual Culture

Magazines operate in a visual culture that systemically devalues and erases age. Its biases towards youth and beauty are long-established, reaching back at least to the Renaissance and its Platonic ideal of beauty. I noted earlier Pollock's (2003) analysis of the meaning of the idealized female nude in Western art. In the late twentieth and early twenty-first centuries, however, this visual culture has taken on new significance with the exponential growth of the modern media. As a result culture has become saturated with images of bodily perfection, supporting a growing reflexive preoccupation with appearance in which individuals—typically women—measure themselves up against unattainable standards, pursuing self-worth and status through work on their bodies (Shilling 2003). These processes increasingly affect older women, who find themselves in a visual culture that systemically erases the signs of age, regarding them as a disruption in the visual field, something to be removed by systematic selection of images or by artificial enhancement. Older female bodies are rarely on view in modern visual culture; and such images, particularly if they involve nakedness, are strongly transgressive, as Tulle-Winton (2000) showed in her analysis of the photo essay *Pretty Ribbons*, in which a model in her eighties was depicted in conscious glamour shots photographed in hard, clear light. The commercially driven visual culture that surrounds older women thus devalues age and treats it as something shameful that needs to be hidden, presenting anti-ageing practices as the prime means of retaining social acceptability.

Magazines are by their nature strongly visual. Their messages—and pleasures— lie as much in the images as in the text. But this sets up tensions for those aiming at the older market. How can they reflect back the lives of readers when these are located within a visual culture that has its own values and hierarchies that systematically devalue the appearance of age? Magazines, if they are to succeed, need to relate directly to the readers and to reflect their lives, at the same time as operating within a visual culture in which status is linked to youthfulness. This tension is illustrated very clearly in the presentation of fashion in the magazines.

Fashion forms the central part of a classic women's magazine. It is at the heart of the element of 'treat' that is fundamental to their appeal. Women's magazines sell on their capacity to be a purchase, like a bar of chocolate, aimed at personal enjoyment, often snatched in the midst of the demands made by others (Hermes 1995).

They offer a moment of escape, a space for fantasy and for imagining different and better lives. This is a central part of their upbeat aspirational appeal. Reception studies show that women do not consume these messages uncritically (Winship 1987; Hermes 1995). They recognize that the visions offered are tangential to their real lives, but they still enjoy the space for fantasy and escape. Beautiful fashion images are an important part of this. They offer readers what the fashion editor of *Woman & Home* described as: 'a lift…a bit of a tonic'. The element of aesthetic pleasure is important here. For many women, fashion, together with home decoration and craft work, provides access to creative, aesthetic dimensions of being denied in the rest of their lives. It often does not matter that the clothes featured are far from what readers might actually wear: indeed many of the most popular spreads are those that feature garments and settings distant from the lives and experience of readers, such as couture evening wear. It is the visual pleasure and element of fantasy that matters. Magazines need to retain this. Featuring older women threatens to undermine it.

Models, Makeovers and Celebrities

Magazines negotiate the tension around images of older women in a number of ways, of which three are particularly prominent: models, makeovers and celebs. The three magazines differed in the approach they took to the age of models. Under the fashion editor, *SAGA* had pioneered the use of older models, employing only those over forty. They were, however, still models, and presented characteristically idealized and aspirational versions of the older woman—typically ones that show little in the way of age, though some did have grey hair. *Woman & Home,* by contrast, did not use older models in its fashion shoots. The fashion editor explained this through her characterization of fashion as a 'beautiful, inspirational moment'. Seeing older models, she argued, would erode this, disturbing the visual field of fashion, which is essentially youthful (a view with which the editor of *Vogue* concurred). Older models would undermine the element of fantasy projection central to magazines in which readers identify with the youthful images:

> They know they're fifty-five, but they just still see in their head this, you know, other woman.

In this way fashion is preserved as a site of fantasy and youthfulness.

Yours, aimed at a distinctly older market, gets round the issue of older models by avoiding fashion shoots altogether. They are expensive and produce images readers find difficult to relate to. Instead the magazine shows fashion through spreads that illustrate garments and accessories, but without the bodies containing them. It is an approach widely used in magazines generally, though in the case of *Yours* it has a specific function in avoiding discordant images the reader might find alienating, either because they were too impossibly young or because they were disturbingly old.

The most prominent way the magazines address the visual presentation of age is through makeovers. These allow magazines to relate directly to the lives of readers, getting round the difficulties posed by classic fashion shoots. They are a particularly important element in *Woman & Home.* The fashion editor explained how they are a

> very big thing of the magazine. It's our USP. So I get very, very involved with the four or five women every month that we feature in the fashion section. So we have our glamorous fashion. Then we have our five women, who wear those clothes themselves, and they're across the ages…That's really why our magazine is so successful, I think, because it's real in that aspect.

Makeovers thus relate directly to the reader through the use of real women, but showing them in a glamorous, transformed way. To this degree they offer older women the promise—or the fantasy—that they could do the same.

The magazines also relate to their readers through the use of celebrities who are themselves older. Over the last decade all magazines have increasingly featured celebrities on the covers and inside. The magazines presented here drew heavily on a relatively small range of older female celebrities, including at the time of the fieldwork, Helen Mirren, Judy Dench, Cherie Lunghi, Felicity Kendall and Emma Thompson. Their function on the cover, where they frequently featured, is the classic one of drawing the reader in and reflecting back to her a woman's gaze that is powerful, calm and contained (Winship 1987). In particular they are there to present a successful version of the older woman: looking good (and part of this means younger) and at the centre of attention. They assert the continued value and status of the older woman, placing her fully in the public eye, styled up in glamorous clothes and make-up, fully integrated with younger celebrity culture. The image is designed to draw the reader in and confirm her—idealized—identification with the magazine through its image of the older woman.

On occasions, however, particularly in relation to older and less affluent readers, such strategies backfire. Glamorous celebrities can provoke resistance and annoyance if their images seem too unreal or too privileged. Readers of *Yours,* as the editor recounted, can observe that these women are rich and lead easy lives and react by saying: 'Don't tell me to get the style secrets of somebody who has got lots of money, time and energy to spend on themselves, and to spend looking young, that's not reality for me.' As always, magazines have to tread a fine line between fantasy, self-identification and the real lives of their readers.

Negotiating Age

Much of the presentation of fashion in the magazines takes the form of guidance and support in relation to the difficult matter of self-presentation, something all three editors recognized was increasingly important. Even the editor of *Yours,* which is read by working-class women in their seventies and over, comments: 'We've all got so much more conscious of what we should be wearing and what we shouldn't be wearing.' It is much less clear today how to be older. As a result women often lack confidence. Clarke and Miller (2002) argue that dress, though a realm of pleasure, is also one of anxiety with, in Simmel's (1904/1971) terms, the competing desires to stand out and to fit in weighted significantly towards the latter. In relation to older women, there are added pressures of dressing in an age-appropriate way, in which the fear of being inappropriately dressed is strong. All three editors referred to the old cultural trope of 'mutton dressed as lamb' and women's fears in this regard (Fairhurst 1998); even the editor of *Vogue* mentioned it obliquely. Many older women lose confidence in how to dress as their bodies change and as cultural expectations in relation to age bear in on them. As the fashion editor of *Woman & Home* commented: 'I've seen a lot of women who...have lost their way.' The editor of *Vogue* concurred with this sense that women found themselves lost as styles that had once worked no longer did:

> There are things that you might have always looked good in and thought was your style, and...you find that suddenly that just doesn't work anymore. I think that's a big kind of problem for women, that suddenly they can't wear what they always looked really kind of lovely in, and they don't know what to do, how to change.

Offering guidance on how to negotiate the difficult cultural territory of being older was thus a central part of what the magazines do. As the fashion editor of *Woman & Home* explained: 'It's our job to edit for people. That's what we do.' Part of this means steering women away from unflattering styles:

> I want to shoot them all, these women who are really elderly and they've got puffed sleeves. You know you actually can't do that over the age of eighteen. (Editor of *Yours*)

At the same time, the editors see their role as encouraging women to be more adventurous and to recognize that they need not be as restricted as they think:

> You know the word that is vital in all this is *permission*. And I honestly believe that you know when all these lovely things come out and you're going down the rail and saying, 'It's not for me, it's not for me, I'm not allowed this.' And then you suddenly come across an absolutely stunning shirt...And you think I love that, but you know there's still this nagging thing, but it's not for me...Somebody has to say to these women...You have the right to join in. (Fashion editor of *SAGA*)

Joining in, not feeling excluded by age, is the important message here.

For these fashion editors, it is axiomatic that there is always a way for older women to wear the latest styles—though the fashion editor of *SAGA* concedes that certain trends, for example, 'Neon, Boudoir', were very difficult. The purpose of the fashion sections is to concentrate on what can be worn by older women and to show readers how to do it. They thus help construct an older woman still linked into mainstream consumption, but in what is felt to be an appropriate way.

The editors recognize that fashion has a role to play in counteracting cultural exclusion. To this degree it is a form of resistance. Engagement with dress is presented positively in the magazines as a means of counteracting cultural invisibility. It is significant that the editor of *SAGA* used the language of 'joining in'. Fashion is seen as part of asserting that the individual is still part of the social world, still aspires to look good and be noticed. As the editor of *Yours* commented in explaining why the magazine, though targeted on a significantly older age group, features fashion:

> That's one of the reasons why we do fashion. Because it's saying you're not disappearing, you're out there in the community. Whether you're a Gran, whether you're a carer, you might still be working, whatever you're doing, wanting to make the best of yourself is part of that. And that's what fashion helps you do.

Fashion—or rather dress—also performs an additional distinctive function in *Yours*. The magazine often runs features in which readers send in pictures of themselves in the past wearing glamorous clothes. Or it takes a current look—for example, bubble skirts—and shows how 'we' did it first, and by implication better, in the 1950s. These strategies allow the reader to imagine herself back in her youth and to assert her value as someone who did once look different and better. They draw on the evocative nature of remembered clothes and the power that lies in such material artefacts of the past with their intimate, embodied connections (Weber and Mitchell 2004). The magazine thus offers an opportunity to assert the memories and values of the group in the face of the cultural erosions of age, of what Vincent (2003) has described as the sense of becoming exiled in one's own culture. As the editor comments:

> We are a positive magazine. We are about somewhere—you know, if you want to go somewhere that is a better place, and that's going to make you feel better by the end of reading this magazine, then come here.

Yours offers a space into which older women can escape.

Not all women, however, welcome this renewed emphasis on fashion and appearance. *Woman & Home* is largely bought by women who do still want to engage with these fields; and they form a prominent part of its appeal. But both *Yours* and *SAGA*, possibly because of their older age groups, have experienced more ambivalent responses from readers. Some readers of *Yours* have responded with annoyance, seeing the inclusion of fashion as an imposition:

> 'Oh, for goodness sake! I really don't need all that. I'm fine in elasticated trousers... I really don't need all this silly nonsense.' (Editor of *Yours*)

The spread of fashionability to older women thus represents the spread of new demands as well as new opportunities, making it harder to abdicate from these areas of life.

Ageism and Age Slippage

Across the adult magazine sector is a systemic pattern of age slippage in which target readership is described as significantly younger than the actual age profile. This reflects the desire to maintain the status of the magazine in a commercial culture in which younger represents better. It allows the magazine to position itself in an aspirational space, presenting the reader with a visual world younger than the one they inhabit, allowing them to identify with a younger, generally more successful self. This pattern was evident in the magazines analysed here, all of which described themselves as targeted on significantly younger age groups than the ones reported by the readership data. For example *Yours* describes itself as 'targeted on the over 50s', whereas as the readership data shows, it is predominantly bought by those in their late sixties and older. Partly this is about lifting the status of the magazine in ways complicit with the desires of readers, reflecting back a significantly younger world. The fashion editor of *SAGA,* for example, divided readers into the 'new old' and the 'war old'; and saw her task when appointed to respond to the interests of the first through the use of mainstream fashion shoots as part of a process of lifting the magazine visually.

At times, however, the journalists themselves seemed to be drawn into this world of self-delusion, imagining their readers as significantly younger than they in fact are. The fashion editor of *Woman & Home* commented: 'Theoretically our magazine is aimed at the thirty-five plus, but I expect our median age is probably forty-five.' In fact, as the data show, it is significantly older. This is a phenomenon not confined to journalists, but evident also in the retail sector generally where there is a systematic bias towards regarding core customers as younger than they in fact are. An element of this age slippage relates to the status of the cultural mediator—whether journalist or designer—for, as in other jobs, there is a halo effect in which an individual's status is affected by that of the groups they serve. Writing—or designing—for the older market lacks status, and there is a systematic desire to move younger to counteract this.

Against these processes of age slippage, however, I should note that journalists also believed their readers are in reality more youthful than their chronological age might suggest. The fashion editor of *Woman & Home* certainly subscribed to the thesis that middle and later years were changing and that 'fifty is the new forty', so imagining the reader as younger was, in her view, the correct strategy for the magazine. *Woman & Home* had been successful because it recognized this:

We've actually changed the magazine quite radically to move with the times, because women of fifty-five are not the same as women of fifty-five a few years ago. And obviously everybody knows this, and we've taken this onboard.

The tensions are also reflected in the responses of manufacturers and advertisers who are reluctant to be associated with this sector of the media. To cover fashion, editors need to borrow samples. All three editors, however, had had difficulties doing this. Initially when the fashion editor of *SAGA* attempted to include fashion, she found manufacturers would not lend, and she was forced to buy the clothes on a credit card and return them the next day. Manufacturers

considered that it wasn't a market. I think they thought at a certain point in a woman's life she didn't go out and buy clothes. Well, she might buy a sweater but she wasn't interested in fashion.

Even more significant was the fear that the clothes would be identified as aged:

There is a tearing worry at the brand manager's level that their brand could be associated with this age group. So they didn't want to be...seen in it, and certainly didn't want me put it on older models.

The other editors experienced similar problems. The editor of *Yours* believed that retailers have 'delusions of grandeur about who is buying their clothes'. All three reported they had had some success in bringing round some retailers through their capacity to show how the magazine could deliver sales. This is a market often neglected by retailers, and as a result featured items were often taken up very strongly. The editor of *Yours* noted that the magazine had a 'response level that other magazines would kill for...there's an awful lot of money out there from these people.'

A similar dynamic works in relation to advertising. None of the magazines secured high status or even extensive fashion advertising. They attributed this partly to the fact that the British fashion industry did not spend much on advertising, expecting to get its coverage free; but more strongly to systematic biases in the advertising industry which is dominated by the young, who do not want to deal with magazines aimed at older readers (Lee 1997; Long 1998; Carrigan and Szmigin 2000). Status for the brand and the brand manager lies in securing space in magazines like *Vogue,* even though these might not sell the goods in the way an advert in one of their magazines might. As a result the advertising the three magazines did secure was noticeably older and less fashionable than the image presented in the editorial pages. Adverts were often for garments that were strongly age coded: in *SAGA* for example, leisure suits in pastel colours, with machine-embroidered floral detail. These were typically shown on very young models, again contrasting with the editorial policy, who would not conceivably wear such garments. As a result they struck a discordant note, but clearly one that did not disturb advertisers. There is thus a notable disjunction between the message about age conveyed in the editorial pages and the advertising.

The High Fashion Magazine: *Vogue*

We now turn to a very different magazine, *Vogue,* to explore how a high fashion magazine negotiates the issue of age. *Vogue* is the premier British fashion magazine (together with the trade paper *Draper's Record*), though it is also a lifestyle magazine aimed at well-off women. One of a stable of glossy journals produced by Condé Nast, it is part of an international publishing empire, with editions in fifteen countries. Each is distinctive and reflects local commercial and visual culture, though in recent decades they have together become carriers of a globalized style that supports international branding (Moeran 2004; David 2006; Borelli 1997; Kopina 2007). *Vogue* is notable for an almost perfect match between editorial and advertising, with the high production values of its fashion spreads reflected in the adverts for major perfume and garment houses. Its high advertising revenue means it is one of the most profitable women's magazines. The current UK circulation is around two hundred twenty thousand, with an attributed readership of 1.2 million. Its target readership is described as 'concentrated in the ABC1 20–44 demographic group. A high proportion are in some kind of job or profession and are in the higher income groups.' The sociodemographic profile confirms this, with a preponderance of As (BRAD 2008). In terms of age, the profile is heavily biased towards those in their twenties and thirties, with a clear falling off from the mid fifties.

How Does *Vogue* Negotiate Age?

Vogue is not aimed at older women. As the marketing data shows, its readership is heavily biased towards those in their twenties and thirties. In recent years, however, it has made attempts to relate to the older market. This partly arose, as the editor explained in the interview, from the realization that older women represented a growing and affluent part of the market. Women in their fifties and sixties have particularly high disposable incomes, and *Vogue* is interested in capturing these for the fashion industry. It also resulted from comments from readers, for, though *Vogue* does not normally attract reader's letters, on the issue of the absence of clothes for

Table 6.4   *Vogue*: Readership by age and socio-economic status.

15–24	23–34	35–44	45–54	55–64	65+
215	124	92	88	52	39
A	B	C1	C2	D	E
201	136	110	70	68	52

older women, it does. Lastly, the editor herself, like many senior journalists, is encountering dilemmas of growing older while still retaining an active interest in dress and fashion.

The editor was aware of the visual tension presented by attempting to relate to older readers in a magazine focussed on high fashion, but for her using older models was impossible.

> I don't think people do really want to look really at older women as kind of exemplars of fashion and beauty. I don't think they find them as such. You could say why? Although I think it's quite obvious really.

Turning to a copy of *Vogue,* she explained:

> Let's just have a look—you can't see many pictures there that wouldn't look really slightly ridiculous…This [pointing to a shoot] would look horrible. Not just strange, absolutely hideous, I think. This, which looks rather lovely on a very young model, would all look rather sad and tired on an older person. You know [shrugs]. That's life.

Through the interview, she naturalized ageism. She reflected the view that this is just how things are. There is no point in trying to pretend otherwise or to attempt to challenge it. This reflected her own position in the media world where her task is to reflect the values of readers, and these are predominately ageist.

In relation to fashion shoots there is an additional problem in using older models that arises from the visual values of the photographic community which are strongly influenced by wider movements in art and photography. This is most noticeable in magazines like *Vogue* where fashion shoots over the last two decades have increasingly deployed highly sexualized, edgy noir imagery (Jobling 1999). Ruggerone (2006) argues this reflects a masculine hegemony in which women are constructed as if intended for a young male spectator's gaze, embodying his expectations of women and male-female relationships. This aesthetic culture presents difficulties for the depiction of fashion in relation to older women who by and large do not respond positively to such images. They would indeed be transgressive if presented in these terms, but not in a way that chimes with current visual values. As a result, the editor explained, it is difficult to get cutting-edge photographers to do work in relation to age.

> I think photographers that we work with don't particularly want to do it, because they're interested in sort of making sort of edgy fashion images, and in the main they can't see how they're going to do that if they're photographing it on an older person.

The way she deals with the visual tension is by adopting a concept of 'ageless style' wherein age is itself decentred, replaced by a concept of stylishness that transcends age. But, in significant ways, it achieves this by effacing and obscuring ageing itself.

Up until 2007, age only featured sporadically in *Vogue;* and it was wholly absent from its covers. The pattern was broken in July 2007 with an issue that addressed 'Ageless Style'; which has been repeated in subsequent years. The cover of the 2007 edition featured eight models integrated into unity through being dressed in white. None showed any visible signs of age, though close scrutiny of one slightly blank face might suggest cosmetic enhancement. Inside, however, their ages are revealed as nineteen to fifty-three. The cover conveys lightness (white with touches of red), glamour and youth. There are no visible signs of age. The sell lines include: 'Vogue celebrates Ageless Style'; 'working the trends: from seventeen to seventy'; 'forever young: insider beauty tricks'. In 2008 the cover depicted a single image, of actress

Figure 6.1   Cover of *Vogue*: The first Ageless Style issue (2007). Photo: Patrick Demarchelier/*Vogue*. Courtesy The Condé Nast Publications Ltd.

Uma Thurman, described in the sell line as 'facing forty with glamour.' (She was in her late thirties.) Again there are no visible signs of age on her face or hands which are airbrushed to perfection. There is, however, a slightly sombre quality to the cover with predominant colours of grey, black and gold. The sell lines include: 'Ageless style: the best pieces at any age' and 'How to grow old fashionably.' The latter, though it echoes the phrase *growing old gracefully,* is notable for its direct reference to growing old, something rare in magazine culture. The covers that followed in 2009–12 continued this evolution away from the initial use of multiple images, with its diffusionary effect, towards a more classic approach focussing on a single individual, though always a celebrity, reinforcing the way age is dealt with through actual women not models.

Vogue had on occasion addressed age before 2007, though not on the cover. Notably in 1998 it was the topic of a *Vogue* Debate. There were four such, which took the form of round table discussions by eight or so invited guests. The subjects were ultra-slim models; appropriate dress for professional women; the absence of black models; and ageing. Each carried a sense that it was a topic where *Vogue* was under fire for promoting malign versions of the female body that supported the culture of anorexia; for failing to acknowledge the changes in women's lives resulting from entry into work where ultra-fashionable, frivolous or overtly sexual dress was inappropriate; for endorsing implicit racism through its promotion of an exclusively white model of beauty; and for excluding older women from view. The model and work debates were mentioned on the cover; the ageing one was not. The panel for the ageing debate included the deputy editor of *Vogue* (42), the beauty director (age not given), a novelist (Fay Weldon, 66), the director of a model agency (54), a property administrator (66), a retailing director (48), a designer (Edina Ronay, age not given) and a private GP (50). The discussion mostly turned around appearance rather than dress, with particular attention paid to cosmetic surgery and HRT. The tone was largely upbeat, with a characteristic magazine emphasis on feeling good and the importance of positive thinking and inner beauty. This last note was somewhat punctured, however, by the intervention of the beauty editor: 'I have to say that it's an irony to listen to us all sitting around saying it's great to be older, when I know that the phones are ringing in the beauty department with women our age asking "Where can I get Botox injections?"' (266). The discussion ended with an editorial note that explained that, unlike the other three debates, this one produced 'no clear conclusions', and it was described as 'not an easy topic'.

Inside the pioneering issue of 2007 was a brief preface by the editor defining her approach:

> When I first thought about putting together an 'ageless style' issue of *Vogue* I was obsessed with what I didn't want it to be: something that told you what to wear at what age. The whole point of style and fashion is that it should be ageless…we have concentrated on what you can wear at *any* age, whether you are in your teens or your seventies. (12)

In the 2008 special issue she wrote more directly on the experience of becoming fifty. She states that she is unwilling to get involved in battles that she is going to lose: 'You can't win a battle against time.' She notes how it is easier to face age if one has been nice looking but never beautiful: 'For those whose identities are completely bound up in their good looks, the diminution is terrifying' (143). In relation to age she comments:

> There is no doubt that the question of what you *can* wear becomes more charged and complex as you age...The fear of dressing inappropriately lurks like some ghastly spectre around the wardrobe: the insecurity about whether you are heading into a mutton-alert territory hovers determinedly.

She concludes the article on a note confirming continuity of identity and pleasure in dress:

> At some point we all think that we lose the person that we were when younger and become somebody old. But we don't, and our clothes, and the pleasures we take in them should reflect that. (185)

Localization, Dilution and Personalization

A systematic examination of the editorial pages of the magazine reveals three main strategies deployed by *Vogue* to finesse the difficulties of representing age: localization, dilution and personalization. *Localization* refers to the strategy whereby older women are confined to certain parts of the magazine. Typically, and most strongly, they feature in the beauty pages where anti-ageing strategies are a central concern. They are never represented visually here. As the editor noted in the research interview, skin products are always sold on perfection; though she did express a slight qualm when she saw they were doing an anti-ageing shoot with a nineteen-year-old model. In terms of covers, age only really features in text, not images: *Vogue* avoids compromising the visual appeal of this key sales feature. Beyond this, questions of age are confined to the features pages. They are never included in the fashion spreads that form the heart of the magazine and are its most prestigious part. These pages are dedicated to mainstream fashion. One exception did occur in 2005 with a fashion spread featuring glamorous Charlotte Rampling as the heroine of a noir film, but it was shot in such low light that her features (and signs of age) were almost wholly disguised. Older women are thus localized in the features and beauty sections and remain largely absent from the mainstream, core fashion pages.

Dilution strategies are pursued through a number of classic journalistic techniques. The first of these, widely used across the magazine sector, is the decades approach, in which fashions are illustrated on women in their twenties, thirties, forties and so forth. Until recently such decades tended to stop at the forties, with the fifties being a daring extension. The 'endpoint' of fashionability is, however, being pushed later in *Vogue* and in other magazines. From 2005 *Vogue* included—exceptionally—a woman in her seventies. The article illustrated key trends, showing how these could be worn by all ages; the woman in her seventies featured 'white'. She did, however, look somewhat different from the earlier decades—more distinctly old. By the time the format was repeated in 2008, *Vogue* managed to illustrate a woman in her seventies who, presumably through cosmetic surgery and airbrushing, was fully integrated with other images, almost wholly devoid of any appearance of age.

Another classic dilution technique is that of generations. The July 2007 issue featured Jane Birkin accompanied by her glamorous daughter in her twenties. It is a strategy often used by advertisers who want to show their clothes as relevant and sellable to all ages without compromising their fashionability, and so illustrate them in family groups. Calvin Klein and Ralph Lauren pioneered such lifestyle advertising, featuring elite WASP pseudo-families. Dilution can also be achieved by features that show stylish women of all ages, typically illustrated by small pictures. These contrast with the full-page fashion spreads. Here the images of older women are diluted by small images and a predominance of younger women. Such pages enable the magazine to reach out to and relate to older readers by showing something of their lives, but without defining the magazine as aimed at this group. Another dilution strategy rests on showing style icons or famous designers such as Mary Quant. This enables the feature to include pictures of these in their heyday as well as now. *Vogue* has an incomparable archive of past images which it deploys with great skill to make up spreads that address current visual interests. Older women can be integrated into this as part of the wider engagement with the history of style.

The third strategy is that of *personalization.* In every case where an older woman is featured in *Vogue,* she is a named individual. These are always real women, not models, living real lives, though with the proviso that these are *Vogue* lives and, as a result, far from the lived reality of most people, even most readers. There are parallels here in the emphasis on actual older women in less elite magazines through the use of makeovers and celebrities, though *Vogue* does also use the latter. The editor noted, however, that it has proved difficult to find powerful or senior women prepared to be photographed in *Vogue* because they see it as threatening to their standing: 'They think that it will be seen as trivial.'

This account of the treatment of age and ageing should not lead us to think that these are central themes for UK *Vogue.* They are not. They are marginal and sporadic. We noted how age-themed issues are always published in July, a dead period for fashion magazines; though the editor in the research interview confirmed that these put on readership. Otherwise features on older women are infrequent and older women only appear occasionally. But this was not always so. During the 1950s, older women had a regular slot in *Vogue* in the guise of Mrs Exeter.

The Lost World of Mrs Exeter

Mrs Exeter was a character developed by *Vogue* in the late 1940s to represent the older woman (Halls 2000). In 1949 she was described as 'approaching sixty' (March 1949). She appeared twice on the cover of *Vogue* (1948 and 1951), including in a glamorous shot by Cecil Beaton, and was a regular and successful feature through the 1950s. Initially represented by drawings, including by the artist John Ward, she developed a distinctive photographic image in the 1950s. By the end of the decade, however, Halls notes that she was getting steadily younger; and she eventually disappeared in the mid 1960s, killed off by the rise of youth fashion. The styles of the 1960s were particularly youth-oriented, with very short skirts and a body ideal that valorized the prepubescent teenager. A quotation from Margot Smyly, the model most closely associated with the character of Mrs Exeter in the United Kingdom, conveys the pressures of the time, as fashion became more youth-oriented, as well as the anger and pique of an older woman cast aside. Describing the 1960s, she says: 'It was a terrible time, a nasty, catty, horrible decade with a lot of ill feeling. Nothing blossomed' (November 1982: 154).

One of the things that is striking about Mrs Exeter from the perspective of today is how old she is and how unrepentantly so: *Vogue* writes in 1949, 'Approaching 60, Mrs Exeter does not look a day younger, a fact she accepts with perfect good humour and reasonableness.' This is in marked contrast to the dominant discourse today, where the aim is to look ten years younger. It is true that the cover images in the 1940s and 1950s do cheat slightly, showing her with grey hair but a smooth face, but at least she does feature clearly as an older woman, and on the cover. This is in contrast to today when even the age-themed issues of 2007 and subsequently show much younger women and erase the signs of age. One area where *Vogue* has always refused to compromise, however, is weight. Halls notes that *Vogue* never addressed the problem of middle-age spread: Mrs Exeter was always shown as extremely slim. Today, of course, slimness is a significant anti-ageing strategy.

The phenomenon of Mrs Exeter is an interesting one; and we can ask why, despite remaining something of a memory in *Vogue*'s collective consciousness (she features from time to time in articles), she has not been—and indeed could not be—revived. Part of the reason is that she is so much a figure of her times, the 1950s, and she remains confined by that period. Her identity is heavily inflected with class and gender. With her elegant, restrained clothes, she epitomizes the bourgeois lady of the period. Always referred to by her married name, she remains encased within her marriage. It is inconceivable that she could have a job. She thus represents a way of life that has ceased to exist for the majority of middle- and upper-middle-class women who are the main audience for the magazine.

There are, however, other reasons why she is beyond revival, and these relate to the changed ways age is experienced, understood and imagined today. Though

Figure 6.2   Cover of *Vogue*: Mrs Exeter (1948). Photo: Cecil Beaton/*Vogue*. Courtesy The Condé Nast Publications Ltd

Mrs Exeter was a minor figure in *Vogue* in the 1950s, she was a regular one, and to that degree occupied an acknowledged position within the magazine. She appeared on two covers, featured as a distinctively older woman with white hair. This is in contrast to today when age features on the cover only through text, not image. Though she is more defined—and confined—by her age than would be the case today, she is oddly also more visible. She has a clear presence within the structure of the magazine, reflecting her secure place in the age structure of society. She occupies a distinctive slot in the age hierarchy, as she does in the gender and class ones, reflecting an era when identities were more fixed culturally in terms of social categorizations and structures.

Since that period, however, a series of social and cultural shifts, outlined in Chapter 3, have reconstituted the meaning and experience of age. As a result the cultural position of older women has shifted. Reflexive modernity has weakened the structures of age, as it has those of gender and class, so that the clear and defined certainties of Mrs Exeter have gone. Instead *Vogue* now promotes an ideal of age-less style in which seamless integration is the goal and in which older women—if they pursue the ideal of fashionability—can remain part of the mainstream. And yet this integration is based in significant ways on an effacement of age. The covers that featured ageless style show no signs of age at all. *Vogue* consistently features older women who look decades younger than their age, and achieving that state is valorized as the ideal. Here the aim is not to move graciously on to the next stage of life like Mrs Exeter, but to look ten years younger and to remain actively integrated into the world of appearance and consumption, reflecting a cultural ideal in which success is ageing without showing the visual signs of doing so.

Conclusion

Magazines for older women—as for younger—are a deeply ambivalent cultural phenomena, reflecting the wider cultural of ageism, and to that degree endorsing its meanings, at the same time as offering forms of escape from and resistance to it. The wider culture prizes youth, and it is not surprising that magazines present themselves in ways that reflect that valuation. This is why *Woman and Home* shows its fashion shoots on younger models, enabling the magazine to present images consonant with wider visual culture. That is why *Vogue,* in line with other high fashion magazines, limits images of older women—and older for *Vogue* means over thirty—only to certain parts of the magazine. As the editor explains in the next chapter, being older, like being fat or poor, is something no one wants to be. Pre-senting material in relation to age in *Vogue* thus rests on a concept of ageless style that transcends the element of age, and in doing so effectively effaces it. As Katz (2005), Kathy Woodward (1991, 2006) and others have noted, successful ageing in modern consumer culture is ageing without giving the appearance of doing so. The visual imagery of mainstream magazines endorses this aspiration, and in doing so entrenches it.

The upbeat character of the magazines is particularly evident in the makeover pages which include a prominent part of the fashion coverage, and the place where the magazines connect very directly with the readers and their aspirations for them-selves. These features centre on making the best of yourself and on being positive. They are about countering the pervasive negativities of later years and the erosion of confidence that can come with these. All three magazines aimed at the older market emphasized this, though in the contexts of their different demographics. They thus offer older women ways of operating more successfully in an ageist culture. But the response remains an individualistic one that does not attempt to challenge the underlying structure of values.

At the same time, like most women's magazines, they contain strongly escapist elements, presenting an idealized, aspirational world that allows older women to escape from the day-to-day limitations of their lives. As Hermes (1995) showed, we need to acknowledge how women recognize the escapist element, looking at magazines as diversions, times of pleasure unconnected with reality. Women do not read magazines to be depressed or reminded of the cultural tensions of their lives; nor do they believe or act out their messages uncritically. Fashion and fashion spreads are central to this element of escapism. Magazines can also offer other forms of escape in relation to age. *Yours* makes a point of taking readers into spaces where their values are endorsed and shared by a community of others and where, despite the cultural erosions around them, their memories are shared and appreciated. Again dress can be part of this, reminding readers of their past and of the young and attractive people they once were, thereby enabling them to make a claim for attention on that basis. But once again the message is an essentially conservative one endorsing the wider cultural estimation of age, even in a way that attempts to soften the pain.

Women's magazines are not radical publications. We should not be surprised by this, given their location within capitalist production and their close relationship with consumption culture. With their bright, consciously positive tone, they have to be read against the realities of older women's lives and the interpretations and evaluations within which these are embedded. In this context what they offer is an idealized, aspirational world that allows older women to imagine a different self and to escape from the day-to-day limitations of their lives. To this degree they send conservative messages to older women about the meanings of their lives and situations. But they do so in conjunction with advice and techniques that aim to allow older women to survive more successfully in that culture and, to a degree, challenge it.

Magazines—like other cultural productions—thus need to be understood not simply as reflectors of the culture, but creators of it. As such, they contribute to a particular discursive construction of later years. As we have seen, it is one that emphasizes being positive, remaining part of the mainstream, presenting yourself well and engaging in beauty practices and anti-ageing strategies. It rests on an active engagement with consumption. It is clearly attractive to readers—and advertisers. But in doing so, other discursive constructions are implicitly silenced—those, for example, of giving up, of not bothering to keep up appearance or 'making the best of yourself', of radical disassociation from material possessions or concerns with appearance, not trying to look younger, but accepting being and looking old. These are absent from their pages.

$-7-$

The High Street Responds: Designing for the Older Market

The fashion industry is a schizophrenic trade: at one end imbued with the values of high fashion and with the glamour and froth of an industry based on fast-moving styles of cultural elites; at the other pursuing the day-to-day task of providing clothing for the population as a whole. This tension lies at the heart of many of the difficulties the industry faces in responding to the older market. In this chapter I explore how the high street conceptualizes or imagines the older customer, and how it designs and markets specifically for her, though in doing so I also address the view that it fails to do so adequately. I focus in particular on the ways it adjusts the cut and style of its offer to respond to the ways the body alters with age and the challenges this presents for fashionability. I also explore the use of colour and the wider significance of this in relation to the changing cultural location of older people. But first I need to explore briefly the nature of the Fashion System and some of the changes that have occurred in it over the last twenty years.

Changes in the Fashion System

As Braham (1997) and others have emphasized, fashion is a hybrid subject encompassing both material and cultural elements. Du Gay (1997) theorizes this dual quality in terms of a 'cultural economy' in which cultural meanings are produced at economic sites such as factories and shops and circulated through economic processes and practices such as adverts, marketing and design. Theorized by Fine and Leopold (1993) as the Fashion System, this represents the nexus of commercial, design and media influences that together provide the principal source of changing aesthetic judgements about clothing, determining the choices available in the market and providing goods to satisfy those. It is a complex system that links highly fragmented forms of production with equally diverse and often volatile patterns of demand.

The predominant language within this commercial sector is that of 'fashion': this is the 'fashion' industry; 'fashion' is what it sells and the changing cycle of 'fashion' is what drives it. But as I noted in Chapter 2, fashion is a somewhat problematic term in the context of this study, where the prominent approach draws on sociological and anthropological traditions that emphasize clothing and dress as part of the lived ordinariness of people's lives. Clothing and dress are treated here as universal aspects of social being, applying to everyone, rather than to special or elite features as promoted by parts of the fashion industry, where fashion can be an exclusionary term denoting the styles of the ultra-fashionable core. This approach is particularly important in relation to older people who are frequently perceived—and often perceive themselves—as beyond fashion. Better terms in many ways for this field of production are the garment trade or apparel industry, where large parts of its production are taken up with fairly unfashionable clothing, often in the forms of standard, relatively unchanging lines. Many of the dress items of older men in particular fall into this category. It remains the case, however, that fashion and fashion industry are the terms used of and by this cultural field, and I adopt them in this chapter.

Over the last fifty years a number of changes have occurred within the fashion industry in the United Kingdom. One of the most significant has been the steady acceleration of the fashion cycle and its extension to larger parts of the market. In the postwar era, British fashion was dominated by the major multiples, such as Marks & Spencer (M&S), operating in close conjunction with the Leeds-based manufacturers, effectively forming an oligopoly that dominated retail. In the late 1990s, however, the industry was restructured as manufacturing moved to the Far East to exploit supplies of cheaper labour, moving from vertically integrated systems to ones dominated by managed supply chains (R. Jones 2006). Supermarkets and other value retailers emerged as rivals to the traditional high street, using their buying power to produce a mass of cheap, fashion-oriented clothes, with the result that the real cost of clothes in the United Kingdom has declined since the 1960s by 70 per cent (Twigg and Majima 2013).

In the past, large sectors of the clothing market took the form of stable, little-changing lines, relatively unaffected by fashion. But with the new world of short production runs, quicker time scales and flexible batch production, more of the market has been drawn into the orbit of fashion (Braham 1997). Clothes have shifted from being durables, expensive items required by everyone and bought infrequently, to consumables, cheap items bought frequently as part of active engagement with consumption (Majima 2006). In this period, consumers move from a world when a coat in the 1960s was a major item of expenditure expected to last several years, to one in the 2000s where single-season coats of fashionable cut and colour became widely available in supermarkets and other low-cost retailers.

This intensification of the fashion cycle has resulted in a further stage in the democratization of fashion. This has been conceptualized by Elizabeth Wilson (1985) as the process whereby the mass production of fashionably styled clothes made possible the use of fashion as a means of self-enhancement and self-expression for the majority. The point at which this transition occurs has been the subject of debate. Some economic and dress historians locate it in the late nineteenth and earlier twentieth centuries, with the emergence of the mass clothing industry; others in the 1960s, with the rise of the youth market. Majima (2006, 2008), however, argues that the true democratization of fashion only occurs in the late twentieth century with the influx of mass cheap clothing, which for the first time allowed the majority to be drawn into the fashion cycle. This majority now includes older people.

The expansion of productivity in the Far East has produced a search for new markets. Among these, increasingly from the 1990s onwards, have been older people and children. The extension of ideas of 'fashionability' has been particularly successful in relation to children, especially girls, who have been drawn into the fashion cycle with the development of parallel collections that replicate adult fashions for young girls. Monsoon in the United Kingdom provides a successful example of this. These developments fit into the wider commodification of juvenile femininity, analysed by Russell and Tyler (2002) in terms of the spread of 'pink'.

Older women have also been drawn into the faster shopping cycle. Shopping data in relation to the last forty years make clear that older women are shopping more frequently for clothes than in the past. An analysis of spending patterns in the UK Family Expenditure Survey 1961–2005 using pseudo cohort methods shows that women aged fifty-five to seventy-four in 1961 were purchasing clothing on average on about six occasions a year. By 2006 this had increased to more than eighteen occasions (Twigg and Majima 2013). Even among women over seventy-five, there was a growth from about three occasions in 1961 to over ten in 2006. These older groups are not shopping as often as younger ones—across the historical period those aged sixteen to thirty-four are the most frequent shoppers—but they are being drawn consistently into the faster shopping cycle characteristic of the last four decades. As a result, women over seventy-five now shop for clothes as often as those aged sixteen to thirty-four did in the early 1960s. Though some of them are indeed the 'same' women, I have argued elsewhere (Twigg and Majima 2013) that the effect is less one of cohort than of period. What we are observing is the spread across all groups of the habit of more frequent shopping in this historical period. These women are not, however, spending a larger proportion of their income on clothes. This is largely because of the reducing cost of clothes, which have become significantly cheaper over the period. There is thus evidence to support the view that the behaviour of older women has been affected by the general climate; and that they have been drawn into the faster shopping cycle that marks the period. Though this FES data does not allow us to explore class-based patterns of expenditure in the United Kingdom, other studies suggest that socioeconomic status is a significant factor in engagement with fashion, with middle- and upper-class older women more likely to be involved in fashion. Birtwistle and Tsim, for example, in their account of older consumers' behaviour, reported that:

> The higher managerial, professional or administrative group was more likely to view clothes as expressions of their personality and image, found clothes shopping to be a hobby and purchased higher quality clothing. (2005: 459)

Lastly, the mass market that characterized the postwar era has fragmented. There has been a clear trend, pioneered for the United Kingdom by George Davies and Next in the 1980s, towards greater market segmentation based on lifestyle. This has gone with the growth of niche marketing, with increasing numbers of shops on the high street aimed at subsections of the market. Often owned by big conglomerates like Arcadia, they can make gains of scale in relation to capital and production while segmenting their offer through a range of differently focussed outlets. As a result we now have not one fashion system, but many. There has been a growth of polycentrism in the system, with a plurality of style sources producing greater variety and individuation. Some of this is reflected in the growth of an older market.

Researching the High Street

This chapter draws on interviews in clothing retail companies with a significant interest in the older market. British clothing retailing is relatively concentrated, with 70 per cent of garments coming from seventeen retail chains (Easey 2002). Among the largest are Marks & Spencer and George at Asda. Both were selected in the study to represent mass market retailers that include older women within their wider offer. Mintel (2006) identifies them as successful examples of mainstreaming retailing for older people. Viyella, Jaeger and Edinburgh Woollen Mill were chosen as companies that target different sectors of the market, though each, in differing degree, with a focus on older women. A fuller account of the study is found in the appendix.

In the complex of material and cultural production that is the Fashion System, many individuals are involved in shaping the supply chain (Fine and Leopold 1993; Du Gay 1997; Entwistle 2000, 2002; Aspers 2010). The companies featured here represent what Aspers (2010) refers to as Branded Garment Retailers, in which the processes of designing, buying and retailing are fully integrated, though typically by managed supply chains rather than by the classic vertical integration of the past (R. Jones 2006). Though respondents varied in their job titles, each could broadly be characterized as a design director, with overall responsibility for the range. All had extensive experience of the fashion industry, mostly with major UK retailers, though also in centres such as Italy.

Marks & Spencer is the biggest clothing retailer in Britain (Key Note 2008). It has a particularly loyal customer base, with the highest share in the high street of those who only shop at one store (Mintel 2006). M&S aims to cater for the whole market: its slogan in relation to womenswear is 'every woman, every time.' Women in their fifties plus, however, represent a core element of its market; indeed M&S has a 45 per cent market penetration among the over forty-fives buying for themselves (Mintel 2006). The interview was conducted with the head of womenswear.

M&S's offer is segmented, partly through the use of collections or brands, which enable customers to identify products relevant to them. Though the respondent emphasized the importance of lifestyle segmentation, a number of the collections have been developed with middle-aged and older women in mind. The largest is Per Una. This was one of the first brands launched by M&S in 2000, developed for them by George Davies. Originally aimed at younger women, it is heavily bought by those over forty. It was described by the head of womenswear as: 'theatrical, feminine, embellishment'. In 2008 M&S introduced a brand, Portfolio, specifically targeted on middle-aged and older women, responding to the sense that there was a

huge gap in the middle. Of this woman who had nowhere to shop, with a lot of disposable income. But more importantly that loves M&S, but was disappointed that there wasn't something that was for her... She was frustrated.

The range received mixed reviews in the fashion press; in 2010 M&S phased it out. Older women also shop in brands not specifically aimed at them. Limited, which is M&S's main fashion collection, is shopped by some older women: 'That brand isn't targeted for them, but they actually like it, because [some of them are] very confident about fashion.' They might also shop in Autograph, M&S's premier brand. There is a fairly consistent tendency, noted by all the respondents, for older women to trade up in terms of quality.

The brand with the strongest age focus is Classic, targeted on those over sixty-five; and this is clearly reflected in the style and cut. The respondent described it as 'conservative' and 'feminine', with a certain 'pristine' look, with noncrease fabrics. Many of its features indeed conform to the old lady style of pretty femininity—pastel colours, machine embroidery round the neck—described in Chapter 2. As discussed in Chapter 4, the range was regarded with aversion by some of the younger respondents in the study like Kathie, who saw it presenting a future she had no wish to join. The price points for the range are kept relatively low. The respondent described the cut as 'body conscious', but not in the sense normally used in the fashion trade, meaning cut close to the body, but conscious of the body and desiring to hide the changes associated with age. Tunics, for example, are popular, and length is 'very, very important'. Dresses need zips as 'she doesn't want to pull something over her head.' Cut is important 'because the body has changed significantly by this time'. For this age group, M&S is the dominant provider in the high street. Indeed for those in their seventies and eighties, there are few other outlets catering for their requirements.

George at Asda is the most successful of the supermarket-based, value clothing retailers. Verdict (2004) notes the growth of the value sector in clothing, doubling its market share since 1998. One pound in every five is now spent in this sector. Though owned by Wal Mart, George at Asda is designed in the United Kingdom. The respondents were design manager for George brands and the buying manager for ladies' brands. In 2007 George at Asda introduced a specific range, Moda, aimed at middle-aged and older customers. Though, like M&S, it emphasized that lifestyle was as important as age, its offer is clearly structured in age terms. The buying manager described how George at Moda has

> three very clear segments to our offer from a ladieswear point of view. We've got G21, so that's up to twenty-five. We've got Core which is twenty-five to forty-five. And then Moda, that's forty-five plus. And they are bought by separate teams.

Moda is very successful, representing 15–20 per cent of sales. Moda deliberately targeted this group, feeling it was 'a missing gap in our market, and to be honest has been hugely successful since we've launched it.' Its aim was to provide a range that addressed the older customer with a

> contemporary younger feel to it... It's not what probably traditionally people would have seen as an older customer range. It's not the Classic M&S sort of range. It has got a more contemporary feel.

Jaeger is a long-established retailer operating at the top end of the UK high street. After some financial difficulties in the 1990s, it was revamped as a designer brand under the label Jaeger London. The bulk of the collections, however, are pitched lower in terms of price and fashionability. Jaeger is commonly found in better-quality shopping destinations or in department stores. The interview was with the design director for womenswear. Mainstream Jaeger has a loyal following among older women. With the characteristic age slippage of the fashion industry, the respondent described the core customers as, 'in our opinion, thirty-five upwards. But the reality was that, actually, she was probably fifty or fifty-five and upwards.'

Viyella is similar to Jaeger, but cheaper and more clearly aimed at older women. The company was bought by Austin Reed in 2008 to be part of a suite of high street clothing stores aimed at different segments of the market. In an interview with the head of womenswear design for the Austin Reed Group, she confirmed that Viyella is confident about the viability of the market focussed on older customers:

> We are very happy with her age. I mean she's definitely fifty plus, sixty plus, seventy plus. But we had no issues with that at all. And we see it as a big business that's going to get even bigger.

Edinburgh Woollen Mill specializes in the older market. It has moved away from its origins as a factory outlet store and is now a mainstream clothing retailer with 192 high street stores and twenty-eight destination sites. Like Jaeger and Viyella, it does well in prosperous market towns. It is also found in tourist destinations, where it is particularly successful with coach parties. Shopping for clothes for this group is often linked to leisure, pointing to ease of access, but perhaps also to the way in which mainstream shopping has become less rewarding for this group. The interview was with the head designer and the marketing manager.

Addressing the Grey Market

Over the last two decades retailers have become increasingly aware of the grey market; since the mid 1990s, a mass of publications, both popular and academic, have identified the potential of this group (Sawchuck 1995; Moschis 1996; Gunter 1998; Lavery 1999; Key Note 2006; Mintel 2006). Long (1998) describes the over forty-fives as having nearly 80 per cent of all financial wealth and being responsible for about 30 per cent of consumer spending. Moody and Sood (2010) in their account of age branding describe the over fifty-fives in the United States as having twice the discretionary income of younger groups (aged eighteen to forty-nine). Market research reports (Key Note 2006; Age UK 2010) point to the relative affluence of those in their fifties and sixties where, though income may decline on retirement, so too do other financial demands, resulting in relatively high discretionary income. Age UK's analysis also notes that the older market is forecast to grow by 81 per cent from 2005 to 2030, in contrast to the eighteen to fifty-nine market where the forecast is 7 per cent (Age UK 2010: 4). This emphasis on discretionary spending needs, however, to be set against the significant numbers of older people, particularly women, living on low incomes. As Metz and Underwood (2005) and others emphasize, older people are if anything more diverse in income and lifestyle than younger ones.

The repeated burden of this marketing-oriented literature is, however, that retailers have failed to address the market effectively. Older women were frequently identified in the late 1990s and early 2000s as frustrated shoppers unable to find attractive clothes aimed at them; a finding confirmed in Birtwistle and Tsim's (2005) study of older female consumers. As shown in Chapter 4, this view was shared by a number of the respondents in this study who felt alienated from shops that they saw as fixated on the young and failing to cater for their desires. Mintel (2000) has indeed identified a danger among such older shoppers of slipping into what they term the 'anti-shopping abyss.' Such anti-shopping attitudes are held by 25 per cent of the male population and 10 per cent of the female population. The task of retailers—in their view—is to prevent this; and older shoppers are a prime target for such action.

Data from the United States support this sense that the fashion industry has had only limited success in engaging the older market, even where that market does have relatively high disposable income. Hurd and Rohwedder (2010) in their analysis of the US population over fifty found that while clothing was a normal good for the lower end of income, it was only a neutral good for the better off. (Economists divide goods into 'normal' ones in which extra income does not lead to greater propensity to consume, having a spending elasticity of less than one, and 'superior' ones where extra income leads to greater consumption, having an income elasticity greater than one.) This contrasts with 'leisure', which is a superior good for this group. It is true that this finding fits with the perception of Metz and Underwood (2005) and others that older consumers are less interested in things and more in experiences, but the overall pattern suggests that the fashion industry has not succeeded in its attempt to draw more affluent customers in to spending more of their discretionary income on dress.

Lastly the hope expressed by some in the industry that the older market will provide a new engine for fashion is treated with caution by Richard Jones (2006) in his detailed account of the sector. His analysis of the impact of the demographic shift in the 1980s and 1990s suggests that this did not affect fashion sales in the way one might have expected. He suggests that the fact that the youth market is dwindling, as noted in the Age UK (2010) report, may not detract from its importance as the prime engine of the industry.

Framing This Market

Fashion marketing to older women rests on an essential tension: that of building a market centred around a negative identity. The editor of *Vogue* expressed this starkly.

> I think at some level nobody wants to be older. Nobody wants to be fat and nobody wants to be old. You don't want to be poor either. There's lots of things that nobody wants to be, and actually older is just, in general, one of them. So to sort of create a kind of niche whereby if you buy it you're saying, 'I am older,' you can kind of see why people don't necessarily want to do that.

Though she added:

> But I'm not convinced that there isn't a way round dealing with it, that we don't quite seem to have got.

These ambivalences set up problems for brands in signalling that they are relevant to older customers—that they have garments designed for them and their bodies—at the same time as avoiding the negative connotations of being directly labelled as for the old. Fashion is profoundly—perhaps inherently—youth-oriented. At its high fashion core, the system is centred on youthfulness. These values are to a significant degree shared by the customers who have internalized ageist standards, seeking youthful fashions in the attempt to look more youthful themselves. This, however, presents a dilemma. Many women want styles associated with youthfulness, and with this, attractiveness, success and fashionability, but in forms adjusted to their bodies and to the social and cultural interpretation of these. I return to this issue when I discuss adjusting the cut.

Retailers thus face a problem in conveying their relevance to this group, which remains, as a sector, in a vague, undifferentiated state that the clothing companies are often reluctant to define. Some used coded terms such as *classic* to indicate the market. Occasionally a brand will use humour, such as Not Your Daughter's Jeans, to suggest a cut aimed at the older figure. What they all avoid, however, is direct age reference. Of the clothing companies studied here only Edinburgh Woollen Mills referred to age: on its Web site it described its customers as forty-five plus, but it quickly qualified this by saying it offered '"ageless style" whatever your age.' None of the other companies in the study referred to age in their marketing. And indeed in negotiating access for the study, I encountered some resistance to being involved in a study focussed on older people. Some of the refusals came with a sense that the company did not want to be publically associated with this market, whatever the reality of their sales profile might be.

Conceptualizing the Market: Age or Lifestyle?

The grey market is, as we have noted, far from unitary; older people are as diverse in their circumstances, values and lives as younger people, and in some circumstances more so (Metz and Underwood 2005). As a result marketing literature frequently raises the issue of whether lifestyle rather than age is a more appropriate category on which to base market segmentation. A number of such schemes have been developed. Market segmentation is, however, an uncertain field. Though it aspires to scientific rigour, its judgements are fairly rule of thumb, suffering as it does, as Easey (2002) comments, from lack of theoretical or empirical underpinnings. Typically it presents characterizations of sectors of the market, often in the form of vignettes, with the aim of enabling product designers to focus on their customers. (The process is akin to the apostrophizing or imagining of the customer that as we shall see the clothing design teams engage in, though it is usually less detailed or empathetic.) Examples of age-related segmentation are found in Moschis (1996), Gunter (1998), Easey (2002), Lavery (1999), Mintel (2000) and Hines and Quinn (2007)—all attempt to reflect aspects of lifestyle.

Such attempts to divide up the older market are often informed by a sense that there is a new type of older person now. Sherman and colleagues (2001), for example, assert the existence of 'New Age elderly'; and other schemes similarly identify 'younger', more 'forward-thinking' segments. These attempts partly reflect a desire to counteract the pervasive negativity that marks product developers' views of this demographic, typically presenting it as reluctant to try new products, indifferent to advertising and with declining capacity to process new information—'failed consumers' in the language of marketing. (Drolet et al. (2010) contains much in this vein.) But it also comes from a genuine sense that the lives of older people are changing, that these are cohorts whose attitudes to consumption are similar to those of younger people. This is a view shared by many of the respondents in the clothing industry.

Clothing companies in the study clearly drew on lifestyles in thinking about their collections. As the design director at Viyella explained:

> This is a brand that aims clearly at older women. It's very definitely aimed at, we call her either a working professional woman, or a nonworking, more to the point, professional woman, because she's often involved in charities, gardening clubs, professionally looking after her grandchildren, so she is a busy lady.

Age was, however, clearly part of this process of 'imagining'—as indeed was class, as this quotation with its references to 'professional' makes clear.

The head of womenswear at M&S similarly emphasized the importance of lifestyle: 'We don't structure our ranges by age. Much more by lifestyle'. But shortly after, she moved into an account that clearly drew on age:

> So we will build our brand boards and we'll talk about the target customer. So we will have brands that will be referencing, let's say an under thirty customer, a brand that will reference thirty-five plus, another one for forty-five plus, fifty-five plus and then sixty-five plus. And we'll try and keep each of those quite separate.

Lifestyle is clearly important in their thinking and in the wider culture, but as this comment makes clear, this cannot be separated wholly from age because lifestyles themselves reflect age: what people do, how they live their lives, their values and attitudes, in part derive from their age and their position within an age-ordered social structure.

Imagining the Older Customer: Designers as Cultural Mediators

Fashions do not simply emerge from markets, but are the product of complex cultural and economic mediation driven by the selective choices of key players in the system, principally designers, buyers and journalists (Entwistle 2002), who together translate what they perceive as incipient taste into looks promoted by the industry. Du Gay (1997) has analysed the ways designers use their symbolic expertise to create new looks for customers, offering what Lurie terms 'expert knowledges' that shape and form how they see themselves and their lives (Paterson 2006). Designers and retailers are thus not simply responding to market signals, but actively shaping and creating them. They do this partly by internalizing the desires and preferences of their customers, imagining how they think and act, developing a sufficiently close identification with their lives that they can use their preferences as proxies for those of customers (Aspers 2010). This process of constantly imagining the customer, getting under her skin, is an important way the industry deals with the demand uncertainty that marks fashion (Crane and Bovone 2006; Blaszczyk 2000).

In the research interviews, design directors engaged in a constant process of imagining the older customer, apostrophizing her by referring repeatedly to 'she' in their attempt to develop an all-enveloping discourse of her views and desires that would allow them to internalize her worldview.

> So we're always talking about this woman, this woman over forty, who's now going into her fifties. And how can we cater for her. Cos she's the woman that we really believe in.

The customer is thus discursively produced through constant imaginings and reiterations of her desires. Design directors here operate as cultural mediators, presenting customers with new ways of acting and being. Some of those ways relate to age.

This process of imagining the customer, however, is more challenging when there is an age gulf between the designer and the customer, as is the case with much of the older market. As I noted earlier in relation to the advertising industry, fashion is primarily populated by young people, and their values affect attitudes to designing for this group which is regarded as a marginal and low-status field (Long 1998). As Aspers notes, in the status ordering of branded garment retailers, 'the elderly' are at the bottom, among those who 'are seldom seen as trend setters' (2010: 45). This reflects the wider values of the fashion world, which is strongly youth-oriented and in which the engine of fashion and the core of high status is the youth market. Some of these ambivalences emerged in the interviews. While all the clothing company respondents were clear in their minds about the age profile of their market, and spoke positively of it, they acknowledged the tensions catering for this group entailed for them as designers. It imposed, in fashion terms, something of Goffman's (1968) 'spoiled identity', as the marketing director of Edinburgh Woollen Mills recognized. Speaking with heavy irony, he commented:

> It's lovely isn't it! Being in a really sexy business which is very, very high fashion!? But the reality is that isn't necessarily what our business is about and we have to, we're very proud of what we've got. You know we accept that it isn't a really, really sexy brand. And if it was a really, really sexy brand, then perhaps people, the volume of people who come and shop with us would stop. Because clearly what we're doing is, we're delivering something to the public that they want.

In general the design directors interviewed were in their middle years, and could thus draw on their own experience, as the head of women's wear at M&S explained:

> The majority of my buyers out there are all under thirty-five...And I feel in a very lucky position actually to do the job that I do, because I'm forty-seven, I've had two children and I'm size 14, but quite confident about body shape and what's happened and everything else. And I can talk to my buyers,...I will wear product that goes right across the brands to talk to the guys about what works and what doesn't work, and try to get them understanding that.

By wearing the product herself she could show how it was important to adjust the cut of clothing to reflect the ways the body changes.

'Moving Younger'

Across this field there is a pervasive language of 'moving younger'. Partly this reflects the aspirational nature of consumption itself. Clothes are part of consumption culture, goods promoted in terms of a dream of an idealized self. This is the central dynamic that fuels the constant pursuit of goods, and it is of particular significance in the case of clothing where retailers are selling in a saturated market. That idealized self is typically younger. This produces a dynamic whereby everyone in the field wants to 'move younger': describing their ranges as aimed at women decades younger than the actual purchasers; using young models to display the clothes; selecting promotional settings that emphasize youthful zest; weeding their ranges to lift the offer visually. As we saw in previous chapters, a similar dynamic operates in the field of fashion magazines, where target readership is systematically described as younger than the age profile in the marketing data.

But companies also want to move younger because they perceive that the market itself has changed and that people in their sixties and over no longer want the sorts of clothing they once did. They believe the current generation of older people is in some sense different, wanting younger-looking styles that no longer label them as old. As the design manager for George at Asda explained:

> When I first started working, thirty years ago, there was a point in time when people, the majority of people, would switch into that way of dressing, into classic dressing, because they felt that was appropriate to their age. But that is gone...This is a massive change, I mean it's a huge change in my lifetime.

Her younger colleague agreed, and saw it as a generational shift:

> I don't feel middle-aged at all. And I don't think it's even because I work in clothing that it's necessarily just me. All my friends who are in different industries are all similar to me...We do all wear fashionable things. And I think we don't feel like we're middle-aged yet. And I know my mum, you know my mum is in her sixties now, and the way that she dresses is—she dresses in an older way to me, but it's not how my Nana used to dress at sixty. So I think it's this generational thing, that we're all feeling younger.

Even Edinburgh Woollen Mill, the most strongly age-related of the companies, was actively moving younger in its styling and presentation. As the marketing manager explained:

> We're sort of, over the years, discovering that the fifty-five-year-old lady is now demanding more than ever before, in terms of the type of fashion that she's looking for...I don't

think people who are in their fifties see themselves as being fifty. They actually see themselves as being a lot younger...Our customer was telling us, you know, we might be fifty-five, we might be sixty-five but we actually don't wanna look like grannies, you know, we don't feel like grannies in our head. We're looking for something younger, slightly more fashionable.

The testimony of retailers, including some who had worked in the field for many decades, clearly endorsed the reconstitution of age thesis, believing that this genera-tion is in some sense different, younger in spirit and expectations. As a result, they recognize that they need to adjust their responses, learning to imagine the customer differently.

The fashion media, however, are less clear that they have learnt this lesson well, a view endorsed also by marketing analysts. The fashion editors of both *SAGA* and *Woman & Home* felt that retailers were still pitching their clothes too old. The for-mer, for example, felt that M&S's Portfolio range launched in 2008 for the fifties and sixties was 'a missed opportunity'. She felt that it would really suit those in their seventies:

This is going to be a winner, a total winner for their plus-seventy range which is the Classic collection. This is what the Classic collection should be. I don't know how well the Classic collection does because they kept asking me to push it in the magazine so obviously it doesn't do that well, but you know those ghastly granny blouses and those appalling trousers in the most appalling fabrics. This range is going to be wonderful for them.

In a similar way she felt that the Cotswold Collection, a mail order company, was perfect for her mother-in-law who is eighty-seven: 'She loves it to bits. It's perfect... but they're calling it forty-plus.' Some of this, of course, reflects the systematic use of age slippage noted earlier, but some pertains to a sense that the industry still has not got marketing to this group right. The fact that M&S, one of the best-established and professional of clothing corporations, could go wrong with its new line for older women reinforces this sense.

Adjusting the Cut

In designing for the older market manufacturers need to adjust the cut of their clothes to respond to changes in the body that occur with age. Clothes lie on the interface between the physiological body and its cultural presentation. They directly reflect the materiality of the body, although always within a cultural context. Adjusting the cut, therefore, is a complex process that encompasses both the literal fit of the garment and its capacity to reflect norms about the older body and its presentation.

The female body, as it ages, changes: waists thicken, busts lower, stomachs ex-pand, shoulders move forward (Goldsberry et al. 1996; Birtwistle and Tsim 2005).

Typically there is some loss of height and a reduction of length between neck and waist. This process sets in by the middle years, and over time acts to change the body in ways characteristic of age. The body at sixty or eighty is different from at forty, and this has implications for the design of dress. Until recently the garment industry responded to these changes—where it did so—in an piecemeal, individual fashion. An interview with a respondent who had extensive experience as a pattern cutter and design director across UK manufacturing confirmed that there was no systematic industry-wide response to changes in the body with age. It was something manufacturers reflected—or did not reflect—in the individual cut they adopted in response to their market. Apeagyei (2012) similarly notes the tendency for manufacturers to treat the knowledge they gain of sizing through trial and error as private and proprietary. In 2001–2, however, a more systematic approach was instigated by the UK government in conjunction with seventeen leading high street retailers with the

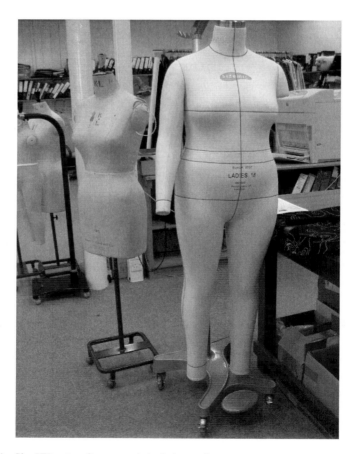

Figure 7.1   Size UK mature fit mannequin in design studio

launch of Size UK, a major study of the UK population based on 11,000 body scans. This revealed that the UK population was larger and taller than in the 1950s, the last time systemic sizing data was gathered (Otieno et al. 2005; Bougourd and Treleven 2010; Apeagyei 2012). Some of the shift towards larger sizes, however, was the product of population ageing. The survey also confirmed the existence of significantly different body shapes in the population; and once again some of the differences relate to age. As a result, new tailors' dummies that replicate the 'mature figure' have been developed and are being used by the industry, including by M&S and EWM.

All the design directors in the study were aware of issues of fit and the way the body can change with age. The head of womenswear at M&S emphasized how

> we fit everything that we buy four times before we agree to it and it goes into production. So we order a sample. We then fit it on a model, who's a real woman, who is fifty, who's had children, so she has the right body shape. And we will make all the necessary tweaks. So we have minimum measurements on areas like the upper bicep, the upper thigh, the mid-thigh, the hips, the waist, the bust, the upper bust, so that all the areas of a woman as she matures. We're very mindful that she wants clothes that flatter.

Clothes do more than just fit the body, they aim to enhance it, presenting it in ways that accord with the body ideal of the period. Part of adjusting the cut is, therefore, about producing garments that assist the wearer to appear nearer the current fashionable norm; in the case of women, nearer the body of a slim, young woman. Clothes have always performed this function, enabling individual bodies with their idiosyncrasies to be presented in a form nearer the current norm. Such adjustments reflect systematic ideals about the body. The history of English tailoring for men, as it developed from the end of the eighteenth century in the context of elite, wool-based clothing, is a testimony to these processes whereby an idealized masculine figure is produced through judicious use of tailoring, cut and padding (Hollander 1995). Men's clothes have traditionally offered greater opportunity for this. But these practices are also present in women's clothes and are used in specific ways that relate to age, with designers sometimes adding or adjusting details in ways that help the older body. For example, as the design director of Viyella explained: 'Older ladies can lose their shoulders, [so a] lot of our blouses still have a shoulder pad.' This restores the body nearer the norm and allows the garment to hang in a more flattering way.

Certain fashions, however, present problems. Both M&S and Jaeger cited the difficulties posed by the fashion for low-cut trousers:

> We were going through a period of fashion where the rise was becoming lower and lower and lower. And we just couldn't follow that fashion because we knew our customer just wouldn't be able to wear it. So obviously we take them lower, but we take them to a level

that's right for our customer. Waists have gone high again, which has been fantastic, because our customers always like that.

Adjusting the cut to make it fit better can, however, have the effect of ageing the garment, writing into its very structure information about the sort of body meant to inhabit it. This is clearest in the ranges distinctly aimed at older women. As the M&S respondent noted, its Classic range is aimed squarely at this group. The bust seams, for example, are adjusted 'because the body has changed significantly by this time'. 'You'd never get a Classic cut customer shopping in Limited, for example. So we know that the fit dimensions that we're working to in Classics are absolutely right.' This means, however, that the range is more clearly age-labelled in terms of fit and appearance, as some of the negative comments by younger respondents in the study showed. Edinburgh Woollen Mill similarly differentiates its ranges to reflect changing body requirements in age, with those aimed at younger customers more closely cut than those aimed at the seventies and eighties. The process of adjusting the cut has, of course, been made harder over the last decade or so in which fashion has dictated that clothes be cut very close to the body, often using materials like Lycra to achieve a fashionable bodycon look. We saw in Chapter 4 how one respondent resented the attempt of TV stylists like Trinny and Susannah to impose such a younger look by making the fit much tighter.

One way retailers can attempt to get round the issue is by featuring softer and looser styling. Some of the more successful and modern-looking ranges for older market use this approach, with companies like Oska or Masai Company managing to cross the age barrier by deploying loosely cut modern styles influenced by a Scandinavian aesthetic. Swedish mail order company Gudrun Sjödén exemplifies this approach with its loose cut, bold colours and patterns, and its use of silver-haired models mixed in with younger ones. Jaeger has considered introducing a range, tentatively called Jaeger Soft, that reflects this different approach.

Certain features in clothing come to be associated with age. In designing, Asda aims to avoid these, trying to find different ways to respond to a problem.

Buying manager:	You do naturally get thicker round your waist…We do take all of those factors into consideration [but…] we try and do them in a gentle way, rather than sort of in a way that historically it might have been tackled. You know, for example, as we say like, classic trousers were always with the elasticated back. So now how we tackle them, we look at drawstrings, and we look at more easier ways, or more fashionable ways, of doing them.
Design manager:	Easy fit, without it looking classic and frumpy. Because of the dreaded elasticated waistband!

But this points to the tension in designing for this group, where changes that make the clothes more comfortable or fit better also label them as old.

Fabric can also have a role to play. Jaeger, for example, avoids sheer or light fabrics that offer little in the way of coverage for the older body

> because a woman when she reaches those more mature years, can't wear sheer clothes. She can't wear very, very fine—if we buy a very, very fine wool, then it's too lightweight to give her the coverage and the confidence, because as you get more mature you want a bit more coverage. So we're very mindful of the weights of our fabrics, of lining things in beautiful linings, so again she feels confident in how she's dressing... If you wear a very fine wool trouser, you know, women do have sort of cellulite and they—you know, and if you start seeing the ripples through this very sheer wool, there's nothing worse. So that's why for us, we believe a good weight of fabric—as long as it's not heavy—the weight gives you the coverage and the confidence.

The repeated emphasis on confidence in this passage is significant. Here the older body is seen as something that can potentially embarrass or betray the customer. Well-designed clothes aim to avoid this.

Adjusting the cut can also be about preventing the exposure of the body in ways that may violate norms about the visibility of older bodies, in particular where this is linked to expressed sexuality. All the retailers were conscious of these issues and the significance of avoiding low necks, exposed upper arms and excessive flesh in general. The design director at Viyella noted how if necklines are too low, husbands comment.

> But I've actually seen a lot of husbands say, 'That's too low'. Because I think this area can get a little bit—I think it can get a bit too thin can't it, so you don't want to show it?

Avoiding such exposure could present difficulties for designers, however, when fashion dictated, for example, sleeveless dresses, so that adding sleeves detracted from its fashionability and aged the garment and, by implication, the wearer.

Here, of course, although the features of the body they are designing to are rooted in physiological ageing, the meanings accorded to them are not. There is no inherent reason why low necks or loose arms should not be displayed, except as part of a desire to hide something deemed culturally shameful. A range of work has explored the ways older, particularly female, bodies are rarely on view within modern visual culture. Dress is, thus, part of a wider set of processes whereby the bodies of older women are disciplined, made subject to cultural assumptions about what may or may not be on view that are internalized by the women themselves and by those designing for them. Particularly sensitive in this are aspects of the body that express sexuality.

Here women's bodies are judged against a cultural norm that equates sexuality with youthfulness and presents older bodies as inadequate, flawed or failed and better kept covered up.

Many women put on weight as they grow older; and one of the marked features of ranges aimed at older customers is that they have 'generous' cut. Indeed one of the ways one can recognize such ranges is through sizing: shops aimed at the teen or young market cut to a smaller size, though all use the standard UK terminology of 10, 12 and so forth. Size 12 is the standard size UK manufacturers design to, grading up and down on either side. M&S, however, which has traditionally had a generous cut, now designs to a size 14. As the design director from Viyella commented:

> We're generous, we're a size up basically...Because I think nobody likes going in and suddenly finding they're a 16, if they think they're a 12. I mean, it's just basic isn't it?

Ranges thus aim to flatter older women and confirm them in their identities by allowing them to believe they still fit into size 12 or whatever their size had been. As I noted in Chapter 3 weight gain is a barrier to fashionable cut; and only the imposition of punishing regimes of dieting can remove the problematic flesh of old age, and not always even then.

Colour and Age

Designers also adjust their designs in term of the colours they choose, once again responding to the interplay between physiological and cultural ageing. In particular they emphasized the need to move away from strong, hard, high-saturation colours, which were deemed unflattering for white complexions as they age. As the design team at Asda explained:

> Design manager: People's skin tone and hair colour, they do naturally get lighter as you age, you know it's a natural process, so we always take that into consideration. But what we do do is still try and give her the colour palette or elements of the colour palette of the season.
>
> Buying manager: We can soften it, it's more like what we would call mid tones rather than full tones, because full tones are very harsh. So it would be like what we call a mid tone which actually is more flattering, but also is more sophisticated. But the ranges are colourful.

They aimed to provide clothes in positive colours that were flattering for this group while still reflecting the dominant fashion mood.

Fashion in colour changes with the fashion cycle. Trends are set up to two years in advance, led by the yarn and fabric manufactures and defined by the cycle of trade fairs and coordinating meetings (Diane and Cassidy 2005). The International Inter-color Committee analyses colour trends every six weeks (Aspers 2010). Some trends are long term; others involve accent colours for just one season. In designing for the older market, retailers aim to pick up these trends, thus integrating older people with the mainstream, but in ways adjusted to be flattering. The team at Asda explained how they did this:

Buying manager: For example on G21 [the younger range] if red is the colour of the season, we might have red with cobalt blue, with bright green. You know, really poppy colours and lots of poppy colours. Whereas with Moda [aimed at women over forty-five] we will take the red...

Design manager: And go more spicy with it, you know, because she likes the spice. So we put it with like a burnt orange. The red might not have so much orange in it, you know, it might be slightly kind of softer, although she would wear black, white and red. But it's about the tone of the red. It's quite a difficult thing to explain without a colour wheel, but it's just like a softened palette, less brash.

Buying manager: Not dowdy, because that's the whole thing, she does like colour. But just softer tones with it as well.

The key terms in this passage are 'softer, 'less brash' and 'not dowdy'.

All the respondents emphasized that these customers embrace colour: 'This is a customer who likes colour' (Asda); 'We can sell bright colours really well' (EWM); 'She likes colour' (M&S referring to Classic range). These views were echoed in the interviews with older women. The liking of colour was thus presented as part of the positive upbeat discourse of the retailers in relation to this group, a repudiation of drab, self-effacing colours that seemed to embody cultural exclusion and depression.

The Meanings of Colour

Such comments need to read against the traditional meanings of colour in dress in relation to older people. There is a long history that associates age with the adoption of darker, drab colours. We can see this historically in Matthaus Schwatz's history of his life in images of dress in which there is a clear trend towards dark clothing in old age that contrasts with the vivid colours of his youth (Braunstein 1992). Lurie (1992) in her account of the meanings of colour in dress similarly associates age with darker colours and with tones of grey and beige.

It is important here to avoid essentializing colour in dress. Its meanings are always socially and historically contingent, complex and multivocal. Drab, low-emphasis colours like beige and grey are also smart neutrals, the core of an elegant urban wardrobe. This is a palette that has increasingly spread to women from menswear as part of the growing involvement of women in white-collar professional work, where they have adopted the same sombre, dark hues worn by men since the nineteenth century, when elite men abandoned brightly coloured dress.

However the avoidance of strong colour is still a significant part of people's ideas about age. These associations can be interpreted as part of the wider process of toning down in dress, the adoption of self-effacing, don't-look-at-me clothes that reflect the imposed cultural invisibility of older people, particularly women. These are colours that make no bid to be noticed, that have retreated from public view. A number of respondents in the study expressed this sense of the need to tone down in terms of colour. Celia, for example, recounted: 'I suppose that just happens really. I don't think perhaps you're completely conscious of changing it. It's just something that happens. You just suddenly feel the bright colours ought to be gone.' Pressure to retreat from bright colours was similarly reported in Holland's (2004) study of women who had consciously adopted dramatic, alternative forms of dress. Iltanen (2005) similarly found in her contemporary study of Finnish designers asked to select garments appropriate for women in their fifties that they predominantly chose muted or dark tones.

Black is an exception here. In the historical past, black was associated with age, particularly through its connection with mourning; and many women adopted black as standard wear from their middle years onwards. The meaning of black in dress, however, was never confined to this; and black also has connotations of drama, romanticism, eroticism and elegance (Lurie 1992; Harvey 1995; Pastoureau 2008). Today the connection with mourning has faded and for the generation discussed here is no longer significant. None of the respondents in the study saw black in that way. Ranges aimed at older women, however, tend not to feature black unless they occupy a middle ground that caters for women who are still working or are involved in formal activities for which black is a standard, smart colour. Edinburgh Woollen Mills, for example, does little in black, and it is not a colour featured in M&S's Classic range, though it is a staple for Jaeger, and is used to some degree in Asda, albeit mainly interspersed with colour.

The neutral colours traditionally associated with age draw their meaning in part from what they are consciously *not*: bright, attention-grabbing colours. Indeed such colours, particularly red, are often presented as unflattering or unsuitable for older women, suggesting as they do an overt sexuality, a brazen, vivid quality well conveyed by the word *scarlet,* with its multiple moral and social referents. We can observe something of this colour system in reverse in the actions of the Red Hat Society, a US based group of women over sixty who meet in public places wearing eye-catching clothes in red and purple (Hutchinson et al. 2008). Though the group represents a distinctly American form of sociality, it does express in *reverse* the pressure felt by many women to become invisible. The use of red here is highly significant, with its brashness, its association with the assertion of sexuality and its repudiation of grey, toned-down, don't-notice-me dress. This is all about being noticed, being present in public space; and it represents a classic example of resistance. Purple is also significant. As Lurie (1992) notes, it is an ambivalent colour associated with royalty and gorgeousness, but also vulgarity and coarseness. These meaning are echoed in Jenny Joseph's (1974) well-known poem, 'Warning', better known as 'When I am old I shall wear purple', which recounts every-day acts of defiance and resistance in age. The poem achieved wide currency and was voted one of the UK's favourites in a BBC poll in 1996. Much of its appeal lies in the meaning of purple and the transgression and excess it conveys. The combination of red and purple indeed has a long history of such transgression, since these are the colours of the Whore of Babylon, 'arrayed in purple and scarlet cloth' (*Revelation* 17:4). This is, of course, not something the Red Hat Society emphasizes, but the associations contribute at a diffuse level to the boldness and assertiveness of the colour choice.

The enjoyment of colour reported in some of the interviews can be seen in similar terms. Not as consciously assertive as the actions of the Red Hat Society, but drawing on some of the same feeling—a repudiation of the self-effacing view of old age and a marker of greater confidence in presenting the self in public view. Anja, for example, rejoiced in the fact that she had 'outrageous colours in my wardrobe.' Gillian similarly embraced the idea of colour: 'I like bright colours.' She pointed to the advances of modern textile technology that meant that strong, clear colours were now in the reach of everyone, including older women. In the past older women 'were drab…they were always the darker colours, whereas as I've said we've got the opportunity to have much brighter colours.' To this degree the dominance of colour in these ranges, and the endorsements of the women in the study, provide further evidence for a shift in attitude to old age. Older women today are brighter-coloured and more visible than in the past and enjoying the fact.

The emphasis on colour is, however, open to an additional interpretation, one that sees it in terms of a retreat from cut. As the body changes, particularly in later old age, it becomes less amenable to the imposition of the normative feminine figure that much cut in dress is designed to display. We saw how Clare in the study reported that she did not want clothes that emphasized curves since she felt hers were not nice curves. Clothes aimed at the older market, particularly the distinctly older market, as in the case of M&S's Classic range, tend to hang in a loose way. In this context, it is hard to make smart, low tones look other than drab. Emphasizing colour is thus one of the ways of injecting pleasure into a range, acting to support a positive presentation of self.

Building Confidence/Keeping Upbeat

The interviews with the retailers were marked by their upbeat, positive tone. In part this reflects the way fashion presents itself in, as Braham (1997) notes, 'breathless and exaggerated language'. But it also reflects what the retailers aim to offer older women—an upbeat positive version of themselves and their lives as embodied in new clothing. The interviews were peppered with references to confidence and the need to support and encourage this. The design directors, like the fashion editors, were very aware of older women who had lost confidence in their dress, so that choosing clothes was no longer an easy or encouraging experience. The design director at Viyella, for example, was conscious of the importance of having the right sales staff, that could support and encourage older customers in making new selections. The style of the changing rooms, with privacy and space, was seen as important, a reminder of Gullette's (1999) vivid reference to shopping as one grows older in terms of '[a] scream came from the dressing room.'

Part of what they aim to offer older customers is a way of being older that is attractive and appropriate, and above all—given the nature of the industry—up to date and new. They aim to do this in ways that are profitable. The Asda respondents, for example, noted how older women were particularly susceptible to buying the whole outfit, looking for a complete look, in contrast to younger customers, who focussed on the single item:

> She's looking for something which is more co-ordinated, which again is an opportunity for us, because we do try and sell her the outfit. So she's less inclined to go for the item. I think that's the key difference, that perhaps the younger customer would be thinking, oh my God, I've got to have that new cobalt blue, drapey top for this Friday's club.

Providing the whole outfit took the pain out of shopping, helping to resolve the loss of confidence characteristic of some mature shoppers:

> The most successful ranges are the ranges that take the pain out of it... What Moda does is it cuts out that. You know you're able to find at that moment exactly what to go with it, even the necklace, so it's a less painful experience... It is the duty of a co-ordinate brand to kind of dispel all that, and say actually, that does look good together. And, hey, you can wear it!

Consuming, Imagining, Responding

There is always a danger in arguing for the relevance of consumption in the constitution of later years of presenting an unduly celebrationist account—particularly so in a chapter that foregrounds the views and values of large commercial retailers. They, after all, are in the business of selling goods; and this inevitably means presenting a vision of later years that is upbeat, optimistic and forward-facing, in which the purchase of things is regarded as empowering. As a result they present a particular vision of how later years might be lived. There is an implicit normativity underlying their offer. This process of imagining the customer, of course, contains biases, bleaches out significant differences between older women, underplays their diversity. We can see this in the implicitly middle-class vision they present: something reflected more generally in accounts of the Third Age, particularly those that emphasize the role of consumption. In part this reflects the dynamics of capitalist production focussed as it is on the most profitable sectors of the market. Both Jaeger and Viyella are targeting the better off; and though Asda and M&S trade across a wider range that includes the 'value' sector, discretionary income is still required to enter into their vision of later years.

There is, however, a second reason for the implicitly classed nature of these accounts, and this relates to the aspirational character of consumption itself. Consumption goods typically contain a promise that reaches beyond their use value. This is particularly so of clothing where what is on offer, as well as clothing for day-to-day use, is the promise—to some degree at least—of a transformed self: a version that is younger, slimmer, smarter, richer, more attractive, of higher social status than the reality. This aspirational dynamic is at the heart of consumption and is reflected in the accounts presented here. Part of this entails 'moving younger', presenting a body image from which age is to some degree effaced so that the customer is potentially integrated into the younger mainstream. Design as we noted earlier is a normative process, so that clothing retailers are not simply responding to market signals, but also shaping and guiding them, presenting new visions of what it might mean to be older.

Conclusion

Fashion is part of the cultural economy in which meanings circulate in and through material production. In this, design directors, like journalists and advertisers, operate as cultural mediators, shaping the aspirations of customers, proposing new ways of being and providing the material means of achieving these at a directly bodily level. Increasingly such activities encompass older people. Clothing retail companies, therefore, need to be understood as part of the wider set of cultural influences shaping the ways ageing is imagined, performed and experienced in contemporary culture. In foregrounding these sources, this chapter argues for a wider understanding of the cultural forces shaping later years than is normally presented in social gerontology, though one that does not need to support a celebrationist account of consumption.

Design directors, of course, respond to the market. Their task is to provide goods people want to buy; and a central part of their skill lies in sensing what these will be. They do this through imagining the lives, wishes, aspirations—and to some degree anxieties—of their customers. But they are not simply responding to demand, but also shaping and creating it, stimulating the market for new goods. This is especially so in relation to fashion, whose nature is that it evolves and develops beyond the reach of customers, constantly presenting to them new ways of dressing, new ways of being. Older people are increasingly integrated into this aspirational culture.

Clothing retailers are interested in the older market. The massive growth in productivity, the reduction in the cost of clothes and the speeding up of the fashion cycle have produced a situation where the youth market is, to some degree, saturated. As a result retailers have sought to develop new markets, including those for older people. This has meant extending the idea of fashionability beyond its traditional reach, to older people. This has entailed rewriting some of the traditional scripts that have informed old age in the past, presenting later years within a new set of cultural meanings.

These meanings, however, cannot be entirely detached from bodily change. Though clothes are wholly cultural artefacts, their design intersects with the materiality of the body. There is an inevitable interplay between elements of cultural and bodily ageing, and this is carried through into the design—and wearing—of clothes. We have seen how the designers adjust the cut of clothes so that they fit and flatter; how they select colours that enhance the skin as it ages; how they avoid forms of bodily exposure deemed culturally shameful or that expose the body as failing to meet the cultural norms of youthfulness. But they are also increasingly using positive colour for this group, which is no longer confined to the low, drab tones of the past; and they have moved designs towards a younger, more relaxed body style that reflects the norm pertaining in the mainstream market. All the respondents in the study recognized the pervasive cultural aspiration of looking younger. Clothes have become part of the wider culture of anti-ageing. 'Moving younger' is a central part of what design directors, particularly for ranges aimed at women in later middle age, are doing. But they have to balance this against the realities of bodily ageing. Extremely youthful styles do not necessarily make the wearer look younger; they can point up the mismatch in expectations, the discrepancy between the ageing body and the youthful style. Designers thus find themselves treading a careful path between proposing new, more youthful ways of being and offering styles that expose the customer to cultural failure.

Evidence from the study does support the idea that the lives and experiences of older people are changing and that spheres like consumption and the wider cultural economy are playing a part in this. Design directors clearly believed, on the basis of their commercial experience, that current generations of older people are 'different', and have aspirations that mark them apart from earlier ones; though I also noted reasons to be cautious in accepting these views uncritically, registering in particular the danger of confusing the processes of 'moving younger' with processes of style diffusion itself, outlined in Chapter 2. The design directors presented these developments in positive terms; and the interviews were imbued with an upbeat, celebratory tone that lauded the new cultural opportunities opening for older women. This is unsurprising. Like other actors in the sphere of consumption, they are in the business of selling goods and this means selling attractive lifestyles. But these cultural developments, like many others in relation to older people, are Janus-faced. The spread of fashion opportunities to older women also entails the colonization of their bodies by new expectations, new requirements—ones that demand that they be fashionable or well-dressed, and present the body in such a way that age is—as far as possible—effaced. Clothes thus take their place as part of wider process of governmentality, whereby the bodies of older people are disciplined, ordered and made subject to new cultural norms.

−8−

Conclusion

In the previous chapters I have outlined some of the ways the field of dress is intertwined with that of age. I have noted how clothes are still age ordered as they were in the past, though this patterning is changing under the impact of wider social and cultural shifts. I have explored the ways dress interacts with the body, so that the two cultural fields cannot wholly be separated, but are in constant dialogue with each other. I have examined the ways age operates within the Fashion System, noting how fashion as a cultural field is constituted around youthfulness, and the ways this presents difficulties for individuals—particularly older women—who wish to engage with it, as well as for the industry that seeks to co-opt them into its commercialized dreams. In this last section I want to draw together some of these themes and use them to address questions around the changing location of later years and the role of consumption in this.

The Role of Consumption in the Reconstitution of Age

I noted how old age has traditionally been explored academically through the lens of frailty and dependence, emphasizing the role of areas like medicine and social welfare in shaping its discourses. I noted how this imposes limitations and how later years encompass a great deal more than this account in terms of marginalization and decline suggests. One of the purposes of this book has been to shift the focus of analysis and to expand the account of age, encompassing a wider set of influences shaping the ways it is performed at an embodied level. Consumption, and within that the field of fashion and dress, provides an arena in which to do this.

It was clear from the study that consumption does indeed play a role in the constitution of age, and that it acts to integrate older people culturally with the mainstream. Many older people feel as much a part of consumption culture as younger cohorts. Later years thus need to be understood, as Öberg and Tornstam (1999) suggest, as an increasingly unified plateau of extended middle years, integrated through shared lifestyle. This is a central part of the meaning of the emergence of the Third Age as a new cultural space. I noted how the terminology of the baby boomers is also often used to characterize this shift; though I also noted the limitations of this sort of cohort analysis and the better characterization in terms of a longer-term historical shift in the position and nature of later years. I suggested earlier that these cultural shifts have resulted in age being read academically back into the fifties and how this process is helping to widen the academic agenda in relation to age, exemplified in the emergence of cultural gerontology as a field and an approach. These processes can, of course, also be read in reverse, marking the trend whereby middle age is increasingly read forwards, colonizing sections (and sectors) of what was previously labelled old age. This approach reflects the widely held view that age is being experienced later (by some at least), that is captured in the popular reprise that 'sixty is the new fifty' or—optimistically—forty.

These general trends need, however, to be qualified. There are significant differences among individuals in later years: indeed, as many commentators have noted, older people are more, rather than less, diverse in their circumstances and values than younger people. Where an individual falls on this new age categorization is also crucially affected by structural factors such as health, gender, income and social class. Ill health, despite the advances of modern medicine, retains its capacity to define the status of individuals, precipitating them early or late into the Fourth Age of 'real' old age. Gender similarly affects judgements about the onset and meanings of age, with women in general described as ageing earlier than men, particularly middle-class men. The Third Age is an implicitly classed term, evoking an aspirational version of middle-class later life that reflects a capacity to maintain mainstream status through patterns of consumption. Age status also reflects other significant patterns of advantage such as ethnicity and relationship status. The lifestyle patterns that underlie the Third Age are, therefore, selective and sectional.

They operate very powerfully, however, within consumption culture. Retailers and marketers increasingly see the world through the medium of lifestyle, believing that this is more significant now in determining choices than traditional forms of market segmentation in terms of age or socioeconomic circumstances. To this degree, their testimony does support the argument that under the impact of postmodernism we have seen a dissolution of traditional identity boundaries and their replacement by ones more determined by choice, self-expression and individualistic values. But I also noted the ways lifestyle categories often obscure and overlay more structural ones. Lifestyles are, indeed, in part determined by factors related to age, so that behind lifestyle factors are often age-related ones, as we saw in the discourses of the design directors with their easy slippage into age categorization. There are parallels to be drawn here with the way class has systematically been obscured within the discourses of consumption culture, collapsed into lifestyle. These underlying, deeply rooted structures, however, remain powerfully significant in shaping the patterns of culture and with them the lives of individuals.

Within the commercial world of consumption there is increasing awareness of the significance of the grey market. Trend reports, market analyses and newspaper articles in the business press repeatedly attest to the potential of this sector; and indeed retailers in the study were very aware of and positively oriented to the older market, which they saw as a profitable and growing sector that they aimed to colonize. In doing so, they were not simply responding to demand, but actively shaping and forming it in ways profitable to them, creating new markets driven by newly created desires. Design is a normative process that involves imagining the customer in ways that reflect her lifestyle and desires, but at the same time proposing new, different versions of them. Design directors thus act as cultural mediators, presenting new ways of being an older woman. Magazines are also in this business, taking up and interpreting the trends found in fashion, giving permission to their readers to try new looks, at the same time as steering them away from ones likely to be unsuccessful. Makeovers perform a distinctive role here, showing older women new ways of presenting themselves, integrating them into the cycle of the fashion renewal represented by the seasons. Through this cyclic process, they aim to lift and renew their appearance in ways that counteract the erosive trajectory of age.

Despite these processes of imagining and proposing, there are signs that the fashion world has not been wholly successful in its attempt to co-opt the older customer. I noted the discourse of the 'frustrated shopper' that has emerged in recent years and the way it was reflected, to some degree at least, in the comments of the older respondents. Many older women felt disengaged from and neglected by the fashion industry; and a number who had money to spend found little to tempt them. The fact that M&S, one of the most successful and knowledgeable of clothing retailers, could still get its offer specifically aimed at older women wrong is testimony to the difficulties retailers face in this area. Of course, fashion is by its nature a volatile field; and its notorious instability and unpredictability of demand mean that many efforts to address a market will be unsuccessful. But the uncertainly of retailers and the critical comments of journalists and market analysts reported in the study are indicative of particular difficulties in this area.

Systematic tensions within the field of fashion make it harder for the industry to address the older market successfully. Fashion has traditionally been constituted as a youthful field; its values are expressed visually in young faces and young bodies. The high fashion core is centred on youth. Age here is a dereliction, a falling away from the ideal, something to be pushed away. These values are carried forward in the attitudes of the personnel who people the industry, who are themselves differentially young. These institutional biases are also reflected in advertising, where brand managers similarly tend to be young and reluctant to compromise their own or the brand's status by placing adverts in media targeted on older people. Designing for the older market also imposes something of a 'spoiled identity'. Of course the majority of design is not taken up with the high fashion core: most mainstream clothes are slow-moving standard items that involve limited fashion input. But the dream is still there, affecting how the industry perceives itself and its activities. Status lies in designing for the young, and this crucially affects the quality of design and the capacity of designers to respond to these customers successfully. Youthist values are, moreover, shared and internalized by customers, whose relationship to clothes directly aimed at the older market remains ambivalent, so that defining this market, sending the right signals to potential customers, presents an additional set of problems for retailers.

New Freedoms, New Disciplinary Demands

The spread of fashionability to older women can—rightly—be interpreted positively, suggesting an erosion of the restrictions that have traditionally limited their lives, cutting them off from the mainstream. Being fashionably dressed implies being visible and present in the public world, asserting that you are still part of things. Engagement in dress thus reflects new cultural freedoms that have expanded the possibilities open to older women. This interpretation is reflected prominently in popular journalism, where the theme of the defiant older woman refusing to abandon the pleasures of shopping has become a recurrent motif. This account, however, is often driven by the particular preoccupations of women journalists in their forties, fifties and sixties. Reflecting their own social world—though also that of many of their readers—they are determined not to give up the cultural practices of consumption and they refuse to accept the cultural invisibility imposed on many older women. Still in employment, often with relatively high disposable incomes, their responses are characterized by defiant resistance.

But consumption is Janus-faced. It also comes with a darker, more negative side. New cultural freedoms impose new requirements, new disciplinary demands in relation to appearance and the body. The spread of fashionability to older women can thus be seen as part of a wider colonization of their bodies by new forms of governmentality, an imposition of new normativities in relation to later years, whereby women are increasingly enjoined to engage in anti-ageing practices in relation to dress, as in other fields. Consumption culture, in proposing new ways of being, implicitly silences other ways of being that involve giving up, not bothering, of sourcing clothes in a limited way focussed largely on comfort or utility. It can mean opting out of the fashion cycle altogether, refusing its dreams of renewal, choosing instead to use up the old stock of clothes most people already have. It can mean ceasing to bother if one looks old, refusing to be drawn into the commercialized world of anti-ageing, embracing invisibility, indeed seeing it indeed as a state that offers new forms of freedom. We saw how some women were happy to retreat from the realm of fashion and display, seeing the invisibility of age as proving an escape, a screen or, in Biggs's (1997) terms, a masquerade behind which they could develop a new sort of life.

Age Ordering in Dress

I noted at the start of this book the long-established phenomenon of age ordering in dress: the systematic patterning of clothing styles according to an ordered and hierarchically arranged concept of age. I also noted the widely held idea that such patterning has gone, or is at least in steep decline. It was clear from the study, however, that age ordering is still operative, so that the dress of the majority of older women remains strongly shaped by ideas about what is age appropriate. Such discourses are recognized and internalized by women, who engage in continuing self-interrogation as to the suitability of their dress as they age, weeding their wardrobes of clothes that no longer flatter, standing in the dressing room asking if the garment is now too young, looking regretfully at younger colleagues in their pretty, youthful dress. Magazine editors also endorse the view that dress remains age ordered and that certain styles are best avoided. A central part of their role, as they see it, is to advise and warn in relation to these norms. In doing so, however, they help entrench and naturalize them, reinforcing them as common sense, something simply to be accepted. Clothing manufacturers and retailers are similarly aware of the ways dress is located in systematic cultural assumptions about age, and they construct their ranges accordingly.

These discourses of age-appropriate dress are rooted in cultures of ageing that are long-established, so that the current features of age-appropriate dress echo older traditions. Despite significant historical shifts, there are clear continuities in the norms governing dress and age that reflect an enduring set of—largely negative—ideas about the body in age and about the social value of older people, especially women. These centre around the need to cover up, hiding the failure of the body to meet the youthful norm; the avoidance of clothes that make claims to sexual allure in the form of low necks, short skirts or exaggerated fit; the adoption of self-effacing, darker styles that make no claim to visibility; the avoidance of highly fashionable dress, or girly, seductive, ultra-feminine styles. These 'rules' are largely expressed negatively in terms of forms of dress no longer appropriate; there is little positive in these norms.

There is, however, also clear evidence for change and for the weakening of norms around age ordering. These reflect wider shifts in the surrounding culture and are not confined to the clothing lexicon, though clearly reflected in it. As we saw, the majority of respondents in the study felt that their lives and attitudes were different from those of women in the past; and they contrasted their experience of being fifty or sixty with that of their mothers or grandmothers. Even with the proviso noted earlier about the difference between later years as seen from the perspective of a young person and as an older subject, their testimony was clear: things have changed. Many asserted that they did not want to dress in the ways traditionally assigned to older women. They had had jobs and had the confidence that derived from remaining in the public sphere as middle-aged women. They were not going to don the mantle of age or accept the drabness and dowdiness they associated with dress for older women in the past. They refused to give up their jeans or move in pleated skirts. Above all they were determined to eschew Crimplene.

The magazine editors also believed that this generation was 'different'; and they had changed the character of their magazines to reflect this. They believed that older women were still interested in fashion and in looking good. *Woman & Home* had made a special feature of this, giving over large parts of the magazine to glamorous images and makeovers showing older women how to achieve a more modern, up-to-date look. Even *Yours,* a magazine aimed at distinctly older and more working-class women, now includes fashion as part of its offer. *Vogue,* a magazine aimed at a very different sector and largely focussed on the younger fashion core, has also endeavoured to incorporate older women into its offer, reflecting the belief that many middle-aged and older women have high spending power and remain interested in dress and self-presentation.

Clothing retailers similarly recognize that the market is changing. Many of the old assumptions about clothing and age have eroded, with older customers seeking out more fashion-conscious, younger styles. As a result retailers are shifting their offer, with design directors looking for ways to integrate older customers in their mainstream collections. Even Edinburgh Woollen Mill, the most age-defined of the retailers in the study, was conscious of the ways customers are changing and the need to reflect this in its ranges, which it aims to move in a younger, more stylish direction.

The symbolism of colour also offers evidence of cultural change. The dress of older people in the historical past was marked by darker, self-effacing colours. Today, by contrast, ranges aimed at older women are often characterized by the active use of colour. M&S's Classic range, for example, makes a feature of clear, bright tones, avoiding black, greys or drab colours formally associated with age (though widely used in smart office dress). Across the board, retailers endorsed the idea that older customers like colour; and this was supported in the interviews with the women themselves, many of whom embraced colour positively in their dress. There is, thus, clear evidence for a shift in the colour palette in relation to older women that reflects a wider shift in their cultural evaluation: older women now expect to be brighter, more colourful, dressed and present in the public eye and, with that, less self-effacing and less invisible.

The Meanings of 'Moving Younger'

At the start of this book I noted the pervasive language of 'moving younger' that marks this cultural field. Retailers aim to lift their ranges by displaying their goods on youthful and attractive models, shown in zestful and upbeat contexts. They weed their ranges for age-coded styles. Magazines describe themselves as targeted at a significantly younger readership than is the reality, presenting to readers a visual world much younger than the one they inhabit. There is also evidence that older women themselves are seeking out fashions that are less age-coded, more modern and younger in feel.

A complex of forces underlies this. First, and most notable, is that of ageism. We cannot understand these impulses unless we recognize the degree to which age is a stigmatized state. Moving younger is thus part of a set of processes that are about maintaining advantage and resisting the negative connotations of being old.

'Moving younger', however, also needs to be understood in a second way, as part of the aspirational nature of consumption. Though clothes are in some degree utilitarian goods, they are more significantly consumption ones, promoted in terms of a dream of an idealized self. This is the central dynamic that fuels the constant pursuit of goods, and it is of particular significance in the case of clothing where retailers are selling to a saturated market. Part of that dream is a younger self. As a result retailers persistently present their goods as aimed at a younger market than is in fact the case; and they certainly avoid association with an older one. This produces a dynamic in which everyone in the field is 'moving younger'. A similar process operates in relation to magazines, where the target readership is systemically described—and imagined—as younger than the actual age profile. This allows the magazine to perform its classic role of reflecting back to readers a visual world that is an idealized version of the one they inhabit, allowing them to identify at fantasy level with a self that is younger than the reality—just as it is slimmer, smarter and richer.

There is, however, a third—and different—way we can understand the phenomenon of 'moving younger'. This is in terms of the processes of fashion itself, in particular the dynamics of style diffusion, so that it is not that older people are 'moving younger', but that styles are 'moving older'. The dynamic of style diffusion shifted in the twentieth and twenty-first centuries away from its earlier basis in social class towards more plural and complex sources, reflecting both the wider democratization of fashion and its relocation among cultural, rather than social, elites. As part of this, age has assumed a new significance in the dynamics of style diffusion, becoming one of the engines of fashion change. Age coding in clothing, rather than simply denoting position in the social order as in the past, has now become integrated into the processes of fashion, part of the fashion system itself, as styles pass from the centre of fashionability in the youth market to the periphery in the older one. It is this process that underlies some of the sense in which ultra-fashionable dress is 'unsuitable', 'discordant' or 'sad' on older women. The shine of its fashionability needs to have worn off before it is acceptable for older women to adopt it.

These processes of 'moving younger', however, meet structural limits in the form of the body and its interpretation. Very young styles do not necessarily create an appearance of youthfulness; rather they point up the discrepancy between the expectations of the style and the ageing body that wears it.

The Interplay of Cultural and Bodily Ageing

Dress is a field in which I can explore the complex interplay between cultural and physiological factors in ageing. We saw the systematic ways the body alters with age and the challenges this poses for designers focussed on this market. We noted how retailers adjust the cut of their clothes to meet these requirements and how this affects the appearance and commercial scope of their ranges. Those aimed at the significantly older market are cut in a way that is distinctive and that testifies to the bodies that will inhabit them. For the 'younger' old market questions of fit are more subtle, a matter of slight adjustment in fit and style. There are thus significant differences in relation to dress in age that reflect not just cultural evaluation but also bodily change. The dress of women in their eighties is different from that of those in their fifties, and this affects how we understand the issues of dress and age. Expanding 'later life' back into the fifties thus requires us also to recognize significant distinctions in the category of the aged.

Many of the adjustments made in relation to age, however, reflect not so much bodily change as the cultural evaluation of it. Norms around age ordering reflect a set of ideas about the body in age which interpret it negatively in terms of falling away from the youthful ideal. There was evidence in the study to support Featherstone and Hepworth's (1991) contention of estrangement from the body as a bearer of identity in age. This feeling underlay the sense of regret and sadness seen in some of the interviews, as respondents found that the body could no longer perform in relation to dress in the ways it had in the past. As a result, clothes were less an area for pleasure and expressivity. For some respondents, this estrangement was experienced as a loss of femininity itself. I noted how femininity is to a significant degree constituted around youthfulness, which becomes a core element in its definition. As a result ageing can be experienced as a form of exile in which the body becomes less able to perform the cultural practices of normative femininity, many of which are enshrined in dress. As a result many older women retreat from this sphere. Why spend time and effort on an aspect of life that offers declining rewards? Other dimensions of life promised more.

Retaining a good appearance, however, was still important, but this is not necessarily a fashionable appearance. I noted the ways neatness and order were still important values for many respondents, particularly working-class ones, reflecting their earlier upbringing in which they were an important element in respectability and indeed stood for a species of self-respect. In old age, however, these values took on new significance where their exercise could stave off the threat of dereliction or of becoming a pitiable old woman. Being well-presented in the sense of clean and neat was an important part of remaining socially acceptable. Here the normative structures are not so much those of fashionability as of avoiding dereliction. I noted how older people cannot risk looking down at heel or scruffy in ways that the young can, and how such lapses threaten their wider moral status. Gilleard and Higgs (2000) suggest that retaining some control over one's public identity is a key element in Third Age identities; those in the Fourth Age lose this power of agency, so that keeping clear of this 'identity hazard' marks one of the fault lines of old age.

Dress and the Changing Structures of Age

Finally, changes in regard to ageing and dress need to be located in the context of wider social shifts. The modernist life course has given way to a new postmodernist version organized around the priorities of late capitalist society, the overpowering influence of the cultural sphere and the proliferation of contingent life strategies (Katz and Marshall 2003). As a result, the old cultural scripts that once guided the process of becoming older have become less clear. In relation to dress, it is no longer so obvious what the 'rules' are or in what ways they still operate: there is a new fluidity and reflexivity in relation to identity that extends to identity in dress. We saw this in the comments of the magazine editors who saw a central part of their role as helping older women negotiate the increasingly uncertain cultural territory of being older. This is no longer just a question of steering them away from inappropriate styles, but of moving them towards younger, more fashionable looks that integrate them into the larger fashion system and its cycle. Such processes assist older women in achieving new standards of appearance, but they also impose new disciplinary norms. It is no longer enough to avoid shabbiness or dereliction in old age; the new requirement is to be positively integrated into the mainstream through active consumption.

This represents a shift from the period of the 1950s, when Mrs Exeter appeared in *Vogue* representing the older woman. She expressed no wish to look younger than her sixty years, something in marked contrast to current aspirations. She was more defined—and confined—by her location in the age structure, as she was in the class and gender ones, and yet also paradoxically more visible in that period. The current treatment of age is different, based around the ideal of agelessness in which the dream is one of transcending age categorization. This vision does offer real gains to older women. They are less confined by assumptions about what older women should wear. The new ageless style also offers greater integration, a lessening of the cultural marginalization that has traditionally marked old age, so that older women are now more free to buy their clothes and cultural styles generally from the same market as everyone else. The boundaries that marked out the state of age have thus weakened. But the dream of agelessness rests on an ultimately impossible demand: that people grow older without showing the visible signs of doing so. Katz and Marshall (2003) have analysed the tension presented by such an ideal in the field of sexuality where remaining 'forever functional' has become a new standard against which successful ageing is judged. Similar critiques have been made in relation to fitness, exercise and appearance, all of which have imposed new disciplinary demands and new forms of governmentality in relation to the body and its presentation. Dress is also implicated in this aspiration to agelessness, as women use clothes as a means of staving off the devalued status imposed by the visual appearance of age. But such dreams, as critics through the ages have noted, are ultimately unachievable. The Fountain of Youth is a mythic trope. It is not possible to transcend the bodily effects of ageing, and the dream of doing so is ultimately self-defeating, undermining both the cumulative gains of being old and the dignity of age.

Lastly it would be a mistake to view clothing and later years solely through the lens of anti-ageing. Clothes are about a great deal more in the lives of older women than simply the attempt to meet or transcend regulatory structures in relation to age. Dress remains for many older women, despite the cultural limitations, a source of enjoyment and a site of aesthetic pleasure.

Appendix

This book draws on a series of empirical studies exploring the theme of ageing and dress. Further details of these can be found on the Web site www.clothingandage.org.

The main study was funded by the UK Economic and Social Research Council (ESRC) under grant RES 000 22 2079 entitled Clothing, Age and the Body. It was based on qualitative interviews with older women, content analysis and interviews in relation to magazines, and interviews in the fashion industry. Those with a sharp fashion ear will recognize that the fieldwork was undertaken in the 2008/9 season.

Interviews with older women: twenty older (fifty-five and older) women were interviewed, mostly in east Kent. They represent a range in relation to age, social class, relationship circumstances, sexuality and employment. It was, however, an all-white sample. They were recruited through a variety of routes: items in the local paper; a university Web site; visits to clubs and associations with different social backgrounds. The names of the respondents have been changed. Additional interviews exploring a longer historical perspective were undertaken with three respondents.

Interviews in the media: three women's magazines, *Woman & Home, Saga Magazine* and *Yours* were selected from BRAD as having different readerships in terms of age and social class. Interviews were conducted with the fashion editors of the first two and the editor of the third. *Vogue* was selected as representing the premier UK fashion magazine. The interview was with the editor.

The main interviews in the fashion industry were with design directors and others in branded garment retailers. The retailers were selected either for having a focus on the older market or for being mainstream retailers who included older customers in their offer. The main interviews were with M&S, George at Asda, Jaeger, Viyella and Edinburgh Woollen Mills. Some additional interviews were undertaken with individuals with specific experience of the fashion industry.

Two smaller empirical studies provided background. The first was a small-scale secondary analysis of the UK Family Expenditure Survey from the 1960s to the mid 2000s funded by the British Academy. This study was undertaken with Dr Shinobu Majima. The second was a scoping study funded by the Nuffield Foundation exploring the role of clothing in the care of frail elders. This has formed the basis for a subsequent study funded by ESRC on Dementia and Dress.

References

Abrams, D., Eiola, T. and Swift, H. (2009), *Attitudes to Age in Britain 2004–08*, Research Report 599, London: Department of Work and Pensions.

Age UK (2010), *The Golden Economy: The Consumer Marketplace in an Ageing Society,* London: Age UK.

Ahmed, S. (2002), 'Racialized bodies', in M. Evans and E. Lee (eds.), *Real Bodies: A Sociological Introduction,* Basingstoke: Palgrave.

Aldridge, A. (2003), *Consumption,* Cambridge: Polity.

Anderson, M. (1985), 'The emergence of the modern life cycle in Britain', *Social History,* 10, 1: 69–87.

Andersson, L. (ed.) (2002), *Cultural Gerontology,* Westport, CT: Auburn House.

Andrews, M. (1999), 'The seductiveness of agelessness', *Ageing and Society,* 19: 301–18.

Andrews, M. (2009), 'The narrative complexity of successful ageing', *International Journal of Sociology and Social Policy,* 29, 1/2: 73–83.

Anthias, F. (2001), 'The concept of "social division" and theorising social stratification: looking at ethnicity and class', *Sociology,* 35, 4: 835–54.

Apeagyei, P. R. (2012), 'Application of 3 D body scanning technology to human measurement for clothing fit', www.researchgate.net/publication/220670311, accessed 12 October 2012.

Arber, S. and Ginn, J. (1991), *Gender and Later Life: A Sociological Analysis of Resources and Constraints,* London: Sage Publications.

Aronson, A. (2000), 'Reading women's magazines', *Media History,* 6, 2: 111–13.

Ash, J. (1996), 'Memory and objects', in P. Kirkham (ed.), *The Gendered Object,* Manchester: Manchester University Press, 219–24.

Ash, J. (2010), *Dress behind Bars: Prison Clothing as Criminality,* London: I.B.Tauris.

Aspers, P. (2010), *Orderly Fashion: A Sociology of Markets,* Princeton, NJ: Princeton University Press.

Baker, L. and Gringart, E. (2009), 'Body image and self esteem in older adulthood', *Ageing & Society,* 29: 977–95.

Banim, M. and Guy, A. (2001), 'Dis/continued selves: why do women keep clothes they no longer wear', in A. Guy, E. Green and M. Banim (eds.), *Through the Wardrobe: Women's Relationships with Their Clothes,* Oxford: Berg, 203–20.

Banister, E. N. and Hogg, M. K. (2007), 'Consumers and their negative selves, and the implications for fashion marketing', in T. Hines and M. Bruce (eds.), *Fashion Marketing: Contemporary Issues,* Oxford: Butterworth-Heinemann, 217–29.

Barnard, M. (1996), *Fashion as Communication,* London: Routledge.

Barthes, R. (1985), *The Fashion System,* London: Cape.

Bartky, S. L. (1990), *Femininity and Domination: Studies in the Phenomenology of Oppression,* New York: Routledge.

Bartky, S. L. (1999), 'Unplanned obsolescence: some reflections in aging', in M. U. Walker (ed.), *Mother Time: Women, Ageing and Ethics,* Boulder, CO: Rowman & Littlefield, 61–74.

Basting, A. D. (1998), *The Stages of Age: Performing Age in Contemporary American Culture,* Ann Arbor: University of Michigan Press.

Bauman, Z. (2000), *Liquid Modernity,* Cambridge: Polity Press.

Beaujot, A. (2012), *Victorian Fashion Accessories,* Oxford: Berg.

Bennett, T., Savage, M., Silva, E., Warde, A., Gayo-Cal, M. and Wright, D. (2009), *Culture, Class and Distinction,* London: Routledge.

Biggs, S. (1997), '"Choosing not to be old?" Masks, bodies and identity management in later life', *Ageing and Society,* 17: 553–70.

Biggs, S., Phillipson, C., Leach, R. and Money, A.-M. (2007), 'The mature imagination and consumption strategies: age and generation in the development of a United Kingdom baby boomer identity', *International Journal of Ageing and Later Life,* 2: 13–30.

Birtwistle, G. and Tsim, C. (2005), 'Consumer purchasing behaviour: an investigation of the UK mature women's clothing market', *Journal of Consumer Behaviour,* 4, 6: 453–64.

Blakie, A. (1999), *Aging and Popular Culture,* Cambridge: Cambridge University Press.

Blaszczyk, R. L. (2000), *Imagining Consumers: Design and Innovation from Wedgwood to Corning,* Baltimore, MD: John Hopkins University Press.

Bordo, S. (1993), *Unbearable Weight: Feminism, Western Culture and the Body,* Berkeley: University of California Press.

Borelli, L. O. (1997), 'Dressing up and talking about it: fashion writing in *Vogue* from 1968 to 1993', *Fashion Theory,* 1, 3: 247–60.

Bornat, J. (2002), 'Doing life history research', in A. Jamieson and C. Victor (eds.), *Researching Ageing and Later Life: The Practice of Social Gerontology,* Buckingham: Open University Press, 117–34.

Bougourd, J. and Treleven, P. (2010), UK national sizing survey—Size UK, www.fashion.arts.ac.uk/sizeuk.htm, accessed 11 April 2012.

Bourdieu, P. (1984), *Distinction: A Social Critique of the Judgement of Taste,* London: Routledge Kegan Paul.

BRAD (2008), *British Rate and Data* (October), London: Emap Media, 559.

Braham, P. (1997), 'Fashion: unpacking a cultural production', in P. du Gay (ed.), *Production of Culture/Cultures of Production,* London: Sage Publications, 119–76.

Braunstein, P. (1992), *Un Banquier Mis a Nu: Autobiographie de Matthaus Schwarz, Bourgeois d'Augsbourg,* Paris: Decouvertes Gallimard Albums.

Breward, C. (2000), 'Cultures, identities, histories: fashioning a cultural approach to dress', in N. White and I. Griffiths (eds.), *The Fashion Business: Theory, Practice, Image,* Oxford: Berg, 23–36.

Breward, C. (2003), *Fashion,* Oxford: Oxford University Press.

Breward, C., Conekin, B. and Cox, C. (eds.) (2002), *The Englishness of English Dress,* Oxford: Berg.

Brown, H. and Smith, H. (eds.) (1992), *Normalisation: A Reader for the Nineties,* London: Routledge.

Bruner, J. (1999), 'Narratives of aging', *Journal of Aging Studies,* 13, 1: 7–9.

Butler, J. P. (1990), *Gender Trouble: Feminism and the Subversion of Identity,* London: Routledge.

Butler, J. P. (1993), *Bodies That Matter: On the Discursive Limits of 'Sex',* London: Routledge.

Butler, R. (1969), 'Ageism: another form of bigotry', *The Gerontologist,* 9, 3: 243–6.

Bytheway, B. (1995), *Ageism,* Buckingham: Open University Press.

Calasanti, T. M. (2003), 'Theorising age relations', in S. Biggs, A. Lowenstein and J. Hendricks (eds.), *The Need for Theory: Critical Approaches to Social Gerontology,* Amityville, NY: Baywood, 199–218.

Calasanti, T. M. (2008), 'Theorizing feminist gerontology, sexuality, and beyond: an intersectional approach', in V. Bengtson, D. Gans, N. Putney and M. Silverstein (eds.), *Handbook of Theories of Aging,* 471–85.

Calasanti, T. M. and Slevin, K. F. (2001), *Gender, Social Inequalities, and Aging,* New York: Alta Mira Press.

Calasanti, T. M. and Slevin, K. F. (2006), 'Introduction', in T. M. Calasanti and K. F. Slevin (eds.), *Age Matters: Realigning Feminist Thinking,* New York: Routledge, 1–17.

Carrigan, M. and Szmigin, I. (2000), 'Advertising in an ageing society', *Ageing and Society,* 20: 217–33.

Chamberlayne, P., Bornat, J. and Wengraf, T. (2000), *The Turn to Biographical Methods in Social Sciences,* London: Taylor & Francis.

Clarke, A. and Miller, D. (2002), 'Fashion and anxiety', *Fashion Theory,* 6, 2: 191–214.

Cohen, A. S. (2012), *Advanced Style,* Brooklyn, NY: Powerhouse Books.

Cole, T. C. (1992), *The Journey of Life: A Cultural History of Aging in America,* Cambridge: Cambridge University Press.

Coleman, P. G. (2011), *Belief and Ageing: Spiritual Pathways in Later Life,* Bristol: Policy Press.

Connell, R. W. (1995), *Masculinities,* Cambridge: Polity.

Cook, D. T. (2004), *The Commodification of Childhood: The Children's Clothing Industry and the Rise of the Child Consumer,* Durham, NC: Duke University Press.

Coupland, J. (2003), 'Ageist ideology and discourses of controlling skin care product marketing', in J. Coupland and R. Gwyn (eds.), *Discourse, the Body and Identity,* London: Palgrave, 127–50.

Coupland, J. (2009), 'Time, the body and the reversibility of ageing: commodifying the decade', *Ageing & Society,* 29: 953–79.

Craik, J. (1994), *The Face of Fashion: Cultural Studies in Fashion,* London: Routledge.

Crane, D. (2000), *Fashion and Its Social Agendas: Class, Gender and Identity in Clothing,* Chicago, IL: University of Chicago Press.

Crane, D. and Bovone, L. (2006), 'Approaches to material culture: the sociology of fashion and clothing', *Poetics,* 34: 319–33.

Crossley, N. (2001), *The Social Body: Habit, Identity and Desire,* London: Sage Publications.

Daatland, S. O. (2007), 'Age identifications', in R. Fernández-Ballesteros (ed.), *Geropsychology: European Perspectives for an Aging World,* Göttingen: Hogrefe & Huber, 31–48.

Daatland, S. O. (2008), 'Self perceived age and ageing: are women less defensive than men', paper given at 60th Meeting of Gerontological Society of America, San Francisco.

Daly, M. (1979), *Gyn-ecology: The Meta-ethics of Radical Feminism,* London: Women's Press.

Dant, T. (2007), 'Consuming or living with things?/ Wearing it out', in M. Barnard (ed.), *Fashion Theory: A Reader,* London: Routledge, 373–83.

David, A. M. (2006), '*Vogue*'s new world: American fashionability and the politics of style', *Fashion Theory,* 10, 1/2: 13–38.

Davis, F. (1992), *Fashion, Culture and Identity,* Chicago, IL: University of Chicago Press.

Degnen, C. (2007), 'Minding the gap: the construction of old age and oldness amongst peers', *Journal of Ageing Studies,* 21: 69–80.

Diane, T. and Cassidy, T. (2005), *Colour Forecasting,* Oxford: Blackwell.

Dinnerstein, M. and Weitz, R. (1994), 'Jane Fonda, Barbara Bush and other aging bodies: femininity and the limits of resistance', *Feminist Issues,* 14, 2: 3–24.

Douglas, M. and Isherwood, B. (1979), *The World of Goods: Towards an Anthropology of Consumption,* London: Routledge.

Drolet, A., Schwarz, N. and Yoon, C. (eds.) (2010), *The Aging Consumer: Perspectives from Psychology and Economics,* New York: Routledge.

du Gay, P. (1997), 'Introduction', in P. du Gay (ed.), *Production of Culture/Cultures of Production,* London: Sage Publications, 1–11.

Dyhouse, C. (2010), *Glamour: Women, History, Feminism,* London: Zed Books.

Easey, M. (ed.) (2002), *Fashion Marketing,* Oxford: Blackwell.

Edmunds, J. and Turner, B. S. (2002), *Generations, Culture and Society,* Buckingham: Open University.

Entwistle, J. (2000), *The Fashioned Body: Fashion, Dress and Modern Social Theory,* Cambridge: Polity.

Entwistle, J. (2002), 'The aesthetic economy: the production of value in the field of fashion modelling', *Journal of Consumer Culture,* 2, 3: 317–39.

Estes, C. L. (1979), *The Ageing Enterprise,* San Francisco, CA: Jossey Bass.

Estes, C. L. and Binney, E. A. (1989), 'The biomedicalization of aging', *The Gerontologist,* 29, 5: 587–96.

Evans, C. (1997), 'Street style, subculture and subversion', *Costume,* 31: 105–10.

Evans, C. (2003), *Fashion at the Edge,* New Haven, CT: Yale University Press.

Evans, C. and Thornton, M. (1989), *Women and Fashion: A New Look,* London: Quartet.

Fairhurst, E. (1998), '"Growing old gracefully" as opposed to "mutton dressed as lamb": the social construction of recognising older women', in S. Nettleton and J. Watson (eds.), *The Body in Everyday Life,* London: Routledge, 258–75.

Featherstone, M. and Hepworth, M. (1991), 'The mask of ageing and the postmodern life course', in M. Featherstone, M. Hepworth and B. S. Turner (eds.), *The Body: Social Process and Cultural Theory,* London, Sage Publications, 170–96.

Feinberg, R. A., Matero, L. and Burroughs, W. J. (1992), 'Clothing and social identity', *Clothing and Textiles Research Journal,* 11, 1: 18–23.

Fine, B. and Leopold, E. (1993), *The World of Consumption,* London: Routledge.

Finkelstein, J. (1991), *The Fashioned Self,* Cambridge: Polity Press.

Flugel, J. C. (1930), *The Psychology of Clothes,* London: Hogarth Press.

Foucault, M. (1990), *The History of Sexuality: Volume I An Introduction,* New York: Vintage Books.

Franklin, A. (2001), 'Black women and self presentation: appearing in (dis)guise', in A. Guy, E. Green and M. Banim (eds.), *Through the Wardrobe: Women's Relationship with Their Clothes,* Oxford: Berg, 137–50.

Freitas, A., Kaiser, S, Hall, C., Kim, J.-W. and Hammidid, T. (1997), 'Appearance management as border construction: least favourite clothing, group distancing, and identity...Not', *Sociological Inquiry,* 67, 3: 323–35.

Friedan, B. (1963), *The Feminine Mystique,* London: Gollanz.

Friese, S. (2001), 'The wedding dress: from use value to sacred object', in A. Guy, E. Green and M. Banim (eds.), *Through the Wardrobe: Women's Relationships with Their Clothes,* Oxford: Berg.

Furman, F. K. (1997), *Facing the Mirror: Older Women and Beauty Shop Culture,* New York: Routledge.

Furman, F. K. (1999), 'There are no old Venuses: older women's responses to their aging bodies', in M. U. Walker (ed.), *Mother Time: Women, Aging and Ethics,* Boulder, CO: Rowman & Littlefield, 7–22.

Gell, A. (1998), *Art and Agency: Towards an Anthropological Theory,* Oxford: Clarendon Press.

Gibson, P. C. (2000), '"No one expects me anywhere": invisible women, ageing and the fashion industry', in S. Bruzzi and P. C. Gibson (eds.), *Fashion Cultures: Theories, Explorations and Analysis,* London: Routledge, 79–90.

Giddens, A. (1991), *Modernity and Self-identity: Self and Society in the Late Modern Age,* Palo Alto, CA: Stanford University Press.

Gilleard, C. (2002), 'Women, ageing and body talk', in L. Andersson (ed.), *Cultural Gerontology,* Westport, CT: Auburn House, 139–60.

Gilleard, C. and Higgs, P. (2000), *Culture of Ageing: Self, Citizen and the Body,* London: Prentice Hall.

Gilleard, C. and Higgs, P. (2002), 'The third age: class, cohort or generation?, *Ageing & Society,* 22: 369–82.

Gilleard, C. and Higgs, P. (2007), 'The third age and the baby boomers: two approaches to the social structuring of later life', *International Journal of Ageing and Later Life,* 2, 2: 13–30.

Gimlin, D. L. (2002), *Body Work: Beauty and Self Image in American Culture,* Berkeley: University of California Press.

Goffman, E. (1968), *Stigma: Notes on the Management of Spoilt Identity,* Harmondsworth: Penguin.

Goldsberry, E., Shim, S. and Reich, N. (1996), 'Women 55 years and older: Part I current body measurements as contrasted to the PS 42–70 data', *Clothing and Textiles Research Journal,* 14, 2: 108–20.

Gough-Yates, A. (2003), *Understanding Women's Magazines: Publishing, Markets and Readership,* London: Routledge.

Greer, G. (1971), *The Female Eunuch,* London: Paladin.

Greer, G. (1991), *The Change: Women, Ageing and the Menopause,* London: Hamish Hamilton.

Grosz, E. (1994), *Volatile Bodies: Towards a Corporeal Feminism,* Indianapolis: Indiana University Press.

Gullette, M. M. (1988), *Safe at Last in the Middle Years: The Invention of the Midlife Progress Novel,* Berkeley: University of California Press.

Gullette, M. M. (1997), *Declining to Decline: Cultural Combat and the Politics of Midlife,* Charlottesville: University Press of Virginia.

Gullette, M. M. (1999), 'The other end of the fashion cycle: practising loss, learning decline', in K. Woodward (ed.), *Figuring Age: Women, Bodies, Generations,* Bloomingdale: Indiana University Press, 34–58.

Gullette, M. M. (2011), *Agewise: Fighting the New Ageism in America,* Chicago, IL: University of Chicago Press.

Gunaratnam, Y. and Lewis, G. (2001), 'Racialising emotional labour and emotional-ising racialised labour: anger, fear and shame in social welfare', *Journal of Social Work Practice,* 15, 2: 131–48.

Gunter, B. (1998), *Understanding the Older Consumer: The Grey Market,* London: Routledge.

Guy, A. and Banim, M. (2000), 'Personal collections: women's clothing use and identity', *Journal of Gender Studies,* 9, 3: 313–27.

Guy, A., Green, E. and Banim, M. (2001), 'Introduction', in A. Guy., E. Green and M. Banim (eds.), *Through the Wardrobe: Women's Relationships with Their Clothes,* Oxford: Berg, 1–17.

Halls, Z. (2000), 'Mrs Exeter—the rise and fall of the older woman', *Costume,* 34: 105–12.

Handley, S. (1999), *Nylon: The Manmade Fashion Revolution: A Celebration of Art Silk to Nylon and Thinking Fabrics,* London: Bloomsbury.

Hansen, K. T. (2004), 'The world in dress: anthropological perspectives on clothing, fashion and culture', *Annual Review of Anthropology,* 33: 369–92.

Harvey, J. (1995), *Men in Black,* London; Reaktion Books.

Hazan, H. (1994), *Old Age: Constructions and Deconstructions,* Cambridge: Cambridge University Press.

Hebdige, D. (1979), *Subculture: The Meaning of Style,* London: Methuen.

Hermes, J. (1995), *Reading Women's Magazines: An Analysis of Everyday Media Use,* Cambridge: Polity.

Hibbert, R. (2001), *Textile Innovation: Traditional, Modern and Smart Textiles,* London: Line.

Hines, T. and Quinn, L. (2007), 'Segmenting fashion consumers: reconstructing the challenge of consumer complexity', in T. Hines and M. Bruce (eds.), *Fashion Marketing: Contemporary Issues,* Oxford: Butterworth-Heinemann, 73–88.

Hockey, J. and James, A. (2003), *Social Identities across the Life Course,* Basingstoke: Palgrave.

Hockey, J., Robinson, V., Dilley, R. and Sherlock, A. (2012), 'If the shoe fits: footwear, identity and transition', www.sheffield.ac.uk/iftheshoefits. Accessed 20 September 2012.

Holland, S. (2004), *Alternative Femininities: Body, Age and Identity,* Oxford: Berg.

Holland, S. (2012), 'Alternative women adjusting to ageing: or how to stay freaky at 50', in P. Hodkinson and A. Bennett (eds.), *Ageing and Youth Cultures: Music, Style and Identity,* Oxford: Berg, 119–30.

Hollander, A. (1978), *Seeing Through Clothes,* Berkeley: University of California Press.

Hollander, A. (1995), *Sex and Suits: The Evolution of Modern Dress,* New York: Kodansha.

Holliday, R. (2001), 'Fashioning the queer self', in J. Entwhistle and E. Wilson (eds.), *Body Dressing,* Oxford: Berg, 215–32.

Holstein, M. (2006), 'On being an aging woman', in T. M. Calasanti and K. F. Slevin (eds.), *Age Matters: Realigning Feminist Thinking,* New York: Routledge, 313–34.

Hoskins, J. (1998), *Biographical Objects: How Things Tell the Stories of People's Lives,* New York: Routledge.

Hughes, C. (2006), *Dressed in Fiction,* Oxford: Berg.

Hurd, M. D. and Rohwedder, S. (2010), 'Spending patterns of the older population', in A. Drolet, N. Schwarz and C. Yoon (eds.), *The Aging Consumer: Perspectives from Psychology and Economics,* New York: Routledge, 25–49.

Hurd Clarke, L. (2011), *Facing Age: Women Growing Older in Anti-Aging Culture,* Lanham, MD: Rowman & Littlefield.

Hurd Clarke, L. and Griffin, M. (2007), 'The body natural and the body unnatural: beauty work and aging', *Journal of Aging Studies,* 21: 187–201.

Hurd Clarke, L. and Griffin, M. (2008), 'Visible and invisible ageing: beauty work as a response to ageism', *Ageing & Society,* 28: 653–74.

Hurd Clarke, L., Griffin, M. and Maliha, K. (2009), 'Bat wings, bunions, and turkey wattles: body transgressions and older women's strategic clothing choices', *Ageing & Society,* 29: 709–26.

Hutchinson, S. L., Yarnal, C. M., Staffordson, J. and Kerstetter, D. L. (2008), 'Beyond fun and friendship: the Red Hat Society as a coping resource for older women', *Ageing & Society,* 28: 979–99.

Iltanen, S. (2005), 'Constructing the image of a user through design', paper delivered at British Society for Gerontology Conference, University of Keele.

Iltanen-Tähkävuori, S., Wikberg, M. and Topo, P. (2012), 'Design and dementia: A case of garments designed to prevent undressing', *Dementia,* 11: 49–59.

Inglehart, R. (1997), *Modernization and Postmodernization,* Princeton, NJ: Princeton University Press.

Irwin, S. (1999), 'Later life, inequality and sociological theory', *Ageing and Society,* 19, 6: 691–715.

Jeffries, S. (2005), *Beauty and Misogyny: Harmful Cultural Practices in the West,* London: Routledge.

Jobling, P. (1999), *Fashion Spreads: Word and Image in Fashion Photography since 1980,* Oxford: Berg.

Jones, I. R., Hyde, M., Victor, C. R., Wiggins, R. D., Gilleard, C. and Higgs, P. (2008), *Ageing in a Consumer Society: From Passive to Active Consumption in Britain,* Bristol: Policy Press.

Jones, I. R., Higgs, P. and Ekerdt, D. J. (eds.) (2009), *Consumption and Generational Change,* New Brunswick, NJ: Transaction.

Jones, R. M. (2006), *The Apparel Industry,* Oxford: Blackwell.

Joseph, J. (1974), *Rose in the Afternoon,* London: Dent.

Kaiser, S., Chandler, J. and Hammidi, T. (2001), 'Minding appearances in female academic culture', in A. Guy, E. Green and M. Banim (eds.), *Through the Wardrobe: Women's Relationships with Their Clothes,* Oxford: Berg, 117–36.

Karisto, A. (2007), 'Finnish baby boomers and the emergence of the Third Age', *International Journal of Ageing and Later Life*, 2, 2: 91–108.

Katz, S. (1996), *Disciplining Old Age: The Formation of Gerontological Knowledge*, Charlottesville: University Press of Virginia.

Katz, S. (2001), 'Growing older without aging?: positive aging, anti-ageism, and anti-aging', *Generations*, 25: 27–32.

Katz, S. (2005), *Cultural Ageing: Life Course, Lifestyle and Senior Worlds*, Peterborough, Ontario: Broadwood.

Katz, S. and Marshall, B. (2003), 'New sex for old: lifestyle, consumerism and the ethics of aging well', *Journal of Aging Studies*, 17, 1: 3–16.

Kenyon, G. M. and Randall, W. L. (1999), 'Narrative gerontology', *Journal of Aging Studies*, 13, 1: 1–5.

Key Note (2006), *Market Assessment: Grey Consumer*, fourth edition, London: Key Note.

Key Note (2008), *Men's and Women's Buying Habits*, London: Key Note.

Khan, N. (1993), 'Asian women's dress: from burqah to bloggs', in J. Ash and E. Wilson (eds.), *Chic Thrills*, Berkeley: University of California Press, 61–74.

Kidwell, C. B. and Steele, V. (eds.) (1989), *Men and Women: Dressing the Part*, Washington, DC: Smithsonian Institute Press.

Kitwood, T. (1993), 'Towards a theory of dementia care: the interpersonal process', *Ageing & Society*, 13, 1: 51–68.

Klepp, G. I. and Storm-Mathisen, A. (2005), 'Reading fashion as age: teenage girls' and grown women's accounts of clothing as body and social status', *Fashion Theory*, 9, 3: 323–42.

Kopina, H. (2007), 'The world according to *Vogue:* the role of culture in international fashion magazines', *Dialectical Anthropology*, 31: 363–81.

Krekula, C. (2007), 'The intersection of age and gender: reworking gender theory and social gerontology', *Current Sociology*, 55: 155–71.

Krekula, C. (2009), 'Age coding—on age based practices of distinction', *International Journal of Ageing and Later Life*, 4, 2: 7–31.

Kristeva, J. (1982), *Powers of Horror: An Essay on Abjection*, New York: Columbia University Press.

Küchler, S. and Miller, D. (eds.) (2005), *Clothing as Material Culture*, Oxford: Berg.

Larkin, P. (1988), *Collected Poems*, London: Faber.

Laver, J. (1937), *Taste and Fashion*, London: Harrap.

Laver, J. (1950), *Dress: How and Why Fashions in Men's and Women's Clothes Have Changed during the Past Two Hundred Years*, London: John Murray.

Lavery, K. (ed.) (1999), *The Definitive Guide to Mature Advertising and Marketing*, Shipley: Millenium.

Laws, G. (1995), 'Understanding ageism: lessons from feminism and postmodernism', *The Gerontologist*, 35, 1: 112–18.

Laz, C. (1998), 'Act your age', *Sociological Forum*, 13, 1: 85–113.

Laz, C. (2003), 'Age embodied', *Journal of Aging Studies,* 17: 503–19.

Lee, R. A. (1997), 'The youth bias in advertising', *American Demographics,* 19, 1: 47–52.

Lee, S. and Mysyk, A. (2004), 'The medicalisation of compulsive buying', *Social Science & Medicine,* 58: 1709–18.

Le Wita, B. (1994), *French Bourgeois Culture,* trans. J. A. Underwood, Cambridge: Cambridge University Press.

Linthicum, L. (2006), 'Integrative practice: oral history, dress and disability studies', *Journal of Design History,* 19, 4: 309–18.

Lipovetsky, G. (1994), *The Empire of Fashion: Dressing Modern Democracy,* Princeton, NJ: Princeton University Press.

Long, N. (1998), 'Broken down by age and sex—exploring the ways we approach the elderly consumer', *Journal of Market Research Society,* 40, 2: 73–92.

Lurie, A. (1992), *The Language of Clothes,* London: Bloomsbury.

MacSween, M. (1993), *Anorexic Bodies: A Feminist and Sociological Perspective on Anorexia Nervosa,* London: Routledge.

Majima, S. (2006), 'Fashion and the Mass Consumer Society in Britain, c. 1951–2005', unpublished D. Phil. thesis, University of Oxford.

Majima, S. (2008), 'Fashion and frequency of purchase: womenswear consumption in Britain, 1961–2001', *Journal of Fashion Marketing and Management,* 12, 4: 502–17.

Manning, L. K. (2012), 'Experiences of pagan women: a closer look at croning rituals', *Journal of Aging Studies,* 26: 102–8.

Mansvelt, J. (2009), 'Geographies of consumption: the unmanageable consumer', *Progress in Human Geography,* 33, 2: 264–74.

Marshall, B. L. and Katz, S. (2002), 'Forever functional: sexual fitness and the aging male body', *Body and Society,* 8, 4: 43–70.

Marshall, N. (2008), *Dictionary of Children's Clothes: 1700 to Present,* London: V&A Publishing.

Marwick, A. (1998), *The Sixties: Cultural Revolution in Britain, France, Italy and the United States,* Oxford: Oxford University Press.

McNeil, P. and Karaminas, V. (2009), 'Introduction', in P. McNeil and V. Karaminas (eds.), *The Men's Fashion Reader,* Oxford: Berg, 1–14.

McNeil, P., Karaminas, V. and Cole, C. (eds.) (2009), *Fashion in Fiction: Text and Clothing in Literature, Film and Television,* Oxford: Berg.

McRobbie, A. (2008), 'Young women and consumer culture', *Cultural Studies,* 22, 5: 531–50.

Metz, D. and Underwood, M. (2005), *Older, Richer, Fitter: Identifying the Customer Needs of Britain's Ageing Population,* London: Age Concern.

Miller, D. (1987), *Material Culture and Mass Consumption,* Oxford: Blackwell.

Miller, D. (1998), *A Theory of Shopping,* Cambridge: Polity.

Mintel (2000), *The UK Clothing Market,* London: Mintel.

Mintel (2006), *Fashion for the Over 45s—UK,* London: Mintel.

Moeran, B. (2004), 'Women's fashion magazines: people, things and values', in C. Werner and D. Bell (eds.), *Values and Valuables: From the Sacred to the Symbolic,* Walnut Creek: Altamira, 257–81.

Moody, H. R. and Sood, S. (2010), 'Age branding', in A. Drolet, N. Schwarz and C. Yoon (eds.), *The Aging Consumer: Perspectives from Psychology and Economics,* New York: Routledge, 229–45.

Moschis, G. P. (1996), *Gerontographics: Life Stage Segmentation for Marketing Strategy Development,* Westport, CT: Quorum Books.

Newton, S. M. (1980), *Fashion in the Age of the Black Prince, 1340–1365,* London: Boydell.

Newton, S. M. (1989), *The Dress of Venetians 1495–1525,* Basingstoke: Ashgate.

Öberg, P. (1996), 'The absent body—a social gerontological paradox', *Ageing and Society,* 16, 6: 701–19.

Öberg, P. and Tornstam, L. (1999), 'Body images among men and women of different ages', *Ageing & Society,* 19: 629–44.

Öberg, P. and Tornstam, L. (2001), 'Youthfulness and fitness—identity ideals for all ages?', *Journal of Ageing and Identity,* 6, 1: 15–29.

O'Connor, K. (2005), 'The other half: the material culture of new fibres', in S. Kuchler and D. Miller (eds.), *Clothing as Material Culture,* Oxford: Berg, 41–59.

O'Connor, K. (2011), *Lycra: How a Fibre Shaped America,* London: Routledge.

Otieno, R. B., Harrow, C. and Lea-Greenwood, G. (2005), 'The unhappy shopper: a retail experience exploring fashion, fit and affordability', *International Journal of Retail and Distribution Management,* 33, 4: 298–309.

Pahl, J. (1989), *Money and Marriage,* Basingstoke: Macmillan.

Paoletti, J. B. and Kregloh, C. L. (1989), 'The children's department', in C. B. Kidwell and V. Steele (eds.), *Men and Women: Dressing the Part,* Washington, DC: Smithsonian Institute Press, 22–41.

Pastoureau, M. (2008), *Black: The History of a Colour,* Princeton, NJ: Princeton University Press.

Paterson, M. (2006), *Consumption and Everyday Life,* London: Routledge.

Phillipson, C. (1998), *Reconstructing Old Age: New Agendas in Social Theory and Practice,* London: Sage Publications.

Phillipson, C. (2007), 'Understanding the baby boomer generation: comparative perspectives', *International Journal of Aging and Later Life,* 2, 2: 7–11.

Phillipson, C. and Biggs, S. (1998), 'Modernity and identity: themes and perspectives in the study of older adults', *Journal of Aging and Identity,* 3, 1: 11–23.

Phillipson, C. and Walker, A. (eds.) (1986), *Ageing and Social Policy: A Critical Assessment,* Aldershot: Gower.

Polhemus, T. (1994), *Streetstyle: From Sidewalk to Catwalk,* London: Thames and Hudson.

Polhemus, T. and Proctor, L. (1978), *Fashion and Anti Fashion: An Anthology of Clothing and Adornment,* London: Cox and Wyman.

Pollock, G. (2003), 'The grace of time: narrativity, sexuality and a visual encounter in the Virtual Feminist Museum', *Art History,* 26, 2: 174–213.

Prochaska, F. (1995), *Royal Bounty: The Making of the Welfare Monarchy,* London: Yale University Press.

Ray, R. E. (2000), *Beyond Nostalgia: Aging and Life-Story Writing,* Charlottesville: University Press of Virginia.

Ribeiro, A. (1995), 'Truth and history: the meaning of dress in art', in A. Ribeiro (ed.), *The Art of Dress: Fashion in England and France 1750–1820,* New Haven, CT: Yale University Press, 1–31.

Ribeiro, A. (2002), *Dress in Eighteenth Century Europe,* New Haven, CT: Yale University Press.

Rolley, K. (1993), 'Love desire and the pursuit of the whole: dress and the lesbian couple', in J. Ash and E. Wilson (eds.), *Chic Thrills,* Berkeley: University of California Press, 30–9.

Rublack, U. (2010), *Dressing Up: Cultural Identity in Renaissance Europe,* Oxford: Oxford University Press.

Ruggerone, L. (2006), 'The simulated (fictitious) body: the production of women's images in fashion photography', *Poetics,* 34: 354–69.

Russell, R. and Tyler, M. (2002), 'Thank heaven for little girls: "Girl Heaven" and the commercial context of feminine childhood', *Sociology,* 36, 3: 619–37.

Sandberg, L. (2008), 'The old, the ugly and the queer: thinking old age in relation to queer theory', *Graduate Journal of Social Science,* 5, 2: 117–139.

Sandberg, L. (2011), *Getting Intimate: A Feminist Analysis of Old Age, Masculinity and Sexuality,* Linköping: Linköping Studies in Arts and Sciences.

Sawchuk, K. A. (1995), 'From gloom to boom: age, identity and target marketing', in M. Featherstone and A. Wernick (eds.), *Images of Aging: Cultural Representations of Later Life,* London: Routledge.

Schneider, J. (1994), 'In and out of polyester', *Anthropology Today,* 10, 4: 2–10.

Sherman, E., Schiffman, L. G. and Mathur, A. (2001) 'The influence of gender on the New Age elderly's consumption orientation', *Psychology & Marketing,* 18, 10: 1073–89.

Shilling, C. (2003), *The Body and Social Theory,* second edition, London: Sage Publications.

Shilling, C. (2005), *The Body in Culture, Technology and Society,* London: Sage Publications.

Simmel, G. (1904/1971), 'Fashion', *On Individuality and Social Forms: Selected Writings,* trans. D. C. Levine, Chicago, IL: University of Chicago Press.

Slater, N. (2003), *Toast: The Story of a Boy's Hunger,* London: Fourth Estate.

Steele, V. (1997), *Fifty Years of Fashion: New Look to Now,* New Haven, CT: Yale University Press.

Steele, V. (1989), 'Appearance and identity', in C. B. Kidwell and V. Steele (eds.), *Men and Women: Dressing the Part,* Washington, DC: Smithsonian Institute Press, 6–21.

Stearns, P. N. (1997), *Fat History: Bodies and Beauty in the Modern West,* New York: New York University Press.

Stewart, A. J. and Torges, C. M. (2006), 'Social, historical and developmental influences on the psychology of the baby boom at midlife', in S. K. Whitbourne and S. L. Willis (eds.), *The Baby Boomers Grow Up: Contemporary Perspectives on Midlife,* Mahwah, NJ: Lawrence Erlbaum Associates, 23–43.

Tarlo, E. (2010), *Visibly Muslim: Fashion, Politics and Faith,* Oxford: Berg.

Taylor, L. (2002), *The Study of Dress History,* Manchester: Manchester University Press.

Taylor, L. (2004), *Establishing Dress History,* Manchester: Manchester University Press.

Thane, P. (ed.) (2005), *The Long History of Old Age,* London: Thames & Hudson.

Thompson, P., Itzin, C. and Abendstern, M. (1990), *I Don't Feel Old: Understanding the Experience of Later Life,* Oxford: Oxford University Press.

Tomassini, C. (2005), *Focus on Older People: Demographic Profile,* London: Office of National Statistics.

Topo, P. and Iltanen-Tähkävuori, S. (2010), 'Scripting patienthood with patient clothing', *Social Science and Medicine,* 70: 1682–9.

Townsend, P. (1986), 'Ageism and social policy', in C. Phillipson and A. Walker (eds.), *Ageing and Social Policy: A Critical Assessment,* Aldershot: Gower.

Tseëlon, E. (1995), *The Masque of Femininity,* London: Sage Publications.

Tseëlon, E. (2001), 'Ontological, epistemological and methodological clarification in fashion research: from critique to empirical suggestions', in A. Guy, E. Green and M. Banim (eds.), *Through the Wardrobe: Women's Relationships with Their Clothes,* Oxford: Berg, 237–54.

Tulle-Winton, E. (1999), 'Growing old and resistance: the new cultural economy of old age?', *Ageing and Society,* 19: 281–99.

Tulle-Winton, E. (2000), 'Old bodies', in P. Hancock, B. Hughes, E. Jagger, K. Paterson, R. Russell, E. Tulle-Winton and M. Tyler (eds.), *The Body, Culture and Society,* Buckingham: Open University.

Tulloch, C. (1993), 'Rebel without a pause', in J. Ash and E. Wilson (eds.), *Chic Thrills,* Berkeley: University of California Press, 84–100.

Tulloch, C. (2002), 'Strawberries and cream: dress, migration and the quintessence of Englishness', in C. Breward, B. Conekin and C. Cox (eds.), *The Englishness of English Dress,* Oxford: Berg.

Turner, B. S. (1984), *The Body and Society: Explorations in Social Theory,* Oxford: Blackwell.

Twigg, J. (2004), 'The body, gender and age: feminist insights in social gerontology', *Journal of Aging Studies,* 18: 59–73.

Twigg, J. (2006), *The Body in Health and Social Care,* Basingstoke: Palgrave.

Twigg, J. (2007), 'Clothing, aging and the body: a critical review', *Ageing & Society,* 27: 285–305.

Twigg, J. (2010), 'Dementia and dress: a neglected dimension', *Journal of Aging Studies,* 24, 4: 223–30.

Twigg, J. (2012), 'Fashion and age: the role of women's magazines in the constitution of aged identities', in V. Ylänne (ed.), *Representing Ageing: Images and Identities,* Basingstoke: Palgrave Macmillan, 132–46.

Twigg, J. and Majima, S. (2013), 'Consumption and the constitution of age: expenditure patterns on clothing, hair and cosmetics among post-war "baby boomers", 1961–2006', www.clothingandage.org, accessed 10 March 2013.

Valentine, G. (2007), 'Theorizing and researching intersectionality: a challenge for feminist geography', *The Professional Geographer,* 59, 1: 10–21.

Veblen, T. (1899/1953), *The Theory of the Leisure Class: An Economic Study of Institutions,* New York: Mentor.

Verdict (2003), *Clothing and Footwear 2008: Verdict Forecast,* London: Verdict.

Verdict (2004), *Womenswear Retailers 2004,* London: Verdict.

Vincent, J. (2003), *Old Age,* London: Routledge.

Wadell, G. (2004), *How Fashion Works,* Oxford: Blackwell.

Ward, R. and Holland, C. (2011), '"If I look old, will I be treated old": hair and later life image dilemmas', *Ageing & Society,* 31: 288–307.

Waxman, B. F. (2010), 'Literary texts and literary critics team up against ageism', in T. R. Cole, R. E. Ray and R. Kastenaum (eds.), *A Guide to Humanistic Studies in Aging,* Baltimore, MD: John Hopkins University Press, 83–104.

Weber, S. and Mitchell, C. (2004), 'Dress stories', in S. Weber and C. Mitchell (eds.), *Not Just Any Dress: Narratives of Memory, Body and Identity,* New York: Lang, 3–9.

Weber, S. and Mitchell, C. (eds.) (2004), *Not Just Any Dress: Narratives of Memory, Body and Identity,* New York: Lang.

Weitz, R. (2001), 'Women and their hair: seeking power through resistance and accommodation', *Gender & Society,* 15, 5: 667–86.

Willetts, D. (2010), *The Pinch: How the Baby Boomers Stole Their Children's Future,* London: Atlantic Books.

Williamson, J. (1982), *Decoding Advertisements: Ideology and Meaning in Advertising,* London: Marion Boyars.

Winship, J. (1987), *Inside Women's Magazines,* London: Pandora.

Wilson, E. (1985), *Adorned in Dreams: Fashion and Modernity,* London: Virago.

Wilson, R. A. (1966), *Feminine Forever,* London: W.H. Allen.

Wolf, N. (1990), *The Beauty Myth,* London: Vintage.

Wolfensberger, W. (1972), *The Principle of Normalization in Human Services,* Toronto: National Institute on Mental Retardation.

Woodward, K. M. (1991), *Aging and Its Discontents, Freud and Other Fiction,* Bloomington: Indiana University Press.

Woodward, K. M. (1999), 'Introduction', in K. Woodward (ed.), *Figuring Age: Women, Bodies, Generations,* Bloomington: Indiana University Press, ix–xxix.

Woodward, K. M. (2006), 'Performing age, performing gender', *NWSA Journal,* 18, 1: 162–89.

Woodward, S. (2007), *Why Women Wear What They Wear,* Oxford: Berg.

Worsfold, B. J. (ed.) (2011), *Acculturating Age: Approaches to Cultural Gerontology,* Lleida: Universitat de Lleida.

York, P. (1980), *Style Wars,* London: Sidgwick & Jackson.

York, P. and Barr, A. (1982), *The Official Sloane Ranger Handbook,* London: Harpers & Queen.

Index